Living, Loving, and Loss

The Interplay of Intimacy, Sexuality, and Grief

Edited by

Brad DeFord and Richard B. Gilbert

Death, Value, and Meaning Series

Series Editor: Dale A. Lund

Routledge
Taylor & Francis Group
LONDON AND NEW YORK

First published 2013 by Baywood Publishing Company, Inc.

Published 2017 by Routledge
2 Park Square, Milton Park, Abingdon, Oxon OX14 4RN
711 Third Avenue, New York, NY 10017, USA

Routledge is an imprint of the Taylor & Francis Group, an informa business

Library of Congress Catalog Number: 2012046708
ISBN 13: 978-0-89503-650-6 (hbk)
ISBN 13: 978-0-89503-653-7 (pbk)

Library of Congress Cataloging-in-Publication Data

Living, loving, and loss : the interplay of intimacy, sexuality, and grief / Edited by Brad DeFord and Richard B. Gilbert.
pages cm. -- (Death, value, and meaning series)
Includes bibliographical references and index.
ISBN 978-0-89503-650-6 (cloth : alk. paper) -- ISBN 978-0-89503-653-7 (pbk. : alk. paper) -- ISBN 978-0-89503-651-3 (e-pub) -- ISBN 978-0-89503-652-0 (e-pdf) 1. Death--Psychological aspects. 2. Grief. 3. Loss (Psychology) 4. Intimacy (Psychology) 5. Sex (Psychology) I. DeFord, Brad. II. Gilbert, Richard B.
BF789.D4L58 2013
155.9' 37--dc23

2012046708

Cover Art by Clare Duval Hansen

Table of Contents

Foreword v
Brad Hunter

Preface vii
Brad DeFord and Richard B. Gilbert

Acknowledgments xi

Introduction 1
Brad DeFord

SECTION 1:
Death, Grief, and Differences of
Sexual Orientation. 19

CHAPTER 1
Death and Intimacy Issues in the LGBT Community:
A Gay Perspective 21
Ronald L. Attrell

CHAPTER 2
Young People and Gender Issues: Living with Loss 43
Linda Goldman

SECTION 2:
Loss of Relationship and the
Restoration of Intimacy in Families 65

CHAPTER 3
Momma's Dead and Daddy's on Viagra!: Elder Widowers,
ED Drugs, and New Romantic Relationships 67
Harold Ivan Smith

CHAPTER 4
Grieving a Not-So-Loved Parent: Sinking in the Mud of
Hurtful Memories 87
Richard B. Gilbert

CHAPTER 5
Infertility and Intimacy: Life's Layered Losses 101
Darcy L. Harris

CHAPTER 6
The Tolls of War: Intimacy and Sexuality Challenges for Soldiers and Their Families 119
M. Douglas Harvey

SECTION 3:
Adjusting to Life's Losses by Aging or Illness or Infirmity 127

CHAPTER 7
Birth of a Stranger: Intimacy, Sexuality, and Dementia 131
Sara Sanders and Joelle Osterhaus

CHAPTER 8
Love, Life, and Losses After 50 151
Anne Katz

CHAPTER 9
Intimacy, Sex and Hospice: Self-Determination, Dignity, and Intimacy Options at the End of Life 165
Sherri Weisenfluh and Vicki Merrill

SECTION 4:
Religious Bases for Understanding Intimacy, Sexuality, and Healing After Loss 181

CHAPTER 10
Living, Loving, and Losing: A Spiritual Reflection Through the Eyes of a Rabbi 183
Daniel A. Roberts

CHAPTER 11
Engaging the Christian Voice in Defining (and Redefining) What Is Right 199
David Daubert and Robert D. Machamer

Afterword: Toward a Spirituality of Love and Longing 219
Brad DeFord

Bibliography
Richard B. Gilbert 225
Index 235

Foreword

Brad Hunter

As I read this book, I had two sets of thoughts. The first had to do with how death and sex are related. Despite many sincere efforts to bring death education and sex education to the public, there are many forces that continue to gravitate toward the denial and repression of both.

The second set of thoughts involved spiritual associations. Ernest Becker, in his classic *The Denial of Death* (1973), said that no human fear is purely secular; all of it is rooted in holy terror—the fear of death. Despite our cultural saturation and fascination with images of violence, death, sex, and loss—images both real and imagined—how little do we really understand and how truly fearful we still are. Deep within us, sex and death are spiritually related, linked by our fears.

In our consumer-driven economies, we are skilled at turning anything into a commodity, and we should not be surprised at the myriad ways we have devised to elaborate economic systems that manipulate our fears about sex and death. Health care systems and pharmacology both raise our anxieties and claim to be able to calm us. Products are sold to feed what Kabir called "the wanting creature inside." This "wanting creature" constantly confuses the mystery of *being* with the problem-solving *having*. And this having-nature, by definition, cannot stand loss and must deny it at every turn.

The result in our culture is that we suffer the greater loss of alienation from the mystery of our being and the persistent wild nature of our bodies. This is a loss we do not grieve, but it means that we lack an awareness that dying and sexuality are essentially transformative and potentially even transcendent experiences, if held in spaces of wisdom and compassion—and yet held not too tightly.

If this is our spiritual condition, then grieving it could also be our healing. There is a Sufi saying "grief can be the gateway to the garden of enlightenment." In Buddhism (which I subscribe to, not necessarily as a set of religious beliefs but as a spiritual *practice*) sickness, old age, and death are called "the Divine

Messengers." They are considered divine because they call upon us to awaken to the preciousness of every fleeting moment of our very lives—and ultimately to life's spiritual and transcendent dimensions. Regrettably, psychology seems to be shying away from terms like "spiritual" and "transcendent." After all, how could we possibly measure and contain such elements in a quantitative analysis?

As I see it, this is the remarkable challenge faced by the contributors to this book: to walk the path of the mystery of being and appreciate the spiritual nature of intimacy and sexuality and to walk the path of the problematic of having and thus articulate in psychological terms the intimacy and sexuality dilemmas faced by those who grieve. I would encourage readers to hear in the psychological text a spiritual subtext, a layering of tonalities and a harmony of both disciplines.

Rainer Maria Rilke once wrote, "I want to unfold. I don't want to stay folded anywhere, because where I am folded, there I am untrue" (2012). Nowhere are we more "folded" than around issues of loss, grief, death, and sexuality. As a society we seem to be stuck on the extreme edges of either obsession or repression. Amazingly, we can observe both of these extreme positions even within our own hearts sometimes!

It takes courage and compassion to look into those dark spaces, those "folds," where, beyond our immediate awareness, "there be dragons," as on ancient maps. The contributors of this edition enter their explorations of these difficult and often complex topics and exhibit the courage and compassion to "unfold," displaying these two important qualities in their search for truth. May their contributions soften those sharp edges where we are folded; may they encourage our deeper unfolding, opening us onto a more spacious truth, both personally and collectively.

What we are offered here is an opportunity to face our fears—about intimacy, about sexuality, about death, and about loss and grief. If these fears be our "dragons," then perhaps what we need most is to see our "dragons" differently. I am reminded of another Rilke wisdom: "Perhaps all the dragons in our lives are princesses who are only waiting to see us act, just once, with beauty and courage. Perhaps everything that frightens us is, in its deepest essence, something helpless that wants our love" (2012). The contributors to this book bring their love to the "dragons" we have made of intimacy, sexuality, and grief. Here they become, if not "princesses," at least less intimidating and more accessible.

REFERENCES

Becker, E. (1973). *The denial of death*. New York, NY: Free Press.

Rilke, R. M. (2012). Retrieved November 25, 2012 from www.goodreads.com/author/quotes/7906.Rainer_Maria_Rilke

Preface

At first glance, loss occurs to us as a disruption in our lives, a break in our sense of continuity that we must grieve in order to repair and restore homeostasis. This is commonly how we regard loss. And it is why we tend to think of mourning as that time of "recovery" from an event of loss in our lives.

Some losses do indeed occur as events. This is especially true of sudden losses or other trauma. We can point to the date and sometimes even the time of the event to note when the change occurred. We identify this as the change that introduced the period of transition we commonly call mourning. Losses to death are particularly marked this way. We know when the loss occurred and the change came, even when we may not know with the same precision when sufficient adjustments have been made and the period of mourning has ended. In fact, some wonder whether this sort of mourning ever truly "ends." If not, life becomes a living through ever-overlapping periods of mourning as our losses accrue. Most often, we simply tell ourselves that one period of mourning has passed and we go on with our lives.

This sense of living through a series of periods of mourning is especially significant when we consider the point of view that more of our losses occur gradually, without clear beginnings, until they have evolved sufficiently for us to notice. In this process, we might not have noticed that mourning these gradual losses has already begun, for we have just as gradually been making adjustments. Many, if not most, of our losses occur as these "erosions" or as "ratcheting downs" in the course of our everyday lives. And the grief we experience is thus likely to be just as subtle, until one day it occurs to us that we have indeed experienced a loss. Perhaps at the same time we realize that we are experiencing other losses too. We may even realize that we are experiencing a kind of cascade of losses, which in their cumulative effect will be pronounced as one loss, although there actually has been no single event.

The losses of aging, for instance, often occur in this way, as do other developmental losses. At some point in our adult lives, in trying to understand who we have become and why, we might well be able to name particular events, but just as significant will be those losses-over-time that we came to realize only later have had the effects that they have had. The emotional processes of mourning thus course through our lives in two ways: one, explicit, following particular events; and the other, implicit, paralleling our accumulating losses. In combination, it is fair to say that mourning etches the landscape of our lives in rivers and rivulets, shaping our emotional topography.

Two areas of our lives on which losses can have the most impact are our intimate relationships and our sexual sense of our selves. Our experiences of ourselves as intimate or sexual beings transcend most identifiable single events in our lives, and probably more result from those losses-over-time whose cumulative effects are now etched into our lives. Taking both kinds of losses into account, our premise is that it is our *losses*, both the events and the patterns of loss in our lives, that jeopardize our ability to meet our sexual needs and to participate in intimacies of significant depth and thus to experience meaningful belonging.

Our understanding is that, when it comes to our intimacy needs and our sexual desires, we are in two distinctly different but overlapping fields of human experience and that each of them has its own history in us. The threads of our intimacy-seeking and sexual expressiveness may have their origins in our earliest childhood, but they also weave themselves continuously through every phase of our lives. This continuity itself transcends each loss-as-rupture and is an aspect of every loss-as-accumulation. Regardless of the nature of the loss, significant aspects of it are tied to its effects upon our intimacy needs and sexual desires.

Since intimacy and sexuality are significant aspects of loss, it is somewhat incongruous that they have generally been underappreciated and even overlooked as aspects of the grieving process. We are offering the essays that follow with several aims in mind. Our primary aim is to encourage a conversation about the significance of intimacy and sexuality issues within our experiences of loss and grief. Simply growing more comfortable with speaking about matters of intimacy and sexuality will help all of us grieve a little easier.

In order to do this, we will want to become more familiar with what intimacy is and how it relates to our sexuality and yet how intimacy and sexuality are different. Along the way, definitions of each will be offered, and by the variety of viewpoints shared here, we might come to appreciate why we have not talked about intimacy and sexuality as much as we might. In a word, our second aim is to grow in our ability to know more precisely *what* we are talking about when we talk about intimacy and sexuality.

Our approach to appreciating the significances of intimacy and sexuality in grief is to explore a broad spectrum of losses. This is the third purpose of this book: to provide information about a wide range of losses and the effects these losses have upon us. For this reason, "loss" is broadly defined, encompassing both what we might call *events* of loss and *processes* of loss. We hope through this initial offering to provide a springboard for greater appreciation of the extensive impact of loss and, from there, to provide a basis for our listening better to each other and ourselves in both professional and personal ways.

Our perspective is that intimacy and sexuality issues pervade the human experience at many levels. We aim only to speak about some of those levels and to do that within the rather limited context of loss and grief. We are under no illusions—about intimacy and sexuality, there is always much more to say! We are encouraging that "more" be said.

Again, we are not pretending that what we are providing here is in any way comprehensive. Rather, we are aware that what we have gathered are shards of our human brokenness, all related to our capacities for intimacy, our seeking to express ourselves sexually, and our grieving our losses. We seek to look at the effects of loss upon our intimacy and sexuality through this variety of human lenses. Each of these viewpoints will provide its own point of view, yet all of them together might encourage us to see why there is merit to giving further consideration to intimacy and sexuality when considering fully what happens to and within us as we grieve. We hope we have gathered sufficient shards to assemble a kaleidoscope. This is neither a telescope to survey the fields adequately nor a microscope for us to appreciate more deeply the effects of loss on our abilities to be intimate and sexual.

In sum, this book is the testimony of some very gifted people who understand the importance of living lovingly and how loss interrupts our living this way. Grief is how we express the meaning of that loss. Our grasp of the importance of grief is often blocked by our own thoughts and emotions, the ways others define our experience for us (much like Job's friends), and the sociocultural restrictions we find are placed on us. Against this tide, this book is intended to open a love story, a sexual story, a feelings story, a living story. We invite you to step into that story, both professionally and personally.

We extend a tremendous thank you to the people at Baywood Publishing, including Dr. Dale Lund, the series editor. The course of assembling this book became a rather protracted process, for reasons of failures of health and wealth; the kind folks at Baywood have been patient with us. In addition there have been too many to be named who guided us and encouraged us to continue. Above all, we are extremely grateful to the many people who agreed to contribute their knowledge and wisdom to this project. As it turned out, more contributed than could be included in this text. In other words, there are losses behind the losses we speak about here. When it comes to intimacy and sexuality and grief, it would seem there truly is always more to be said.

Beyond the borders of this book, the two of us have enjoyed getting to know each other. Working together has been a joy! We have laughed, we have occasionally disagreed, we have learned to embrace each other's values, and we have grown in understanding of each other. Out of this project, a friendship has been forged—a degree of intimacy for which we are each grateful.

We hope you will have a similar experience as you read. We encourage your responses! Please join us in this conversation.

Brad DeFord
Richard Gilbert

Acknowledgments

Some of the benefits of editing a book together include collaboration and mutual support. What the reader holds here is a testimony to that joint work, and to the friendship that has grown because of it.

Moreover, since this is an expression of many voices beyond our own, we want to thank all of the contributors for their perspectives, their patience, and their persistence in completing this project. Indeed, many were called, and wrote essays, but only a few were chosen. So we are grateful both to those whose contributions are visible, and to those whose are "invisible." Such is the experience of grief manifested, in both what is seen and what is not seen.

Unseen too but not unappreciated are our friends whose support over the process of assembling these essays was unwavering and at times extraordinary. We both faced trials and set-backs as we put this book together, and, like Ringo Starr, we recognize that we could only have gotten by "with a little help from our friends." Too many to name, we hope it is enough to say simply, you know who you are!

We are just as grateful to the staff at Baywood Publishing Co., to Stuart Cohen, President, and especially Bobbi Olszewski, Editorial and Production Manager, for her careful reading and insistence on quality. This is a better book because of them.

Finally, we want to acknowledge our teachers: those who have told us their stories and let us walk with them in their grief, whose shared heartaches were the seeds for the fruit that is harvested here. We hope they see themselves reflected here, and feel gratefully acknowledged. Together we dedicate this book to them. And:

Brad dedicates this book to Clare, *for the love and joy that have risen from our shared intimacy, sexuality, and grief.*

Dick dedicates this book to "*my many friends and colleagues who bear the gifts of love and friendship, often swaddled with care, patience, and forgiveness. The richest treasures of love, encouragement, and even the occasional stern word, come from my family: Sharon, Allison, and Arlen, and for recent gifts of two grandsons, Andrew and Adam. It is fun to be Pop Pop!*"

Introduction

Brad DeFord

Mourning is a period of postloss grieving when we reevaluate our relationships with others and with ourselves. Mourning proceeds as a search. It is a form of "exploring," during which we get to know again a world that has been irrevocably changed by our loss. This "getting to know again" entails sorting out the familiar from the unfamiliar. As we mourn, we learn anew how things work, on whom we can count—and on whom, we discover, we cannot truly rely. Mourning often confounds our expectations.

What motivates mourning is the search for comfort. Because loss often renders us discomforted in ourselves as well as uncomfortable with others, mourning includes getting to know both others and ourselves again.

When our loss is the death of someone with whom we had experienced an emotional attachment, mourning has this inherently paradoxical quality about it: the feeling endures that we *remain* in a relationship with that person even though that person is no longer alive. We are aware that he or she is gone, yet our loved one still seems with us somehow. Emotional connections persist, continuing after the death of the Other. Through these emotional connections, the Other remains "alive" to us, "alive" in us, and "alive" through us. As we mourn, we determine how significant that "afterlife" of the Other is going to be to us now, as we go on living. In that way, the one who is gone continues to be "here," on a feeling level at the very least but also at a cognitive level, occupying our thoughts.

Mourning is thus a unique "self/other" experience, a poignant and often acute experience of what Bromberg (2011) calls our "relational mind." It is one of those times in our lives, on par with falling in love and birthing a child, when we are most aware that we *are* indeed "relational" beings, living what Sullivan (1953) might call "interpersonal" lives.

Moreover, mourning makes us aware of the interpersonal nature of our lives in a way that is unique from our other experiences. Usually when we say we are relational beings we think in terms of dyads—our relationship with others or our relationship with ourselves, our outward relationships as opposed to our inward relationship. Mourning is not entirely like this; it circumambulates a relational *triad*: Self, living Others, and the Other who has died.

What makes mourning unique is that, while other interpersonal experiences are characterized by the *presence* of the Other and the degree of interactivity between one's Self and an Other, mourning is characterized by the *physical absence* of the Other, complemented by the continuing *psychical presence* of the Other. For instance, we can be so aware that the Other has left that we often feel abandoned. Missing the Other, we nearly always feel lonely. One of the most prevalent and persistent feelings of mourning is that hollow helplessness of loneliness. Sometimes what we feel is a "general" loneliness, but more often it is quite specific: we are lonely *for* the One we are mourning. The loneliness of mourning is its own reminder of the relational nature of mourning.

This is the significance of the interplay of intimacy and sexuality in *grief*, as opposed to other times and circumstances in our lives. In the relational flux that follows death, we find ourselves facing personal issues as we live *in the shadow*, as it were, of the one who has died. If perhaps we had thought that we had "settled" our intimacy and sexuality "issues" *before* our loss, we will likely find that they are unsettled anew *by* the loss. And our addressing and resolving them again will now occur within the context of mourning.

This means that during mourning, our intimacy seeking and sexual expressions are also not dyadic but triadic. They primarily coalesce around those three relationships: our relationship with our Self, of course; our relationship with the One who has died, the One whom we are mourning; and our relationships with Others—family, and friends, those we have known, and those people we will come to know. During mourning, the continuing physical absence but emotional presence of the One who has died influences both our relationship with ourselves and the nature of the relationships we pursue with others.

Because after loss much has changed (even though it may appear to be the same), we come to experience the risks of getting to know others and the risks of allowing ourselves to be known by them, again, only now in the unfamiliar context of mourning. Both intimacy and sexuality take on a significance they may not have had before; after loss, we discover that we can no longer take them for granted. In this way, our loss can also precipitate a secondary loss: that of our assumptions and presumptions about what intimacy and our sexuality mean to us. What was true for us before the loss may not be true for us after the loss.

Mourning demands our attention to all three of these relationships. As we mourn, we process the emotional residues of our relationship with the One who has died. In that process, we rediscover ourselves. This rediscovery inevitably entails a reassessment of our needs for intimacy and of our desires for sexual expression with others, in the present and in the future. Ideally what occurs as we mourn is a reasserting of ourselves in relationships with others as we gain familiarity and confidence in our relationship with ourselves, and as we rework our relationship with the One who has died.

Yet seldom is mourning ideal—precisely because of our awareness of the absence/presence of the One who has died. During mourning we often feel torn: we feel lost, perhaps even abandoned; we seek the company of others, yet we also feel unsure of ourselves and how we might behave. Moreover, shaken, we can feel uncertain about our "acceptability" to others. These are just some of the ways in which mourning brings its own relational uneasiness. No wonder we may find ourselves longing for the relationship that was; in contrast to the present possibilities, it was at least familiar, and there would be no small comfort in that. Yet we are aware, sometimes acutely, of the importance of establishing new relationships, at least making new friends. Establishing these new relationships, in turn, makes us aware of what we probably had forgotten or denied: that relationships *do* require risk. Feeling self-protective, we may even choose *not* to risk the relational intimacy that would provide the most comfort, let alone the sexual expressiveness that would bring the most release. Perhaps to our detriment, we may make choices that feel safer to us yet deprive us of precisely the relationships that would be most healing. How we manage the risks of relationships determines the shape of the path our mourning will take.

In order to appreciate the emotional complexity of the intimacy and sexuality issues we face in mourning, we will need to begin with some definitions of terms. For instance, what *is* intimacy? To understand intimacy, we will be helped to learn more about solitude—and how it differs experientially from loneliness. Then, what do we mean when we speak of sexuality? In what follows in this book, we will be glimpsing a variety of ways in which loss is intertwined with our capacity for intimacy and our understanding of our sexuality.

What we are likely to find is that, as we cross the thresholds of our understanding of these experiences, we will have entered into realms of human experience wherein simplicity and perhaps clarity are elusive. Like mourning itself, intimacy and sexuality are their own "rabbit holes": they open worlds where language is inadequate, descriptions are maddeningly general, and exceptions, more often than not, "prove" whatever rules we might imagine there to be. Perhaps this is itself a reason why the interconnections of intimacy, sexuality, and grief have seldom been examined by thanatologists. Intimacy and sexuality are, however, at the very least a common subtext among those who come to bereavement groups for support. There they are spoken of, most often, indirectly but frequently alluded to, if seldom raised explicitly. In other words, it is safe to say that intimacy and sexuality issues are very much on the minds and hearts of those who grieve—but they may be uncomfortable about voicing their thoughts and feelings.

Those of us who would comfort those who mourn would do well to become better versed in matters of intimacy and sexuality and what is psychosocially—and spiritually—at stake during mourning.

WHAT IS INTIMACY?

Intimacy might be best understood as an appreciated *comfort* and *security* with being in relationship. The comfort we feel when a relationship is intimate is directly proportional to how *safe* it is for us. It is the comfort we have in the relationship that encourages us toward developing its potential for intimacy, and the safety we feel supports our willingness to take the risks that intimacy requires. Intimacy in relationship is not a given, nor is it inherently equal or balanced. Each of the parties in a relationship has his or her own sense of when a boundary is established or might be crossed, and the relationship has deepened sufficiently to be deemed "intimate." What one party regards as intimate the other may not. This difference means that intimacy is not necessarily mutual, if by that we mean an equality of risk is taken. Rather, mutuality in intimacy concerns *consent*: the agreement, often tacit, between people that their relationship displays the felt characteristic of being intimate.

One gauge of the depth of intimacy is the significance of the risk overcome in order to have arrived at intimacy. Often the risks of intimacy are underappreciated. Frequently we assume that relationships of a certain kind are inherently intimate, such as the relationships between spouses or partners. But in fact, we have all manner of ways and reasons for remaining strangers to one another. For instance, Bromberg (2011) appreciates the risks that must be overcome in order to be intimate when he discusses the role of "dissociation" among the other psychological defenses we employ because being in relationship is emotionally stressful. What he calls the "gift of intersubjectivity" (2011, p. 14) comes with the task of *not* dissociating and trying to remain present in the relationship. When both parties are up to the task of intimacy, mutuality can be experienced.

When we reflect on the intimacy we have enjoyed, it is likely that we had three kinds of experiences against which we would otherwise have defended ourselves: vulnerability, openness, and a degree of lack of control.

To begin, we know when we are in an intimate relationship because we are able to be **vulnerable**. In other circumstances, our sense of risking vulnerability might be either relatively low or perhaps overridden by our desire to be intimate, or perhaps it is assuaged by the reassurances of the other. But when we are mourning, we are likely to feel vulnerable already—made so by our circumstances. This makes our intimacy-seeking that much more acute, that much riskier. Our confidence in intimacy directly correlates with our confidence in our ability to manage our feelings about being vulnerable. Sometimes this vulnerability is also experienced as dependence, as being able to rely upon the one with whom we would be intimate. Intimacy permits and encourages vulnerability and establishes a confidence in being dependent.

Our vulnerability makes us aware that we are risking an emotional **openness** about ourselves. When we are in an intimate relationship, we experience an opportunity to be less guarded about what we think or feel. Intimacy encourages a kind of freedom and trust, one based upon an assurance of acceptance. Misunderstandings may arise, but they can be addressed and resolved. The process of reaching better understanding itself deepens the degree of intimacy felt in the relationship.

The comfort with openness that accompanies intimacy leads to the third quality we often experience: in intimate relationships, power or **control** is less significant. In intimate relationships, we discover that we can be comfortable with a certain *lack* of control, or at least, we can experience a lack of concern about both self-control and control of the Other. In fact, when *controlling* becomes an aspect of a relationship, it loses what Brenda Schaeffer calls "true intimacy" (1997, p. 57) and instead becomes an addictive relationship. When we are truly experiencing intimacy, we relax our *self*-protections and permit ourselves to *be* ourselves. We can do this because the intimacy of the relationship provides its own assurance that our boundaries will be respected. As we become comfortable with vulnerability, we likewise relax our vigilance. We could even say that only in intimacy can we be helpless and unafraid.

In their discussion of families, Fossum and Mason (1986) suggest another dimension that can be present in our intimate relationships that is especially important as we consider the impact of loss. They say, "our definition of *family* intimacy is the experience of closeness and familiarity between two or more family members in a variety of contexts, with the expectation that the experience and the relationship will *persist over time*" (1986, p. 158). Of course, we may safely presume that our personal capacities for intimacy were initially developed within the context of our families. Within that context, we likely learned what it meant to be intimate—what intimacy was and what it was not. Moreover, what Fossum and Mason identify is that intimacy comes with its own *expectations*, one of which has to do with the relationship enduring. On the one hand, what this means is that brief encounters are probably not intimate, however significant to us they might be. On the other hand, deepening intimacy in a relationship takes its own time, and appreciating that a relationship has developed a level of intimacy leads to our expectation, even desire, that the relationship will persist.

This is true for more than just our relationships with other members of our families. In fact, some familial relationships are less than intimate. But as we mourn, we experience this sense that an intimate relationship would have, or should have, continued over time. In terms of the relational triad, this is one way our relational past influences our present relational choices during mourning. The level of intimacy we enjoyed in our relationship with the One who has died contributes to our sense of its irreplaceability and perhaps to our despair that we might not establish another relationship of similar intimate depth. We realize that time itself was one factor in what made that relationship intimate, and we likely wonder whether we have enough time left in our own lives to take the time to develop a relationship that deeply, with a depth that would engender a similar promise of persistence. One of the questions we ask ourselves as we mourn is "Do we dare hope for intimacy—again?"As we risk that hope, mourning may help us appreciate that intimacy, whether within our families or among our friends and relations, is, to recall Bromberg's word, a "gift."

It may help us hope for intimacy if we adjust our expectations of intimacy. Schaeffer cites Eric Berne, whose definition of intimacy is "a profound exchange of thoughts, feelings and actions in the here and now" and who concludes that "we are fortunate if we experience only three hours of sustained true intimacy in our lives" (1997, pp. 57–58). In other words, we may well *expect* that our intimate relationships are going to last, but perhaps our experiences of intimacy are rather more fleeting. And perhaps our experiences are more rare a "gift" than we had imagined.

There is another aspect to intimacy that might shed some light on this difference between our expectations of intimacy and its reality. This is the notion that **our capacity for intimacy with others is based on and grounded in our capacity for intimacy with ourselves**. James Nelson puts it this way: "Any kind of true intimacy depends on the solid sense of identity of each of the partners. Otherwise a relationship becomes symbiotic, with one person becoming an extension of the other" (1988, p. 53). Differences in "solidity" of identity lead to differences in the ability to participate in intimacy. This is one of the reasons why the mutual comfort of intimacy, meaning its *equal* emotional balance and commitment, is so rare. Moreover, when we are mourning, it is not uncommon to wonder who we are *now*, in the aftermath of loss. Grieving brings its own crisis of identity; we certainly feel less "solid" about ourselves than we likely do at other times in our lives. One of the tasks of mourning is to reestablish an intimate relationship with oneself.

In a paradoxical way, this is one of the reasons why, during mourning, it is important to rework one's relationship with the One who has died *and* to reestablish significant intimate relationships with Others who are living. What Stephanie Dowrick says about *risks* of the emotional dynamics of intimacy becomes more significant as we mourn. She says: "In intimacy you risk being **who you are**, and risk facing who the other person is **in their entirety**—not just in those parts which are socially acceptable or 'useful' to you" (1991, p. 196). That is, Dowrick echoes Nelson's observation that, in order to be intimate, each partner in the relationship must have developed a sense of "self" that they are willing to put forward—to "risk"—in being vulnerable to, dependent upon, emotionally open to, and less concerned about control with the Other. Yet when we are mourning, our sense of ourselves is somewhat shaken; we can feel less sure of ourselves, less "solid" in Nelson's terms. Moreover, our sense of who we are is most likely experienced as who we are *not*—that is, we can find ourselves looking at ourselves and then at others and saying, "I am mourning—and *you* are not!" Certainly, during mourning we find others looking at us and saying to themselves, however tacitly, "I know you are mourning, and I'm glad I am not!" This is why Dowrick's comment that "what matters most in *the way you experience* *others is the way you experience your own self*" (1991, p. 186) takes on its own meaning during mourning. Our grief casts a shade over our attempts to reestablish intimacy both with ourselves and with others.

Moreover, there is a dimension to experienced intimacy that colors one's intimacy-seeking during mourning. This has to do with how the interaction of intimacy can alter one's sense of one's Self. Dowrick says that intimacy "is a matter of tuning into someone else's reality, and risking *being changed by that experience*" (1991, p. 183). She is speaking about one risk of intimacy that is always present. Yet, during mourning, that risk is heightened by the likelihood that one has experienced "too much" change already. One aspect of mourning is the wish to have things be as they were before the loss. When loss destabilizes our sense of ourselves (in Nelson's terms, "de-solidifies" our sense of ourselves), the prospect of further change can feel to the mourner as more threat than comfort. The potential comfort of intimacy will be weighed against the possibility that that intimacy will be its own source of change in one's life.

Of course, the ways in which in intimacy we mutually act as "mirrors" for ourselves and to others means that the benefits of intimacy are likely to outweigh the risks. By (re)establishing intimate relationships with others during mourning, we can better get to know who we are *now*. If in that process, our sense of ourselves is changed, then intimacy becomes a key aspect of our post-loss adaptation. The altered sense we achieve of ourselves, and receive from an intimate relationship with an Other, helps us not only to live into our post-loss life but also to rework and appropriately adjust our relationship with the One we are mourning. In other words, improved capacity for intimacy in one aspect of the triad of relationships we experience during mourning has the impact of positively altering the other two aspects as well.

As a psychotherapist, Bromberg ratifies this understanding that our significant relationships change us. He says that this occurs quite literally through the psychotherapeutic dyad, which brings about a "serendipitous rewiring" of our brains. And he adds that what occurs in the course of psychotherapy is also "what we hope for in a personal relationship" (2011, p. 136). Moreover, Bromberg appreciates that all of our relationships, but especially our intimate ones, have a life of their own. He cites Jessica Benjamin's concept of "thirdness," the "shared reality" of a relationship which "is what makes intersubjective meaning possible and what allows us to trust the process of knowing and being known" (Bromberg, 2011, p. 134). Benjamin's concept of "thirdness" articulates how it is that those who mourn alter, and continue to be altered by, the relationship they have with the One whom they mourn.

We understand from this that intimacy creates a unique form of intersubjectivity that breathes life into our relationships; each one has its own "horizons" of expectations and its own hopes for being deepened and perpetuated. This understanding helps us see that when an intimate relationship is lost, what is mourned is not only the *person* of the Other with whom it was sustained but also the *relationship* itself, its "thirdness," its irreplaceability, its uniqueness. Moreover, what has become lost to the one who survives is the Other's active reflections, the "mirror" before which, or the context within which, the mourner might have continued to know more about herself or himself. The self/other intersubjectivity in an intimate relationship has its own life—and thus can also suffer its own death, one that requires its own mourning.

During mourning, the survivor finds herself or himself bereft of the comfort of the intimate relationship that was. The vulnerability of it comes to feel like weakness. The openness of it comes to feel like exposure. And the willingness to cede control in it comes to feel like a helplessness, an inability to protect oneself. Add to these the disappointment and confusion that follow when a relationship that one had hoped would be timeless because it was intimate turns out to be finite, and one can appreciate the wound to intimacy experienced by those who mourn.

The path of mourning begins with these realizations, acknowledged or not, and the individual mourner experiences being thrown back upon self, *by* self. If the key to true intimacy is having established a consistent yet malleable sense of oneself, then the key to mourning is to reestablish this sense of self after loss. Mourning presents the dilemma of solitude vs. loneliness as the matrix upon which the mourner comes to know herself or himself again. As this is accomplished, those who mourn will be better able to reestablish a capacity for intimacy in their relationships with Others who are also living and to rework the significance of the intimacy experienced in the relationship with the One they are mourning.

SOLITUDE VS. LONELINESS

The distinction between solitude and loneliness becomes experientially significant as we mourn. We would say that **solitude is synonymous with one's capacity for intimacy with oneself**. Thus, one's capacity for solitude is the foundation for one's capacity for intimacy with others. Solitude is experienced as a calmness in one's inner core, a being at peace with oneself especially when one is alone, by oneself, but also when one is with others.

Here we are opposing loneliness and solitude as contrasting experiences of oneself when one is alone. Loneliness is experienced as a form of anxiety or worry—the opposite of the peacefulness that is solitude. Since neither solitude nor loneliness is an absolute, we can think of them as being the poles of a continuum: the greater one's capacity for solitude, the less one is discomfited by loneliness; the more one is distressed by being alone, the less one is likely to seek solitude and the more one is likely to feel isolated.

Our society, in general and through our families, does not readily teach us to be in solitude. It emphasizes togetherness, even as it stresses the importance of individuality and independence. Our culture often regards a capacity for solitude as an attitude of aloofness and being above it all, a sort of snobbery, a poor choice, a withdrawal from the world, form of a disengagement. Because of our culture's suspiciousness of solitude, as one seeks to develop a capacity for solitude, one can experience a kind of "push back" from others; they might even express feelings of having been rejected.

As Anthony Storr says, "contemporary Western culture makes the peace of solitude difficult to attain" (1988, p. 34). He points to society's ubiquitous noise and the multitudes of people, but we could also take note of the omnipresence of technology and the social pressures to be "networked." Our society expects connection, and places a high value on connectivity. When Dowrick tells us that "you and I share a drive toward connection" (1997, p. 135), what she means by "connection" has little to do with contemporary definitions of "connectivity." As measured, for example, by "friends" on Facebook, the latter has become a false substitute for the former.

Perhaps at no other time in our lives do we become more aware of the difference between connection and connectivity than when we are mourning. There is no more common feeling in grief than the fear of being alone or, in loss, of the fear of being singled out, all while one is aware of having been *dis*connected from others. In loss and grief one is distinguished by diminishment and identified by of what or of whom one is bereft. Especially in a gain-oriented society, loss becomes an isolating experience. Quite often others simply do not know how to respond to us. When we are mourning, we look for company yet we commonly do not feel that we fit in. In other words, we look to belong most at precisely the time when we feel least like we actually do belong. Our grief is often infused with the fear that, in fact, we have lost that which enabled us to belong. Mourning makes us acutely aware of our need of each other—in a culture that values our independence from each other and does not readily provide the means for our establishing new, interpersonal relationships.

Not only does our culture fail to appreciate and support the value of solitude, but it may actually contribute to the loneliness and isolation felt by many who mourn because it overvalues individuality. In his now classic *The Pursuit of Loneliness* (1970), Philip Slater made the case that "three human desires that are deeply and uniquely frustrated by American culture" (p. 5) are the desires for community, engagement and dependence. According to Slater, in lieu of community, we prefer competition; in lieu of engagement, we prefer avoidance and un-involvement; and in lieu of dependence, we prefer independence. The result is that, in American culture, "individualism finds its roots in the attempt to deny the reality and importance of human interdependence" (Slater, 1970, p. 26). No wonder the American who mourns feels both psychologically and socially displaced.

Slater subtitled his book "American Culture at the Breaking Point," hoping that it would in fact change for the better. One sad note is that this has not happened, and if anything, the trends he identified have been accelerated by technology. As contemporary a writer as Sherry Turkle, in *Alone Together* (2011), identifies the insidious ways our technology, and its effects upon our forms and patterns of communication, leads to less person-to-person interaction—and more isolation and loneliness.

It is important for us to take this into account when we speak about our capacities for intimacy and the repair of our intimate relationship during mourning because it helps us appreciate the degree to which those who mourn are swimming against the cultural stream. This concerns us here insofar as loneliness and a sense of isolation arise commonly in the aftermath of our losses. Our culture fails to prepare us for mourning. Our capacities for intimacy turn on our capacities for solitude, yet intimacy and solitude are themselves counterpoints to our culture's inculcation of isolation and loneliness.

If we are to turn loneliness into solitude and isolation into the reconnection of intimate relationships on which healthy mourning turns, Dowrick's insights are persuasive. She traces this connection between loneliness and isolation in a way that echoes in the experiences of the bereaved, saying, "At the core of loneliness often lies a fear of abandonment, usually experienced as a fear that the loneliness—the fear of *not being wanted by someone*, of not being recognized, or understood, or sought after, or appreciated—will go on forever" (1991, p. 160). She concludes: "And behind the fear of abandonment is something else: a lack of trust in your own self" (1991, p. 160). For those grieving the loss of both a person with whom they shared intimacy and of that relationship, the experience of having been abandoned, with all of its accompanying fears, arises. Often those who mourn add to their own distress by feeling that they themselves are to blame for feeling the way they do. This is why it is important to remember that our cultural predispositions contribute to making grief an experience of both interpersonal isolation and intrapersonal loneliness.

When we are grieving and threatened by loneliness, we become aware of how well or how poorly we have developed a capacity for solitude. Evelyn and James Whitehead write that "solitude helps us to befriend absence" (2010, p. 153); befriending absence would certainly ease our grief. If we can develop a capacity for solitude, then the loneliness of grief would be mitigated. Befriending the absence would counter our feelings of loneliness and isolation.

How might we go about this? Turning to Dowrick again, we emphasize: "Your capacity for solitude, for feeling comfortable with your own self, exists on a continuum with your capacity for intimacy—being in good contact with others" (1991, p. 135). In other words, she suggests that our capacity for solitude relates not to our autonomy *from* relationships but to our autonomy *in* relationships. She says, "I cannot be together with you unless I have some sense of my own separateness and autonomy. I can't be my own self with you if I am bound to you in dependency. When our togetherness enhances my life but my life does not depend on it—I can be together with you and still be myself" (1991, p. 140).

On the one hand, healthy solitude makes for healthy intimacy. On the other, the aloneness of mourning need not lead to loneliness; if aloneness leads to solitude, then mourning could itself become an opportunity for a greater capacity for intimacy.

In spite of our sociocultural mixed messages about independence and togetherness, we might have had experiences in our childhood that would benefit us in our mourning when we are faced with developing a capacity to be alone—without being anxious. Being able to live Dowrick's "continuum" of solitude and intimacy might entail our having internalized the possibility that we can be *taught* to be alone—but not when we are *left* alone. The psychologist Donald Winnicott observed children at play in the presence of a noninterfering and nonengaging mother. His conclusions are instructive. He identified this paradox: "It is only when alone (that is to say, in the presence of someone) that the infant can discover his personal life" (as cited in Storr, 1988, p. 20). That is, just as we need to be taught to be ourselves, we may also need to be taught to be alone, to be *by* ourselves—and to be comfortable, not anxious. Yet we do not learn this best when we are *left* alone, whether abandoned or simply ignored. Instead, both solitude and a sense of self are learned at the same time and in the same way—*with the appropriate, nonanxious attention of another*. As Dowrick summarizes, we learn to be "alone while someone else is present" (1991, p. 137). (The Whiteheads also cite Winnicott's observations of the developmental significance of our being "alone in the presence of another" and add that Winnicott called this a "holding environment" [2010, p. 155]).

If we are to come to a positive view of mourning, an attitude and expectation counter to our culture's, then we could begin by framing mourning as a "holding environment." It may be that bereavement professionals are the only ones who adopt this attitude, but perhaps a more sanguine perspective would encourage those who mourn to count other persons in their social network as present enough to mitigate their loneliness and encourage their development of a capacity for solitude. Of course, in our culture it is likely up to the initiative of individual mourners to form their own "holding environments." We would be helped to see that as one of the tasks of mourning, for it complements our coming to terms with our solitude.

For instance, validating Winnicott, Dowrick concludes that one's "solitude is likely because you have been comfortably alone with someone else" (1991, p. 137). To emphasize the point, as Storr does, "the capacity to be alone thus becomes linked with self-discovery and self-realization; with becoming aware of one's deepest needs, feelings, and impulses" (1988, p. 21). Perhaps in the very emotional rawness of grief we have an opportunity to develop deeper capacities for solitude—and thereby, for intimacy—if, on the one hand, we allow ourselves to become aware of our deepest needs, feelings, and impulses and if, on the other hand, we provide for ourselves a sufficient "holding environment" of others who are comfortable both with our grieving and with our being ourselves.

SEXUALITY, INTIMACY, AND GRIEF

In some ways, it is easier for us to talk about intimacy than it is to talk about sexuality. "Easier" because intimacy is a less overdetermined topic. Granted, intimacy and sexuality seem to have a lot in common. Both are subjectively defined. Yet, by the same token, intimacy and sexuality are often confused. Common parlance takes sex to be an "intimate" experience. As Dowrick puts it, "for many people, and especially for men, the idea of intimacy is virtually synonymous with sex" (1991, p. 253). On the other hand, we are also aware that sex can be an addiction—a compulsive act expressing no intimacy at all (see Schaeffer, 1997). In Dowrick's words, "sex is just one of many ways to get close—and to push away" (1991, p. 257).

Sexuality is about identity. It is a personal statement of who we *are*: "I am heterosexual," "I am homosexual," and "I am bisexual" being just three of what amounts to a spectrum of statements we might make. Sexuality is one significant claim we make about *who* we are. Using our sexuality, we define ourselves to ourselves and to others.

Sexuality is about behavior. We commonly speak of sexual *drive* or *instinct*—and how that drive is resolved or that instinct is acted upon. Who we are becomes how we act and why we behave as we do. Because sexuality concerns our relationship with ourselves as well as our relationships with others, sexuality is one aspect of the connection between solitude and intimacy. Dowrick says:

> Sex is one of the ways you can bring intimacy to solitude, loving yourself, feeling safe with your memories of being loved by others. Sex is one of the ways you can bring what you have learned through solitude (who I am; what I want) to your experiences of intimacy. (1991, p. 256)

Yet sex and intimacy can sometimes be mutually exclusive—and not just when sex becomes an addiction. There are other times when sexual behavior is not intended to carry implications of intimacy, such as in "hooking up" or similar "just sex" behaviors. And there are relationships wherein intimacy itself may prohibit or inhibit sexual expression. Friendship might be an example of the former—and marriage an example of the latter. Esther Perel (2007) notes that marriage often brings an increase in felt intimacy, accompanied by a decline in sexual activity. "Love seeks closeness," she says, "but desire needs distance" (2007, p. 19f). As a psychotherapist, she seeks to help couples "put the X back in sex."

The point is that sexuality and intimacy function as a grid upon which one can measure the meaning of one's relationships. Some are sexually intense but have little or no closeness or intimacy. Others are intimately intense but lack an explicit sexual component or behavior. This grid becomes its own explanation of our emotional confusion about sexuality and intimacy: when intimacy is sufficiently intense, the closeness itself can feel to carry with it a sexual aspect, whether this is enacted or not. Such is our general social confusion about the connection between intimacy and sexuality that sexual activity alone can be confused with intimacy and that intimacy alone can be confused with or perhaps infused by sexual feelings.

These distinctions carry a certain poignancy and pertinence when it comes to end-of-life care and grief. Much end-of-life care is intimate in name and nature. As we die, the boundaries of privacy and self-control, which we learned earlier in our lives, become difficult to maintain personally. So we rely upon others to do things with and for us that we now no longer can do by and for ourselves. All of the characteristics of intimacy come into play here: we are vulnerable, we are "open" and indeed exposed, and we lack control of our boundaries so we look to others to respect them and maintain them for us. In a word, dying challenges us to be comfortable with being dependent—and to make wise choices about whom to depend upon. Thus, in our dying, we trust to be provided with end-of-life care that is intimate without being sexual—especially when it is being provided by a professional caregiver and not someone with whom we have had a prior sexual relationship.

For those who mourn, the quest for comfort brings forward a range of experiences along the intimacy–sexuality spectrum. In the course of navigating the always unfamiliar and uncertain waters of grief, those who mourn face dilemmas of intimacy and sexuality particular to that time and their loss, and always in the wake of the absence/presence of the One they are mourning.

Stephanie Ericsson (1993) is one widow who has written with emotional clarity about her experience of mourning, intimacy, and sexuality. As do many widows, she came to the milestone question of what to do about her wedding ring:

> When is the right time to take off the ring? For months, I hung on to those rings, not only as a link to my husband, who I was still unready to let go of, but also for the protection of it. I now belonged to nobody. But I had once belonged to someone. This was an important combat I made against the abandonment I felt, and the isolation I was in. (1993, p. 128)

Wearing her wedding ring possibly provided protection against sexual advances, but it also kept out possibilities for intimacy. And it was intimacy as much as anything she felt ambivalent about. On the one hand, she wrote:

> What we once knew so intimately eludes us. We have a hard time remembering the face of the person who died, or the voice of the one who left us. We feel only an empty space next to us. At night, we face our beds, and crawl into the empty space, knowing our dreams will waft through us, and us through them. We ache for one more encounter with the one who is gone, even if it is only in our dreams. . . . Sleep will not be restful, for we no longer have a grip on what it is that we long for. We are in a seemingly perpetual state of longing, without knowing what for. (1993, pp. 140–141)

She added:

> It isn't that depression is so terrible. That I can deal with. It is the loneliness. I don't want to be with anyone and I don't want to be alone. When I have a date around he takes up space. Sure, the loneliness is gone for a while, tucked away, but the space around me is crowded. It isn't a fair trade-off. (1993, p. 141)

This seems to be a necessary dilemma—necessary to continuing to live, to coming back to life, perhaps necessary to being alive. Ericsson puts the intimacy/sexuality dilemma of mourning into its most basic terms: those of touch. She writes:

> The body needs to be touched. It is as fundamental as food, air, warmth. Yet, when sucked into the whirlpool of grief, touch can burn instead of comfort. How strange that we retract so fast from the very touch that can heal us. Yet even a gentle touch can upset the delicate, fragile adhesive that holds together a person touched by death. An embrace could throw us into the treacherous caldron of memories—times when it was there and times when we only yearned for it to be there. (1993, p. 161)

Ericsson comes to this conclusion:

> When there is the death of one, what happens to the other? What happens to the tapestry that was woven over experiences that were shared, points of view that had merged, and emotions that had been grown, year after year? One day we will take the emotional pain of death as seriously as we take physical pain of injury. (1993, p. 162)

Ericsson's husband died suddenly—and at a time when she was pregnant with their first child. She found herself immediately immersed in mourning. For those who provide end-of-life care, mourning begins with an awareness of the inverse relationship between intimacy and sexuality in end-of-life care. The sexual relationship, or what was known as the sexual relationship, is gradually diminished and often lost while the intimate relationship continues and perhaps even deepens. Loss of sexuality is very frequently mourned by both those dying and those providing for their care. But for those who survive, as for all those who mourn, how to experience and express their sexuality become important aspects of their grief. As they reawaken to themselves—or, more accurately, seek to become acquainted with the new selves they have become after loss—they face the challenges of becoming intimate again with others as well as with themselves. Taking comfort in solitude and enduring the ache of loneliness, they learn again, now, in a way appropriate for their post-loss self, who they are as sexual beings and how they are best to express themselves that way.

OUR WINDOWS ON THESE TOPICS

At Disneyland, there is ride of yellow submarines. Guests to the park can board and sit comfortably as the metal vessels slowly submerge, make their way around a track, and show a limited view of what is in the underwater world before the submarines slowly come back to the surface and passengers can disembark.

What follows is like that ride. The topics of intimacy, sexuality, and grief are each in themselves as vast as the oceans in depth and power. It would be impossible to explore each of them, let alone all of them together, in one short book. However, here we can gain significant views that, at the very least, suggest what the worlds of these waters hold. Each section is its own portal; each deserves more exploration and development; each in its own way tells us that there is more to intimacy, sexuality, and grief than we can completely say.

We have chosen to begin with two chapters on sexual orientation and grief. Because much in bereavement literature is written from and for a heterosexual perspective, we thought it might be a helpful departure to hear about the impact of loss upon people who are LGBT—lesbian, gay, bisexual, or transgendered. Ron Attrell speaks about death and grief in the LGBT community—highlighting the lingering impact of the AIDS epidemic. Linda Goldman reminds us that the very process of coming to make the self-affirmation of being LGBT entails its own losses and relational risks. Between them we begin to understand that whenever we think of loss only as a single event, we are likely going to misunderstand the degree to which an event of loss was both preceded by other losses and is framed in the context of contemporary losses. This is a view of intimacy, sexuality, and grief from another portal on our culture, a view that might help us appreciate what is at stake both in this part and in the whole.

The second section addresses four of the many challenges to the "restoration" of intimacy faced by those who mourn. Harold Ivan Smith concerns himself with recent developments in pharmacology, specifically how "erectile dysfunction" drugs have affected the bereavement arcs of men, and the women they would love, and the relationships between fathers (whose wives have died) and their children whose mothers have died). Dick Gilbert speaks an uncomfortable truth: not all parents were beloved by their children, nor were all children loved and treated kindly by their parents. One's emotional history with one's parents affects not only how one mourns their deaths but also how one establishes intimate relationships before, during, and after mourning. Darcy Harris's information concerns another seldom-acknowledged experience: infertility. She discusses the effects upon the intimacy and sexuality of couples who find that conceiving a child is not as "natural" as they might have expected but instead entails expenses and disciplines—and indignities—to suffer both individually and together. Not all of these "losses" are nameable, nor are they easily mourned. Men and women returning from war may also find themselves similarly dismayed by the impact of deployment and combat upon their sexual relationships and capacities for intimacy. Doug Harvey, himself a veteran and a chaplain, describes the toll our nation's conflicts in Iraq and Afghanistan have had on many soldiers and their families. As diverse as each of these four subjects are, they provide their own portals on relational dynamics in our families. If it is in our families that we learn how to be intimate and what it means to be sexual, then we can see, through each of these perspectives, that our families are frequently more cauldrons of emotions than crucibles for exemplary living and grieving well.

Section three offers three views into the effects of aging, illness, infirmity, and dying upon our capacities for intimacy and options for sexual expression. Sara Sanders and Joelle Osterhaus have researched the psychosocial impact of Alzheimer's disease and other dementias upon the persons who have them and upon those who would love them. Issues of identity, sexual and otherwise, arise. Dementia does impair one's capacity both to be intimate and to appreciate and receive offered intimacy. Since it goes without saying that the dynamics Sanders and Osterhaus describe are becoming increasingly common, we would do well to encourage a wider, social adaptation, as Susan and John McFadden do in their book, *Aging Together* (2011).

In addition to dementia, aging can bring physical illness and other challenges to our intimacy and sexuality. It is precisely the "togetherness" issues of aging that Anne Katz addresses. Writing as an oncology nurse, Katz details the effects of specific illnesses upon both our capacities for intimacy and our desires for sex—and more, upon our sense of what "good sex" is. She aims to be both medical and practical. But she reminds us that aging is itself a matter of gradual losses and their mourning. This entails adjustments to who we are and how we think of ourselves and thus adjustments to our relationships with others and ourselves. The Whiteheads have written that "aging offers new invitations to solitude" (2010, pp. 159–160), but we are likely to experience this positively only if we see such physical changes as *invitations* to solitude and not condemnations to loneliness, on the one hand, and as additional opportunities to be intimate with others and not isolated from them, on the other. Unfortunately, many who experience illnesses related to aging find themselves more isolated than connected and more lonely than consoled by intimacy.

This debilitating and alienating experiences of aging may be what we take for granted, if so we may be surprised when we find that the dying and those who would care for them still desire intimacy—and sexual expression. Sherri Weisenfluh and Vicki Merrill, social workers from Hospice of the Bluegrass in Kentucky, present their research and findings with the hope that intimacy opportunities and sexuality issues might be better appreciated and addressed by those providing professional end-of-life care.

Finally, in the fourth section, we offer two chapters with religion's perspectives on intimacy and sexuality. Rabbi Daniel Roberts reminds us that our cultural understandings of sexuality and intimacy are based in the Torah, that is to say, are rooted in thousands of years of religious tradition. And Dave Daubert and

Bob Machamer encourage us to adapt our religious communities as to be more attentive to and caring for those who mourn. More actively and more personally than other kinds of contemporary communities, religious communities can provide the social support, interpersonal contacts, and spiritual grounding that can diminish isolation, mitigate loneliness, and reestablish the personal identity that has been shaken by loss. Although Daubert and Machemer do not use this term, what they are proposing is that religious communities could provide "holding environments" already in place for those who mourn—if they would claim this as part of their purpose and identity.

RESURFACING TO SPIRITUALITY

It is fitting to end in the field of religion because many still seek the counsel of their faith and the consolation of their deepest beliefs when they feel lost during mourning, whether they identify themselves as religious or not. Like dying, mourning *is* essentially a spiritual time, a period in our lives when we do turn inward in the hope of finding something to hang onto, something to keep us afloat, something with which to keep our heads above the flood of our feelings. The three topics we are entertaining are like three different kinds of light. Intimacy, sexuality, and grief overlap each other, and in the space where all three combine, there is a white light that marks what they have in common spiritually.

We can easily find terms that are more spiritual than *psychological* or *sociological* to describe what intimacy is: terms that tell how intimacy is not just about our emotional vulnerability but also about our human frailty and need of each other; not just about our willingness to be open and unguarded but also about our being "exposed" to each other—being "naked" of body, thought, and feeling; and not just about our limitations with what we can control but also about our fundamental desire to *surrender*, to let go, to let be—if we are to gain acceptance from others and serenity within ourselves. To switch metaphors, at their combined core, intimacy, sexuality, and grief are spiritual paths that intersect each other, indeed that intertwine as we journey through our lives.

Thus, all of the challenges of intimacy, sexuality, and grief have at their center *spiritual* choices—and even spiritual solutions. Henri Nouwen, in his book *Intimacy* (1969), names perhaps *the* fear central to all human relationships: "Many are asking themselves if we are doomed to remain strangers to each other" (p. 23). Acknowledging that he addressed his book to adolescents, he says, "today it more and more seems that the struggle for intimacy is not limited to a certain age group, but has become the struggle of modern man" (1969, p. 2).

Contemporary postmodern society not only interposes technology between persons, interfering and substituting for face-to-face relationships, but it also contributes to increasing the awkwardness we have with each other and with interpersonal relationships in general. Intimacy is more of a "struggle" now than it was when Nouwen was writing, and sexuality is now more likely to be divorced from intimacy than deepened by it.

As contemporary culture fragments, it provides fewer guidelines for emotional processes such as grief. Each of us is left increasingly to our own devices when it comes to intimacy and sexuality. In such a world, it is difficult to speak of repairing the fabric of relationships rent by loss, let alone the healing of emotional wounds. That is why, today, recovering spiritual language is just as important as acknowledging psychosocial dilemmas.

Intimacy, sexuality, and grief are all best addressed by affirming our commonality, our mutuality, and our interdependence. Regardless of what our culture tells us, regardless of what our fascination with technology teaches us, we *are* in this together. Our relationships and our relatedness do matter. If the meaning of mourning is basically that we have arrived through loss to a time in our lives when we can better appreciate our need of each other, then we can affirm that mourning might paradoxically be less about loss, than it is about *gain*. And we can take the opportunities of mourning to grow in intimacy, in sexuality, and most importantly, in love.

REFERENCES

Bromberg, P. M. (2011). *The shadow of the tsunami and the growth of the relational mind*. New York, NY: Routledge.

Dowrick, S. (1991). *Intimacy and solitude: Balancing closeness and independence*. New York, NY: W. W. Norton.

Ericsson, S. (1993). *Companion through the darkness: Inner dialogues on grief*. New York, NY: HarperCollins.

Fossum, M. A., & Mason, M. J. (1986). *Facing shame: Families in recovery*. New York, NY: W. W. Norton.

McFadden, S. H., & McFadden, J. T. (2011). *Aging together: Dementia, friendship & flourishing communities*. Baltimore, MD: Johns Hopkins University Press.

Nelson, J. (1988). *The intimate connection: Male sexuality, masculine spirituality*. Philadelphia, PA: Westminster Press.

Nouwen, H. J. M. (1969). *Intimacy*. Notre Dame, IN: Fides/Claretian.

Perel, E. (2007). *Mating in captivity: Unlocking erotic intelligence*. New York, NY: Harper.

Schaeffer, B. (1997). *Is it love or is it addiction?* Center City, MN: Hazelden.

Slater, P. (1970). *The pursuit of loneliness: American culture at the breaking point*. Boston, MA: Beacon.

Storr, A. (1988). *Solitude: A return to the self*. New York, NY: Free Press.

Sullivan, H. S. (1953). *The interpersonal theory of psychiatry*. New York, NY: W. W. Norton.

Turkle, S. (2011). *Alone together: Why we expect more from technology and less from each other*. New York, NY: Basic Books.

Whitehead, E. E., & Whitehead, J. D. (2010). *Transforming our painful emotions*. New York, NY: Orbis Books.

SECTION 1

Death, Grief, and Differences of Sexual Orientation

This starting point is significant. If we are not to remain societal "strangers to each other," then we must learn how the losses particular to our experiences shape who we are, how we see others as well as how others see us. In other words, this starting point is not just about the issues in each chapter but about how by embracing each other in our particular woundedness, we grow in our capacity for intimacy. This strengthens our ability to love, and lets love define and heal us. If loss, however it occurs, is a form of death, then any loss can leave us isolated, singled out. By embracing each other in our losses, we reverse this trend: if we can embrace loss, we can embrace life—and learn to love anew.

When it comes to the losses of LGBT people, a key element in their mourning has to do with whether those losses are socially "sanctioned"—and in what ways. "Sanctions" can express social approval and understanding; they can also express disapproval or rejection. The losses, intimacy-seeking, and sexual expressions of LGBT people remind all of us how *social* our relationships are. Society's reactions to these aspects of our lives tell us whether we "belong" or not, whether what we are feeling is likely to be validated or not, and whether we are likely to be understood and responded to accordingly or not. More important than whether our grief is "disenfranchised" or not is whether we are going to feel better integrated into our society—or more isolated and left to fend for ourselves. The sanctioning of LGBT sexuality, intimacy, and grief speaks to our social beliefs and, in spiritual terms, defines the parameters of our hospitality: whom we welcome and whom we do not. In other words, there are social as well as personal aspects to our being "embraced" as we grieve.

Both of our contributors speak well to the significance of loss, intimacy, and sexuality in the LGBT community. **Ronald L. Attrell, LCSW, CT, CIRT**, is a licensed therapist working on the west coast. He has been working in the grief and loss field for over 20 years, first as a licensed funeral director in Oregon, then as a psychotherapist. He has had a private practice since 2003, first in Connecticut and currently in California. In addition to specializing in LGBTQ issues, he works with the general population on all types of loss and grief, mood disorders, living with chronic illness or pain, codependency, couples therapy, concurrent disorders, and the integration of mind, emotion, body, and spirit. Ronald is certified in thanatology, a certified Imago Relationship Therapist, and a member of NASW, ADEC, LAGPA, AAPC, and CSCSW. He may be contacted at attrelllcsw@gmail.com.

Ronald is integrated in his own beliefs and values so that he is centered when serving as a guest in the story of another person. He knows the perils of these journeys, especially in the frequently "separated" voices of those who follow an other-than-heterosexual orientation.

Linda Goldman, LCPC, FT, NBCC, a licensed therapist based on the East Coast, is a remarkable woman who has never forgotten what it is to be a child or a teenager. She has worked in the field of children and grief and loss issues for over 30 years as a teacher, guidance counselor, and grief therapist. Her many books—those for parents, counselors, and teachers as well as those for children and teens—are among the most respected on these subjects. Her book *Coming Out, Coming In: Nurturing the Well-Being and Inclusion of Gay Youth in Mainstream Society* (2008), on teenagers and their struggle with sexual orientation and gender identity, will set the standard for our teens and those who walk with them.

Linda has also taught courses on working with gay youth at Johns Hopkins University, George Washington University, and the University of Maryland School of Social Work. Linda's website is www.childrensgrief.net, and she can be reached by e-mail at linda.goldman@verizon.net.

Together, Ronald and Linda contribute to our understanding of how our psychological development, through adolescence and adulthood, is shaped not only by loss but also by the responses and reactions of our wider society. This is true for all of us, of course, whether we are LGBT or not. But those whom our society negatively sanctions can teach us more about the importance of our social context than can those for whom social acceptance is more likely a matter of course.

CHAPTER 1

Death and Intimacy Issues in the LGBT Community: A Gay Perspective

Ronald L. Attrell

LGBT people must encounter death and intimacy in their lives as must their heterosexual counterparts. Do these encounters, however, hold some differences? This chapter is a brief, beginning exploration of the differences in these encounters and how consequent challenges to intimacy have an impact on gay people. Suggested differences concern:

- coping with their particular experience of disenfranchised grief,
- inadequate language to describe the loss or loss status,
- the absence of models for grieving,
- the lack of support due to one's identity as a LGBT,
- the history of multiple losses,
- relationship roles,
- the limited availability of professional or self-help support,
- repetitive assaults on the validity of same-sex intimacy, and
- being a closeted griever.

This chapter will examine these topics and point to areas needing further exploration.

First, a look at terminology. LGBT is an acronym for lesbian, gay, bisexual, and transgender. Some would delineate between gay and lesbian perspectives, as between male and female, but labels are more fluid today. Some lesbians prefer *gay*. Younger people often prefer *queer*, so LGBTQ. Others self-describe as bisexual. Transgender people may be gay or straight. This chapter references primarily gay men but holds the awareness that these issues are real for all sexual minorities.

GRIEF IS BLIND

I heard John sobbing and then entered the bedroom. He was lying on the bed next to his partner, who had just died. Cradling and rocking Sam in his arms, tears streaming down his face, John cried out, "No, you *can't* go. I love you so much. How can I get along without you?" As John continued rocking and caressing Sam's body, his cries and sobs quieted until he was gently telling Sam how much he loved him, would miss him, what wonderful times they had, and that he would see him again.

The magnetic intimacy between the two men was palpable. That and the raw, powerful emotions of grief and love etched the scene into my memory as a licensed funeral director. I recall it now as a licensed therapist, over 20 years later, and am transported back to witnessing a sacred intersection of physical and emotional intimacy with crushing grief. It was the same scene I had witnessed with heterosexual couples. How would John find his way back to being able to risk an intimate life with someone again?

Grief is blind. That is what I have observed over 35 years of working with people of all sexual identities, orientations, and relationships through death, sickness, grief, and mourning to rebuild their lives again. It is the experience of loss common among all people widely described in the literature from attachment theory (Bowlby, 1980) to research in grief and mourning (Freud, 1917; Lindemann, 1944; Neimeyer, 2001; Prigerson, Bierhals, Kasl, Reynolds, Shear, Day, et al., 1997; Worden, 2009). Various models of stages (Kübler-Ross, 1969), phases (Parkes, 1972; Sanders, 1989), processes (Rando, 1993; Stroebe & Schut in Doka, 2007, p. 91), or mourning tasks explore how grief presents and then how to cope with it in the mourning process. Using Worden's tasks-of-mourning model (2009, pp. 39–53), the journey is one of accepting the reality of the loss, processing the pain of the grief, adjusting to a world without the deceased, and finding an enduring connection to the deceased in the midst of embarking on a new life.

The experience of loss involves disruption of intimacy among relationships. The disruption is not only with the person who died but with others as well. Initially it feels that the bond with the beloved one is irretrievably broken. The griever gradually understands that there are still continuing bonds (Klass, Silverman, & Nickman, 1996; Stroebe, 2005), yet the enduring connection (Worden, 2009) needs to be adjusted to allow reengagement with life. Knowing which bonds need loosening, for not all bonds are helpful (Stroebe, 2005), can be painful and expands the list of losses. This presents the griever with the challenge of how to risk intimacy with new friends, or another spouse/partner or lover, all while being cognizant of the wrenching pain that occurs when the relationship ends. This challenge is common to all grieving people.

The general absence of social support for gay relationships (Driggs & Finn, 1990, p. 133) means the gay person encounters particular barriers to reestablishing intimacy with the surrounding world. The following composite vignettes from this writer's psychotherapy practice may help bring to life similarities and differences between gay and straight people as they encounter grief, with particular attention to the impact of their families upon their mourning.

Harry and Jim

Harry and Jim loved life and lived it to the fullest. Remodeling their home; gardening; singing in the city's men's chorus; traveling, including a vacation they loved in New Zealand; selling Tupperware; going to the movies; enjoying sex and a real heart-to-heart connection with each other—along with the usual ups and downs and daily challenges of any couple committed for a lifetime. They had a great circle of friends and enjoyed the support of their parents, who loved being part of their lives.

When Harry was diagnosed with a terminal illness in his forties, grief entered their lives in a new way. Like any couple, they made many adjustments: financial planning, wills, taking more time for each other, and planning trips sooner rather than later. Because Harry's illness was HIV/AIDS, other adjustments included how to continue being sexual so it was safe for both of them. Whatever adjustments became necessary, the couple was undergirded by the support and love of family and friends.

Because Harry and Jim were fully accepted by their friends and family, they were not cut off to deal with life's adversities in isolation. They had support throughout their 20 years together. In the months and years after Harry died, Jim could talk of his deep grief with his parents. They understood that Jim was feeling what they would experience when one of them dies. This parental support was uniquely valuable for Jim to adjust to Harry's death. The wider circle of support was also critical for Jim to believe he had a safe container to allow him to loosen connections to Harry, including letting go of pain as a connection, allowing him to find other enduring bonds to Harry. It kept Jim connected to Harry while also allowing him to feel safe to risk intimacy in going on and finding enjoyment in life again.

Susan and Ellen

Susan and Ellen's experience was not the same as Harry and Jim's. Although they felt they were soul mates and had friends' support, neither had family support. Susan's family was openly hostile to two women being a couple. Ellen came out to her family about 4 years into their committed relationship. Her parents listened but never talked about Ellen as a lesbian or about Ellen and Susan as a couple again.

During the 12th year of their relationship, Susan died unexpectedly at age 31. The families' responses only complicated Ellen's devastating grief. Susan's family saw her death as judgment from God for the women's homosexuality and blamed Ellen for "leading Susan astray." Ellen's family tried to be supportive but could not really equate her loss with losing a spouse. They expected Ellen to get over her "friend's" death and move on.

This lack of acceptance or full understanding denied Ellen the experience that her grief was as valid or as real as that of a heterosexual widow's. The family, the first line of support expected when a spouse/partner dies, was unavailable to Ellen. She not only lost her spouse, which is the only term that fully describes how Susan and Ellen thought of each another, but also lost that primal expectation of returning to family for succor when adversity strikes.

DISENFRANCHISED GRIEF INCLUDING INADEQUATE LANGUAGE

These vignettes exhibit the ameliorating or debilitating impact of supportive or rejective families and friends. Susan and Ellen's story demonstrates *disenfranchised grief* as defined by Doka: "grief that persons experience when they incur a loss that is not or cannot be openly acknowledged, publicly mourned, or socially supported" (1989, p. 4). In other words, Ellen's grief was not recognized, nor understood, nor given value by her family or culture.

The vignettes also expose the wider disenfranchisement that gay people encounter. Both Jim and Ellen were still faced with how to *name* their loss to others. What was their identity? Not widow, not widower; their spouse had not died. Without that status, they were often left trying to defend or explain the validity of their grief at work and in daily encounters. Shernoff states, "when a gay man's partner dies, his trauma is often exacerbated by the lack of mainstream culture's recognition of relationship, his loss, and his being a widower" (1997, p. 27).

This lack of appropriately descriptive terminology can surprise the griever who thinks of his partnership as a marriage and is shocked and dismayed to find others do not. "I'm so sorry your friend died" is often what is heard. Use of *friend* or *roommate* may be purposeful due to belief that gay relationships are not equal to heterosexual ones. Gay and lesbian relationships have typically been viewed in our current culture as caricatures of heterosexual relationships (Kaufman & Raphael, 1996, p. 187). Using *friend* is one way that the *sexuality* of a gay relationship is denied. It reflects the shame felt, not by the two people *in* the relationship but by those uncomfortable about it. Or using *friend* may be a vain attempt at kindness. Or it simply may arise out of a lack of understanding or acceptance of what a loving, intimate, sexual gay relationship entails. One of my clients related his sister telling him that "of course" two men are not capable of loving each other as a man loves a woman. Perhaps she had never read the story of King David and Jonathan in I and II Samuel in the Bible. Grieving Jonathan's death, David's lament includes "greatly beloved were you to me; your love to me was wonderful, passing the love of women" (II Samuel 1:26, New Revised Standard Version). The passion of David and Jonathan was so honored that it was recorded and the story retold for thousands of years. Few loves are so remembered (Piazza, 1997, p. 62).

Gay marriage confronts the caricature belief even further. This writer observes how difficult it is for many people who are comfortable with *partner* yet still stumble or omit using *spouse* or *husband* when the couple is legally married. Such invalidation of the relationship's actual status can be a stunning blow to the griever.

If you are a heterosexual man, imagine hearing someone say upon the death of your spouse, "I am so sorry your friend died." Immediate confusion. "My *friend*? Oh no, Mary was my *wife*." You are clear that the person does not understand the depth of your relationship or your loss. You automatically correct them.

For a gay man, the response may not be quite so simple. If he is sure the comment is a misunderstanding, the response may be just as automatic. If he knows it is deliberate, he may be stunned and faced with a choice: take on this battle or, in grief, decide it's one battle too many and let the assault stand. Even when not grieving, gay people may let *friend* stand or use it themselves due to the inadequacy of language allowed them. Disliking the business connotation of *partner*, feeling *lover* can carry a transient meaning without the depth of friendship, and unable to access the legal use of *spouse*, *friend* may be the preferred word even though it does not connote the full extent of the relationship.

The intimacy of relationships with friends, family, and coworkers is immediately degraded when a gay person, in the depths of grief, has to defend the validity of his love. He finds the camaraderie and bonds with those people are not as strong as he thought. Perhaps even worse, the cumulative effect of such invalidation, dependent upon the individual's ego strength, can even cause the griever to momentarily doubt the validity of his own grief and identity as a gay man (Walter, 2003, p. 29). This shreds intimacy with self when grief already provides moments of doubting one's sanity. The usual support that these societal relationships are expected to provide during grief is damaged or lost. Trust and connection are broken. The distance created isolates the person in his grief.

Difficulty in finding peer support or support groups is another barrier to the gay griever rebuilding his world. One gay widower, unable to find a support group, said, "You find yourself asking, 'If there's nothing for me, then where do I fit in? Why am I not a valued member of society?'" (Storey, 2005). Such breaking of intimate supports with resultant isolation places the gay griever at higher risk for developing complicated mourning or prolonged grief (Ingram, Jones, & Smith, 2001; Lamendola & Wells, 1991; Prigerson et al., 1997; Worden, 2009).

Other people certainly experience forms of disenfranchised grief. The difference for a gay spouse is that the death can reactivate emotions experienced when establishing one's gay identity (Walter, 2003, p. 29). The disenfranchisement activated around being a gay griever connects to the disenfranchisement of not being a fully embraced member of society as a gay man. For him, disenfranchised grief goes to the core of his personal identity. This goes beyond not having one's relationship validated due to not being married, which heterosexual couples may also experience. A gay person can be reminded that his break in connection with peers and family is due to *who he is*—or at least due to an integral part of his personhood.

Disenfranchisement can also appear in the workplace. One example is when appropriate policies are not in place to acknowledge the loss. The relationship between griever and employer is damaged when leave for a partner's death is not equal to spousal leave or may be nonexistent since it becomes equated with a friend's death. The gay griever may need to pull himself together to continue with work without time to regroup—unless taking unpaid leave—because his "spouse" has not died.

In *Heavenly Hurts* (Klein, 1998, p. 79), a gay man, Brad, says after his partner, Dan, has died, "when I got to my desk that first day, no one said anything." He relates he was afraid to be fully out at work since a friend was fired after it became known he was gay when his lover died. Brad noticed the loss of potential support from his coworkers. This is evidence to the gay griever and to heterosexual coworkers that his loss is not equal to theirs. He is not a full member of the group. The loss of identity with one's coworkers is another intimate societal connection broken. Klein writes of the importance of workplace acknowledgment: "The recognition that death is a part of life in the workplace as well as in the rest of the life of the mourner helps towards a healthy resolution of grief" (1998, p. 83). Without this, the mourning process is impeded, contributing to higher risk for complicated grief.

For gay parents, not having appropriate leave from work also has an impact upon their children. The time needed to help the family adjust to having a single parent is not available. It is much more difficult for the widower to immediately find childcare or household assistance than to build these supports during spousal leave. The same lack of time challenges gay parents when a child dies and one parent is not the legal father. Reworking and rebuilding family intimacy is always difficult after the death of a parent or child. Not having spousal leave only intensifies the challenge and, again, places the family at higher risk for prolonged grief.

Religions have also, sometimes, been used as a means of invalidation of intimacy between gay people. Bishop Desmond Tutu is quoted to have said of common attitudes toward homosexuals: "we spurn them, we shun them because we are all caught up in an acknowledged or a tacit homophobia and heterosexism" (as cited in Alexander & Preston, 1996, p. ix). Such religious exclusion becomes additionally harmful when it prevents gay people from accessing spiritual support during times of loss. Many people who have not lived closely to particular tenets of their religious traditions still expect and receive solace from these traditions in times of grief. Gay grievers, especially gay widowers, however, may find that their religious communities or local clergy will not reach out to them even in their grief. This disenfranchised grief can be experienced as a deeper loss beyond that of disapproval for being gay. Indeed, some Christian churches deny rejecting people for being gay but do reject them for living it out. The church may allow them to attend but disavow the legitimacy of grief over the death of a spouse or partner. Switzer (as cited in Nord, 1997, p. 93) notes that being unable to obtain active support from one's religious beliefs places grievers at high risk for complicated bereavement.

Just because people are hurt by their religious traditions does not mean they are willing to abandon them. The Rev. Dr. Mel White writes of his grief in the accidental death of his 14-year-old brother:

> We were devastated by his death. . . . When Denny died, I honestly believed it was my fault. I actually thought God was punishing me for my sick and sinful feelings toward other young men. Of course I knew it didn't work that way. I knew in my head that God was loving and forgiving, but I had trouble believing it in my heart. . . . I believed that because of my homosexual thoughts other people had to suffer. I saw my brother's death as the ultimate sign that God had taken his hand of blessing off my life. (Gold, 2008, pp. 19–20)

Although a believer, the griever was cut off from his spiritual supports to somehow make sense of this terrible loss. This making sense of the loss, meaning "reconstruction" (Neimeyer, 2001), and learning how to reshape one's "assumptive world" (Parkes, 1972) are both critical during the mourning process.

A gay person who has not been able to integrate his spirituality or connection to a religious tradition with his sexual identity remains impaired in developing true intimacy with himself or others. Dr. John McNeill, a gay Jesuit priest, states, "to have a stable, healthy relationship, one needs to have a healthy self-love and acceptance, which is psychologically possible only when one can accept one's sexuality as morally good and . . . compatible with God's love" (1987, p. 245). Religious traditions initiate the struggle when they teach shame for gay identity or behavior. This struggle becomes an additional barrier to the intimacy needed by gay couples in coping with life-changing illness or by gay widowers in trying to reshape their world into one that permits the reentry of intimacy. "This is tragic because an active spiritual life is of great benefit in maintaining intimate relationships. We believe that being close to others often requires spiritual discipline and guidance" (Driggs & Finn, 1990, p. 62).

I observed the benefit of such an active spiritual life for a couple within their Episcopal church. The two lived an integrated life as gay men and as a couple in their careers, families, friends, and spiritual community. Life was full and good and they were approaching their 10th anniversary when one became

HIV+ and developed AIDS. They sought and received spiritual, emotional, and practical support from their priest and parish as they dealt with disappointments, anger, and fears. Rather than being driven apart, the couple worked through it all to become much more intimate and caring with one another. It was amazing to behold. They said they would not have made it without being able being able to access their spiritual beliefs and live these out within a community who embraced them as a gay couple. The symbols and familiar liturgies enveloped them. This spiritual intimacy continued to support the widower as he tried to make meaning of his husband's illness and death, became sick himself, and still found ways to reengage with his changed life until his own death. His spiritual community cared for him all the way through to laying his urn to rest next to his partner's.

Klein (1998, p. 151) also mentions a gay couple who used their spiritual beliefs to nurture them as a couple. These beliefs grew to become a continuing bond following the lover's death when the widower related seeing the Bible open to a passage that had been meaningful to them.

As shown above, some organized religions are now affirming gay people. Gay people are reclaiming spirituality in ways that speak to them, finding integration between their sexuality and spirituality (Glaser, 1994). This can foster deepened intimacy with self and others and can facilitate healthy mourning when losses come.

IMPACT TO INTIMACY FROM MULTIPLE LOSSES

In the early days of the AIDS epidemic, from the mid-1980s through the 1990s, many gay men entered the nightmare of multiple deaths. Even if it was not your lover or partner, marriage not even being an option at that time, it was multiple friends or friends of friends. One 1998 study of gay and bisexual men found that within a mean period of 7.87 years, 53% of participants reported up to 6 deaths, 24% reported up to 24 deaths, and 20% reported from 25 to 200 deaths (Oram, Bartholomew, & Landolt, 2004, p. 65). Jason, a friend of mine, reported that he stopped counting after he had crossed out from his address book the names of 100 friends who had died!

The assault on one's ability to risk being emotionally intimate after such mind-numbing loss can be overwhelming. Kastenbaum (1977) wrote of bereavement overload, when so many of one's peers die that mourning for each is incomplete before the next death comes. This loss experience for gay men has been described as AIDS-related multiple loss syndrome by Klein (1998). Nord (1997) wrote of the special trauma and challenges to adjustment that gay men face after multiple AIDS-related losses as existing "in a season of perpetual fall" (1997, p. xx). Mourning became an unending state. Clients and acquaintances of mine told me they stopped going to funerals because they could not stand the retriggered intense grief.

Author Chris Glaser, a graduate of Yale Divinity School, writes, "What saddens me most is that I cannot feel for each friend as deeply as if the death were an isolated event" (Glaser, 1994). The numbness of unending mourning protects but also deadens one's ability to feel. Paul Monette, a prolific writer who was gay, wrote about grieving the death of his second lover: "I understand that a second grief is marked by deafening silence rather than keening, the ashy taste of anticlimax" (1992, p. 27). This deadening brings its own layer of sadness, sadness about the inability to feel as deeply as before or to feel a fresh grief for each person, and requires its own mourning. Odets and Schwartzberg (as cited in Perreault, 2007) also wrote of this grief overload for gay men as well as for those living with HIV. Amidst such devastation, they suggest that it caused these men to question their identity and fundamental values (as cited in Perreault, 2007, p. 42).

In those days before antiviral treatments, an HIV/AIDS diagnosis was hopeless. Survivors thought the end was near and so could not hope for intimacy again; rather, they resigned themselves to life without it. The focus soon became to be reunited with one's deceased lover/partner or friends. This resignation to living without intimacy was seen previously in elderly widowers and widows but not in men in their thirties and forties. Monette wrote of his own experience: "What they don't seem to understand is, I used up all my optimism keeping my friend alive. Now that he's gone, the cup of my own health is neither half full nor half empty. Just half" (1988, p. 1). His experience reminds us that just as for any heterosexual widower or widow, sometimes the block to rebuilding connections to others is just the terrible aloneness. Monette writes: "trying to stay under the Dalmane. Putting off as long as I could the desolate waking to life alone—this calamity that is all mine, that will not end till I do" (1988, p. 342).

In those early years of the epidemic, through ignorance and prejudice, AIDS became identified with gay men. It became commonly thought of as the gay disease (Storey, 2005). Some even announced from pulpits that AIDS was a sign of God's condemnation of homosexuals. Many people still make this identification. Threads of intimacy are broken when one is singled out from the general population and then blamed and shamed for that separation. Becoming "the other" adds another layer of loss for gay men to process. Even if a gay man does not personally know anyone who is sick or has died, he knows he is part of "that group." Men still in the closet experience this too. Yet their hiding in fear brings the further loss of disconnection from coworkers, family, and friends.

Today HIV/AIDS is no longer associated solely with gay men. Multiple deaths of peers within a year are no longer the norm. Survivors of that period, however, still carry the wounds of multiple losses and the impact on how intimate relationships are formed. Monette wrote of this struggle: "And I know better than anyone what I wrestled from the darkness of my dead self: three times I've managed to love another man. My white-knuckle grip on happiness, hoarded against the gloating of my enemies, against the genocide by indifference that has buried alive a generation of my brothers" (1992, p. 172).

As Jim, another gay man, talks of his path to reconnection to the world, he mentions work making the biggest difference and that self-pity about staying in the past goes nowhere. What is central to Jim's successful reengagement is how he has reframed his world. Jim believes he lost the person but that the love continues: "It's that life-source—that spark—it's that connection that was there. It's what worked, that spark of life. . . . That ability to see past the pain, to see past the horrible loss, and to carry that spark with you is what I do now. . . . I do feel strong and capable of doing anything" (Walter, 2003, pp. 140–141).

Such experiences intersect with my work as a psychotherapist. I have seen gay widowers encounter the same roller coaster of grief and mourning on their path to reengagement with intimate connections as their straight counterparts do. Sometimes, they live on as witness to those who died: "For I am the final gleam of Roger and Stephen as well, the two men I am surest of, who willed their stories to me" (Monette, 1992, p. 4).

IMPACT ON SEXUAL AND RELATIONSHIP INTIMACY

Cancer, chronic pain, loss of limbs, paralysis, and HIV/AIDS (now with a prognosis in this country of living with HIV/AIDS as an ongoing battle) all bring challenges to intimacy and sex within any relationship, gay or straight. Loss of interest in sex or ability to function or embarrassment of the change in one's physical appearance can cause avoidance of physical contact. For the partner/spouse who is not ill, fear of causing more pain, decrease in attraction because of the effects of illness, and discomfort being around illness can block touching or being sexual. Both may find being with each other brings the reality of approaching death too close and so avoid each other to prevent "going there." A predominant relational "enjoyment affect" is crucial in maintaining connection in a relationship (Kaufman & Raphael, 1996, p. 195). Enjoyment is sorely tested when illness strikes. Cords of attachment may also be severely stretched. Financial stress may occur from treatment cost or loss of income. This calls for intentionality to keep joy and attachment present so the couple stays connected in the midst of pain and loss.

When the diagnosis is HIV/AIDS, or other diseases communicable by intimate or sexual contact, the challenge to intimacy is even more complex. Fear and shame can both become blocks to intimacy. Fear of transmitting the disease, fear of becoming infected, and fear of increasing the virility of the disease are concerns. The couple questions how to have sex and remain safe for both partners/spouses. For some, whether even to have sex is the first question. Shame can have multiple layers: shame for having the illness, or of the mode of becoming infected, or for transmitting it to one's partner. Of course, anger towards one's partner can occur for having the illness, for how he became infected, or for transmitting it.

Fear, shame, and anger can raise serious barriers to work through before desire for intimacy returns. And there is additional pain if this is not possible.

Tension between desire for sexual intimacy and fear of contracting illness, however, can provide gay or straight couples an opportunity to become more creative. It invites exploring new ways of being sexually intimate while keeping it safe. This can also broaden physical intimacy to increased use of sensuality without always needing to end in physical orgasm. Couples may grow to use all of the senses and the body to experience physical, emotional, and spiritual connection with one another. Coping with illness can actually lead to deeper levels of intimacy and connection. Fear, beginning as a barrier, can be transformed into feeling safe with one another as additional avenues of expression are found. It can be transformed into the assurance that "I will not be abandoned by my reality." The couple can be drawn into deeper levels of physical and emotional pleasure as well as a deeper bond so that the relationship is strengthened rather than diminished.

For gay couples, the developmental state of how "out" the individual or couple is also has an impact upon how fear and shame may present (Kaufman & Raphael, 1996, p. 105). Unrecognized, residual internalized homophobia may become reactivated and need to be addressed. If the illness is HIV/AIDS, it can upset the balance the couple has established around how open they are about being gay or a couple. Potential supports are automatically limited when either or both are closeted (Oram et al., 2004, p. 68). The one who is ill may want to come out, but the other partner may not be ready. Or the other partner may want to come out for increased support, while the diagnosis may have only increased his partner's fear and shame, causing him to retreat further into the closet.

If how the illness was contracted has broken relationship agreements, then anger and betrayal may also be challenges to intimacy. If both are ill, their own grief may make them less available to the other for support and may fracture the intimate connection both need. Processing all of these fears is a major challenge. Open communication is a must and can remind each partner that he is not alone in dealing with these challenges (McWhirter & Mattison, 1984, p. 119).

HIV/AIDS is now present in the wider culture, yet, for many, the diagnosis still carries shame. Whether rational or not, as mentioned earlier, shame for just having the disease can be a block to seeking emotional support. Old cultural messages that diseases are "dirty" can lead one or both of the partners/spouses to shame. For the ill person, shame over loss of control over one's body can be an unnoticed shame (DeFord, 2010). Men are conditioned to be in control. For many, it is evidence of being a man. One's self-image as a sexual being may be lost or inaccessible when control over basic bodily functions is intermittent. Embarrassment about odors, loss of mastery over one's body, and loss of privacy may all trigger shame (DeFord, 2010). This body shame disrupts the relationship with oneself if, as DeFord suggests, the most "primordial" of our relationships is the one with our own body. Our current culture has an extreme emphasis on physical attractiveness. This is often particularly true for gay males. It can be very difficult for a man to believe that his spouse/partner still wants to be physically intimate or finds him attractive emotionally and physically when he is caught in shame about the drastic change in his physical appearance. Loss of stunning beauty may need its own mourning. Growing to accept one's body amidst whatever illness strikes is necessary to continue or rebuild intimacy for the couple. Without this, there remains a broken connection, deepening the sense of isolation and "otherness" for having the illness or for how it has changed one's body.

For men, and therefore gay men, having sex is often the way of attempting to communicate emotion or feel connected. When sex is not an option or is being avoided, other means of connecting may be unknown or unfamiliar. Men often confuse sex and intimacy. They may not know that true intimacy also includes difficult conversations (Driggs & Finn, 1990, p. 67). This means addressing the grief that is present and not just having sex to deny it or try to make it all okay. Without this skill at conversation, partners/spouses will be isolated from one another in dealing with the impact of illness or grieving another family member's or friend's death. A male couple may receive a double dose of the culture's "manliness" messages: men don't cry and don't show emotions except anger and aggression. Arguments may erupt without adequate tools for communicating the feelings fueling the anger. Sadness, shame, confusion, fear, and anger have no place to go. Again, intimacy between spouses/partners is broken when it is sorely needed. Feeling trapped, sexual release and comfort may be sought outside of the relationship without commitment to learning truly intimate communication.

Gay men may also, however, have some advantages over their heterosexual counterparts in dealing with this dilemma. One of these can be freedom from traditional sexual and emotional roles (Driggs & Finn, 1990, p. 127). Gay people often bend and blend stereotypic male and female thinking patterns, emotions, and behaviors as part of their development (McWhirter & Mattison, 1984, pp. 49–50). In society, this can be a lightning rod for fearing, rejecting, and harming gay people. At home, however, it allows gay men more flexibility in relating to one another. They may have broken free from the "real men" straitjacket. They discover they can use their full range of emotions and not lose their manhood. It means that talking about what is going on with each other, rather than just acting it out sexually, is already part of their repertoire. When illness hits, they have other avenues to remain intimate, work through fears, and actually deepen their connection.

Another advantage can come from gay people's bicultural socialization and intragender empathy as defined by Driggs and Finn (1990, p. 128). The first, bicultural socialization, is learning to function in both gay and heterosexual cultures so one can discover freedom from behaving just one way. When routines or household tasks need to be adjusted due to illness, gay people are not restricted by "only women do that" or "men have to do this." With role flexibility, they more easily move into whatever task is necessary without shame or needing to get someone from outside the household to help. Taking on cleaning, laundry, cooking, or whatever the partner/spouse can no longer do, can, again, increase connection between the couple rather than create resentment or anger and distance. The second, intragender empathy, has to do with two people of the same sex finding it easier to understand each other's needs, desires, and longings. This can also make it easier for a gay couple to grow in emotional and physical intimacy. Couples who have nurtured this complementariness (McWhirter & Mattison, 1984, p. 49) can aid connection when grief and loss challenge it.

GRIEF'S OTHER APPEARANCES

Today some gay people are becoming more valued and accepted, while others still feel themselves living in a culture of disapproval and discrimination. This brings an ongoing, generalized sense of disconnection from others. It breaks the bond of security necessary for daily living and engenders a grief response.

The pain and loss of living with disapproval or shame keeps one in unresolved grief. Grief is regularly retriggered with no perceived option or ability to move through this to a life without the ongoing shame and unremitting pain. Such a pattern provides an experience very similar to living with multiple losses. With no end to mourning in sight, traumatic grief symptoms may emerge. Traumatic grief carries higher risk for suicidal ideation and long-term dysfunction (Latham & Prigerson, 2004; Prigerson et al., 1997).

The cluster of recent suicides among gay youth exemplifies this broken intimacy with peers and the general culture. It reflects the hopelessness that can occur when one is frozen in mourning. In an online commentary, Rev. Cody J. Sanders wrote:

> These suicides are not acts of "escape," or a "cop-out" from facing life. When LGBT people resort to suicide, they are responding to far more than the pain of a few individual insults or humiliating occurrences. When LGBT people commit suicide it is an extreme act of resistance to an oppressive and unjust reality in which every LGBT person is always and everywhere at risk of becoming the target of violence solely because of sexual orientation or gender identity. They are acts of resistance *to a perceived reality in which a lifetime of violence and abuse seems utterly unavoidable.* (2010, author's emphasis added)

A sense of community and belonging provides an intimacy of safety that allows us to thrive as we trust others will accept and not harm us. This contract of social intimacy is shattered when teens, or adults, *cannot* trust their community to keep them safe. They may then become caught in a perceived reality that such safety is impossible. The loss of living with this safety can lead to grief that is overwhelming and enduring.

A sense of overwhelming loss is often temporarily present during grief. This becomes particularly complicated for gay grievers, however, when they hear of a LGBTQ person being murdered or dying by suicide because of being gay. They not only grieve that one individual but are reminded that their own personal safety is at risk because of *who they are*. That safe, intimate connection of being one of the pack, whether real in one's experience or a necessary defensive illusion, is broken. A gay couple, or dating teenagers, are jolted back to the reality that simply holding hands in public carries the risk of violence and death. Living in such an atmosphere is an ongoing barrier to natural expressions of affection that nurture relationships. It interrupts romantic intimacy. Needing to remember to ignore the impulse to hold hands or give a quick kiss can become a protective habit (Driggs & Finn, 1990, p. 13).

This protective mechanism becomes part of unconscious behavior, remaining active even when it is not needed. It carries over into the home, so intimacy is decreased even there. Spontaneous emotional expressions are particularly important when trying to maintain or rekindle intimacy in long-term relationships, when living with chronic illness, or when grieving. Witnessing or hearing of violent deaths due to being gay is a reminder of danger. The resultant fear is a recurrent barrier for couples or individuals to break through in trying to build safety and trust. It is a challenge to again risk expressions of fondness and love, knowing the risks. For some teens and adults, it is too great a challenge. Rebuilding a generalized sense of emotional and literal physical safety is crucial for individuals and couples. It is an ongoing process for gay people living in a culture where gay bashing and humiliation are personal reminders of one's own vulnerability.

CLINICAL IMPLICATIONS

In the current culture, the mourning task of making sense of the loss and restoring a sense of safety to allow reengagement is one that gay people must work through again and again. A gay man needs to be assessed not only for any presenting loss but also for past losses and violent experiences. The client's generalized sense of safety and well-being while living in the world as a gay person also needs assessment. This may present more as anxiety than grief. Living with such a sense of threat or danger after witnessing, experiencing, or hearing about violent or humiliating events because of one's sexual identity or orientation can elicit traumatic symptoms. Diagnostically, post-traumatic stress disorder with hypervigilance, increased irritability, and a sense of a foreshortened future, or acute stress disorder, with a subjective sense of numbing, detachment or absence of emotional responsiveness, and increased anxiety (APA, pp. 424–432) may present. Clinicians need to assess for such symptoms that may be masked by grief or that may be an underlying block to couples or individuals having difficulty trusting or reestablishing intimacy.

Teenagers

For LGBTQ teenagers, clinicians need an empathetic understanding of the special challenges to their developmental phase of building a safe, intimate connection with the world. Both straight and gay teens have a sense of invincibility as part of growing power and independence. For LGBTQ teens, this invincibility may be prematurely punctured by experiencing or hearing of gay bashing or murder. These gay teen grievers will need both clinical and practical assistance to make their immediate world free from physical or emotional bullying. They then need help in processing their grief from living in a world where discrimination solely because of sexual orientation is still a reality. This help will include shifting the perceived reality of unremitting physical violence to a more normalized belief that danger is in the world but one is usually safe. As in any grief work, this may include a total restructuring of the teen's assumptive world.

Rebuilding emotionally safe intimacy demands the clinician be fully comfortable with and embracing of LGBTQ people as a normal part of the human sexual continuum. LGBTQ teens, or prepubescent kids, today experience their growing awareness of to whom they are romantically and sexually attracted just as do their heterosexual counterparts. Self-report demonstrates this repeatedly. There are many such stories. Excerpts from four of those told in *Crisis* express this well:

> The Rev. Dr. Mel White writes of being at a Boy Scout Jamboree when "I experienced my first 'crush' on my tent-mate, Darryl, another thirteen-year-old. While all the other boys were whispering about their girlfriends, I was hopelessly infatuated with a boy." (Gold, 2008, p. 26)
>
> Neil Giuliano writes, "He was riding a lime green Sting-Ray bicycle. . . . I knew who he was but seeing him this time was different—I sensed something going on inside me. Just an inner stirring I had never felt before. . . . At thirteen or fourteen, he was older, and I remember looking at his shoulders and arms; I was fascinated. There was something about him drawing me in, and I wanted to be closer to him. That was when I first started noticing my attraction to guys. I was around ten years old." (Gold, 2008, p. 206)

The difference for LGBTQ kids is that their own awareness is usually challenged rather than automatically accepted *without question*, as is the experience of heterosexual kids, or they lose the experience of dating. Two self-reports describe this experience:

> Julia Brindisi writes, "I hadn't even been aware of what the word *gay* meant until seventh grade. Oddly, I never told anyone outright, mostly because I didn't think my thoughts about kissing other girls deviated from societal norms. I didn't even realize I'd have to 'come out.' . . . I just remember arriving home from school one day and being confronted by my mother with a letter I had thrown in the trash; in it, I had written to my boyfriend that I was bisexual. After that, communication ended and mistrust

> set in. I heard a lot of 'it's just a phase' and 'you're doing it for attention.'" (Gold, 2008, pp. 254–255)

> Tony Meyer writes, "My parents may have been okay with me being gay, but they would not let me date. We fought about it constantly. First they said I could date when I turned seventeen; once I was seventeen, they thought college would be a better time. . . . The way my dad put it was he didn't mind my *being* gay; he just didn't want me *living* gay—and risking my safety—while in high school. . . . No matter what I said I could not calm that fear." (Gold, 2008, p. 249)

Such questioning immediately implies that LGBTQ kids cannot trust their own feelings and drives like straight kids can. The message communicated is that they are deficient or not as able to understand themselves. Self-esteem is attacked and shame begins building. When parents seem accepting but cannot let the teenager begin the developmentally appropriate and important experience of dating, shame and fear can still occur. Shame can build from being singled out, not trusted or apparently not able to cope with life. Fear that one is unable to establish a sense of safety in the world may also be the internalized message. The clinician needs to hold in awareness the impact of these messages on one's identity formation.

Teens may present as sad, angry, confused, ashamed, or grieving about their same-sex attraction. Assess for the origination of these feelings and thoughts: are they truly from the teen's own internal uncertainty or are they from conflict between what the teen has been taught and what he or she is naturally feeling? Whichever is present, the teen requires a clinician who can work comfortably with the questioning and process while fully embracing whatever affectional or sexual orientation or gender identity is being discovered and expressed. The National Mental Health Association's website states, quoting a 1998 article by Norton and Vare: "Gay and lesbian teens are at high risk because 'their distress is a direct result of the hatred and prejudice that surround them,' not because of their inherently gay or lesbian identity orientation" (n.d.). One 21-year-old writes:

> I'm so tired of reading about the doomed gay teenager. Hopelessness is not tied to sexual orientation. It's tied to a lack of acceptance and a lack of visibility. I wasn't depressed because I was gay; I was fine with being gay. I just didn't understand why people were being so mean. . . . As a little kid, I didn't have the vocabulary to describe my feelings. But in middle school, when I did start realizing I was attracted to guys, the words I heard in the halls told me it was unacceptable to feel the way I did. Once I understood this, I got scared. I realized I couldn't let anyone know. (Gold, 2008, p. 232)

Grieving will be part of this process for LGBTQ teens. They will need to cope with adjusting their own or family expectations. Although attitudes are changing, they will still have losses from living in a culture where homophobia is present. Depending on their experiences, they will need assistance to rebuild trust and safety with emotional intimacy in a world that can be dangerous. Gay teens grieving the death of a family member or friend bring a constellation of identity or life milieu factors for a clinician consider. If the clinician is unable to trust the LGBTQ teen's internal romantic/affection and sexual identity compass as part of this work, then referral is essential for the client's wellbeing.

Adults

Adult gay grievers need the usual grief assessment but also a careful exploration of their particular life experience as a gay person and how it impacts their grief. A death due to sexual orientation, whether purposeful or by societal neglect or passive discrimination, may shatter the pseudo intimacy and safety the adult thought he had established with the world. Again, grief work will need to address the shattering of a "safe" world, just as one might provide when a spouse is diagnosed with cancer or killed in an accident. The difference for the gay adult, however, is the shattering of safety to *be one's self*. This is different from something happening to you because of where you are or because an illness has attacked your body. The rupture is to the safety of intimacy with one's self in addition to others. Witnessing violence can also trigger unresolved internalized homophobia. Clinicians need to remain aware that rebuilding intimacy for LGBT grievers may need a wide approach before a new sense of safety can be found.

Closeted Grievers

When the surviving lover or partner is still in the closet, prolonged grief is more likely. Fear is often the overriding emotion complicating the grief: fear of being "discovered" as tears; decreased ability to eat, sleep, or concentrate at work or in family or social settings; increased irritability; and all of grief's symptomatology appear. Panic may start driving the urgent question of how to keep people from knowing what is going on. Assessment is crucial to help differentiate between normative fears and anxiety following a partner's or lover's death and the fear of being "outed." This assessment will also expose the client's fear and patterns of protecting from intimate emotional connection in many areas of his life. These blocks to intimacy prevent the griever from obtaining needed support.

Therapy includes assistance with maintenance of compartmentalization of the griever's life while focusing on grief work proceeding within these limitations. This allows the self's sense of security to remain intact and yet permit grieving. For the totally closeted man, the therapeutic relationship will become the one place where his grief can be witnessed and validated. It can be the safety valve for grief's full force that allows stable functioning in the rest of the world. It is also, however, the place where growth around intimacy is occurring as the client risks owning his sexuality and sexual orientation with the therapist. This is sometimes the first time such a client has verbalized this to anyone other than his deceased lover or partner. This witnessing may be all the support the client needs to proceed with mourning. He will remain closeted and return to his life successfully with intimacy blocks and protectors still intact. The therapist should also be available, however, for the grief work to open the door for the client to move toward increased intimacy with himself, with his sexuality, and with others in order to mourn adequately and adjust to life without the person he loved.

Partially Out or Out Grievers

Men who are out to some and not to others may present with some fear. They will also, however, reveal a struggle or desire to be more open in mourning and search for supports. A thorough bio-psycho-social assessment will help identify fears, shame, and protective patterns. Assessment will also reveal where the person is on the gay man's developmental path (Isensee, 1991, pp. 20–23). It will give insight into the level of integration in the griever's personal, professional, and social lives.

This can be used to help differentiate between grief anxiety due to his partner's/spouse's death from fear of risking more intimacy in his relationships. Would he like to be able to be more integrated? Is he ready to include that process as parallel to his grief work? If he is, focusing on grief work in the first sessions before going on to complicating factors is a valid approach (Worden, 2009, p. 156). This may also depend on where the client is in the mourning process. If the death has been recent, the primary work is certainly experiencing the pain and facing the reality. Establishing some sense of stability is indicated so that this strength is available to assist deeper work (Freud, 1917, p. 140).

Living with grief as a semi-closeted gay man is not always so orderly, however. The question posed above may well be stated at your intake session. I have worked with clients who made it through the funeral or memorial service by letting the relationship be seen as only that of a friend. The truth of the relationship as that of a lover or partner is ignored or denied. As weeks have proceeded, however, their grief symptoms are not in alignment with what others expect following the death of a friend. This becomes a trap of not knowing how to explain their grief. Parenthetically, grief over a friend's death is certainly another type of disenfranchisement, for both straight and gay people, which is addressed elsewhere in the literature (Folta & Deck, 1976; Smith, 1996, 2002).

This bind may well be the unconscious impetus for seeking therapy. If the client is ready to explore this, there can be a parallel process of grief work and self-growth. A linear progression from grief to self-growth is not likely. Work will interweave between the two. Focus may shift session to session, but there will be a continued thread toward a more complete integration of self. This opens increased intimacy with self while allowing and reaching for more authentic and intimate connections with others. Loosening of bonds with the deceased can be a metaphor of the griever releasing the "closeted self" and forging new bonds within oneself to allow engagement with a more integrated life just as the griever is forging different bonds with the deceased that allow movement into a full life without that person's physical presence. The client's work has achieved risking intimacy with self and with the wider world.

RECOMMENDATIONS

Given observation and anecdotal and self-report data, mourning outcomes with restored capacity for intimacy are generally more successful among gay widowers and other gay grievers when they have accepting and nurturing support systems. Data need to be gathered for statistical analysis to reveal if this conclusion is accurate. Markers could include validating support from family, friends, workplace, marriage or other legal recognition of the relationship, health-care, legal and funeral providers, and spiritual community. Measurements would compare these data to those of grievers without such supports.

Collection and publication of stories exhibiting gay couples, widowers, and single men coping successfully when grief enters their lives are needed. Such "primers" (Lindemann, 1944, p. 220) are necessary to help the gay griever see and incorporate new ways of thinking and behaving to reenter the world. Gay people need these visible role models from within their own community to internalize that mourning can lead to finding intimacy and joy in life again. Our general culture needs these models to continue to build awareness of their similarities in these struggles with gay grievers and to see barriers needing removal so that gay grief is no longer disenfranchised.

More support groups need to be developed where gay people are not just tolerated but fully welcomed. These group members will treat the gay person's grief as real and as valid as their own.

Another area needing statistical analysis could be the following hypothesis: **The atmosphere of discrimination and invalidation where physical violence against gay people is tolerated or encouraged precipitates symptoms of multiple loss syndrome and grief overload in gays who are grieving.** Whether traumatic grief is also a result of such an atmosphere could be included in the analysis or explored in a separate study.

The challenges to intimacy that death and other losses bring to gay people are daunting: questions of their sexual identity, a reexamination of what it means to be a gay in their culture, alienation because of their grief as well as for who they are, challenges to their identity as valid widowers, the reestablishment of emotional safety within society by working through grief from fear of violence because of sexual orientation, and aching for the touch of their beloved while unable to name the intimacy of their relationship for fear their closeted world of work or school and family will also explode. Yet the resilience of gay widowers and other gay grievers is also astounding. Increased competency is needed among mental health providers in understanding the sameness and the uniqueness for gay people as they encounter grief and mourning in our culture. Such competency would better help them as they assist with the rebuilding of connections so gay grievers may find their way back to intimacy without prolonged grief.

Lastly, grief therapists who are not comfortable with LGBT people should refer them out when they first mention being gay. It is not ethical to expect that one can focus on the grief work and not get into "the gay stuff." The emotional journey of grief will not be that easily controlled. It floods the entire system and needs someone who can sit comfortably, supportively, and with unconditional positive regard for the *whole* person. Grief does not heal when merely tolerated. It needs full expression and acceptance of its entire voice.

REFERENCES

Alexander, M., & Preston, J. (1996). *We were baptized too: Claiming God's grace for lesbians and gays*. Louisville, KY: Westminster John Knox Press.

American Psychiatric Association. (1994). *Diagnostic and statistical manual of mental disorders* (4th ed.). Washington, DC: Author.

Bowlby, J. (1980). *Attachment and loss. Vol. 3: Loss: Sadness and depression*. New York, NY: Basic Books.

DeFord, B. (2010, April). *Transforming shame: Understanding how stories heal*. PowerPoint/paper presented at Association for Death Education and Counseling 32nd Annual Conference, Kansas City, MO.

Doka, K. (Ed.). (1989). *Disenfranchised grief: Recognizing hidden sorrow*. Lexington, MA: Lexington Books.

Doka, K. (2007). Challenging the paradigm: New understandings of grief. In K. Doka (Ed.), *Living with grief: Before and after the death* (pp. 87–102). Washington, DC: Hospice Foundation of America.

Driggs, J. H., & Finn, S. E. (1990). *Intimacy between men*. New York, NY: Dutton.

Folta, J., & Deck, E. (1976). Grief, the funeral, and the friend. In V. Pine, A. Kutscher, D. Peretz, R. Slater, R. DeBellis, R. Volk, & D. Cherico (Eds.), *Acute grief and the funeral* (pp. 231–240). Springfield, IL: Charles C. Thomas.

Freud, S. (1917). Mourning and melancholia. In J. Rickman (Ed.), *A general selection from the works of Sigmund Freud* (pp. 124–140). Garden City, NY: Doubleday by permission of London: Hogarth Press.

Glaser, C. (1994). *The word is out: The Bible reclaimed for lesbians and gay men*. San Francisco, CA: Harper.

Gold, M. (Ed.). (2008). *Crisis*. Austin, TX: Greenleaf Book Group Press.

Ingram, K., Jones, D., & Smith, N. (2001). Adjustment among people who have experienced AIDS-related multiple loss: The role of unsupportive social, interactions, social support, and coping [Abstract]. *Omega: Journal of Death and Dying, 43(*4), 287.

Insennsee, R. (1991). *Growing up gay in a dysfunctional family*. New York, NY: Prentice-Hall.

Kastenbaum, R. (1977). *Death, society, and human experience*. Boston, MA: Pearson/Allyn and Bacon.

Kaufman, G., & Raphael, L. (1996). *Coming out of shame*. New York, NY: Doubleday.

Klass, D., Silverman, P., & Nickman, S. (Eds.). (1996). *Continuing bonds: New understandings of grief.* New York, NY: Routledge Taylor & Francis Group.

Klein, S. J. (1998). *Heavenly hurts: Surviving AIDS-related deaths and losses*. Amityville, NY: Baywood.

Kübler-Ross, E. (1969). *On death and dying*. New York, NY: Macmillan.

Lamendola, F., & Wells, M. (1991). Letting grief out of the closet. *RN Journal, 54*(5) (May), *23*(3). *General Reference Center Gold.* Gale Document Number: A10761882.

Latham, A., & Prigerson, H. (2004). Suicidality and bereavement: Complicated grief as psychiatric disorder presenting greatest risk for suicidality. *Suicide and Life-Threatening Behavior, 34*(4)Winter, 350. Abstract from *Health Reference Center Academic* [Web]. Gale Document Number: A126852193.

Lindemann, E. (1944). Symptomatology and management of acute grief. In R. Fulton (Ed.), *Death and identity* (Rev. ed., pp. 210–221, 1976). Bowie, MD: Charles Press.

McNeil, J. J. (1987). Homosexuality: Challenging the church to grow. *The Christian Century,* (March 11), 242–246.

McWhirter, D. P., & Mattison, A. M. (1984). *The male couple*. Englewood Cliffs, NJ: Prentice-Hall.

Monette, P. (1988). *Borrowed time: An AIDS memoir*. New York, NY: Harcourt Brace Jovanovich.

Monette, P. (1992). *Becoming a man: Half a life story*. New York, NY: Harcourt Brace Jovanovich.

Monette, P. (1994). *Last watch of the night*. New York, NY: Harcourt Brace Jovanovich.

National Mental Health Association. (n.d.). *Bullying and gay youth.* Retrieved from http://www.nmha.org/index.cfm?objectid=CA866DCF-1372-4D20-C8EB26EEB30B9982

Neimeyer, R. (Ed.). (2001). *Meaning reconstruction and the experience of loss*. Washington, DC: American Psychological Association.

New American Standard Bible (reference edition). (1971). I and II Samuel (pp. 420–442). Glendale, CA: Regal Books.

Nord, D. (1997). *Multiple AIDS-related loss: A handbook for understanding and surviving a perpetual fall*. Washington, DC: Taylor & Francis.

Ocamb, K. (2008). Gay men seek intimacy. *The Bilerico Project Newsletter,* April 20, 5:32 p.m. *Web Group Blog*. Retrieved January 1, 2012 from http://www.bilerico.com/2008/04/gay_men_seek_intimacy.php

Oram, D., Bartholomew, K., & Landolt, M. (2004). Coping with multiple AIDS-related loss among gay men. *Journal of Gay & Lesbian Social Services, 16*(2), 59-72.

Parkes, C. (1972). *Bereavement: Studies of grief in adult life*. London: Tavistock Publications.

Perreault, Y. (2007). *The presence of absence: The effect of HIV sero-status on the bereavement experiences of long-term survivors of multiple AIDS-related losses.* Toronto, ON, Canada: AIDS Bereavement Project of Ontario. Available at www/abpo.org

Piazza, M. (1997). *Holy homosexuals*. Dallas, TX: Sources of Hope.

Prigerson, H., Bierhals, A., Kasl, S., Reynolds, C., III, Shear, M., Day, N., et al. (1997). Traumatic grief as a risk factor for mental and physical morbidity. *American Journal of Psychiatry, 154*(5), May, 616. Abstract from *Health Reference Center Academic* [Web]. Gale Document Number: A19495415.

Rando, T. (1993). *The treatment of complicated mourning*. Champaign, IL: Research Press.

Sanders, C. J. (2010, October 2). Why anti-gay bullying is a theological issue and the moral imperative of anti-bullying preaching, teaching & activism. *Religious Dispatch Website,* Sexuality/Gender: Opinion.

Sanders, C. M. (1989). *Grief: The mourning after: Dealing with adult bereavement.* New York, NY: Wiley.

Shernoff, M. (1997). *Gay widowers: Life after the death of a partner*. New York, NY: Harrington Park Press.

Smith, H. I. (1996). *Grieving the death of a friend*. Minneapolis, MN: Augsburg.

Smith, H. I. (2002). *When your friend dies*. Minneapolis, MN: Augsburg.

Storey, N. (2005, June 11). Man to write about how gay men cope with loss of partner. *The Santa Fe New Mexican,* C-1. *General Reference Center Gold.* Gale Document Number: CJ180137950.

Stroebe, M. (2005, April). *Continuing bonds in bereavement towards a theoretical understanding*. Paper presented at Association for Death Education and Counseling 27th Annual Conference, Albuquerque, NM.

Walter, C. (2003). *The loss of a life partner: Narratives of the bereaved*. New York, NY: Columbia University Press.

Worden, J. W. (2009). *Grief counseling & grief therapy: A handbook for the mental health practitioner* (4th ed.). New York, NY: Springer.

CHAPTER 2

Young People and Gender Issues: Living With Loss

Linda Goldman

Life is a lesson of love and intimacy for children as well as adults. The losses that come to us through the course of our lives influence our capacity for intimacy. Childhood development, family systems, social constructs, and internalization of cultural indoctrination have an impact upon gender issues that begin in childhood and reach fulfillment through one's sexual orientation and gender identity. Loss related to gender identity, sexual orientation, and sexual stereotyping can ultimately converge to create low self-esteem, difficulty in relationships, inability to see a future, and lack of protection of the adult world–all of which influence one's capacity for intimacy.

THE YOUNG CHILD AND GENDER ISSUES

Young children quickly discover that there are certain attributes society dictates, such as "girl colors and boy colors, girl games and boy games, and girl toys and boy toys, determined by gender" (Goldman, 2010, p. 72). All too often, standards include pink for girls and blue for boys, boys playing football and girls playing with dolls, and girls becoming nurses and boys becoming doctors. Many of our children are limited to and by cultural constraints that rob them of their innocence and may lower their self-worth.

Five-year-old Joey was playing with his sister's doll. Joey's father ran over to him, grabbed the doll out of his arms, and shouted "Boys don't play with dolls." That was the last time Joey did. The message was clear: "If I want Dad's love, dolls are out." This simple interchange created a profound loss for Joey, the loss of intimacy with his dad. He wondered how he could ever share with his father all the things he liked to do, fearful that it would make Dad angry and not like him. Joey decided at that young age there were many things he could not tell his father if he wanted his love and approval.

Eight-year-old Sarah was given a baby carriage for her birthday. Sarah began using the carriage as a go-cart and thought it was so much fun. Mom gave her a similar message: "Girls play with dolls, not go-carts. Change it back to the way it was." Sarah tried to play with dolls but was not really interested. However, around her mother she pretended to like dolls. Sarah gave up being her authentic self at a young age to gain her parent's approval.

These two scenarios highlight gender stereotyping for young children that begins with the color of their room, the choice of baby toys, and the way a dad hugs a son or a daughter. Very early in life children learn to conform to gender stereotyping in order to gain the approval and love of parents, teachers, and friends. When girls and boys venture outside the box of conformity, they are often met with disapproval, rejection, and harassment, which lead to the loss of innocence and self-esteem. When they exhibit atypical gender behaviors, parental approval diminishes even more, as parents often perceive these children as *too different* and challenge them to change and conform. These admonishments are particularly painful outcomes when they come from parents.

"Gender binary" can be defined as the cultural construction of male and female roles based on perceived gender. "These constructs are assumed to speak to the ability of everyone to function within perceived boundaries" (Goldman, 2008, p. 18). Susan, age 7, commanded her 4-year-old brother Todd, "Go away! We are talking girl talk now!" Messages early in childhood imprint false norms of gender stereotyping and constraints that begin with messages like "boys don't cry" and "girls don't climb trees" and develop into "only boys fly airplanes" and "only girls clean the house."

Mary and Michael were twin 9-year-olds. Their father died. Mary was urged to express her feelings, and Michael was reminded: "Be brave like your dad, because you are the man of the house now." Mary's aunt reminded her she needed to take care of her mother now because her mom needed her. These stereotypical gender responses to grief burdened both children with over-responsibility and diminishment of feelings due to cultural norms. The results of these responses were the loss of the world of childhood as well as a parent.

Many children and adolescents in today's world cannot or do not want to conform to the preconceived notions of this gender binary. Heightened awareness of cultural constructs can uncover the limits of false perceptions that restrict thinking and actions for our young people before they ever enter the school system. As one self-assured 8-year-old, Tyler, told his Mom: "I'm a real man and I still wear a pink tie."

GENDER IDENTITY AND LOSS

A child's internal sense of what it is to be male or female is his or her true gender identity. As one young person transitioning from male to female explained, "It is the gender our brain tells us we are, not our body. Our gender identity is something we feel in our soul. But it is also a continuum, and it evolves" (Brown, 2006, p. 2).

There is an increasing trend by parents and professionals to support gender identity rights. New York City ruled to allow the sex listed on a birth certificate to be altered and some children allowed to be "who they are" to reduce depression and suicidal ideation. In a *New York Times* article, "Supporting Boys or Girls When the Line Isn't Clear," Patricia Brown (2006) explains a growing advocacy for children who do not conform to gender norms in clothing and behavior.

Brown explains a shift in trends: "First we became sensitive to two mommies and two daddies, now it's kids who come to school who aren't gender typical" (2006, p. 1). Reaction in school systems to situations such as a boy wearing a dress range from a teacher blaming parents and stating it just was not normal to an 8-year-old elementary school boy being thrown into a large trash can by his peers and constantly teased for *acting like a girl*. The school counselor told his parents it was their fault for not teaching him to *act like a man*:

> Parents and teachers can model a dialogue free of gender bias for all children that includes jobs, toys, clothing, and colors. Caring adults can create gender-neutral conversations, eliminating phrases like "girls do this" and "boys do that" and present broader statements such as "children can play this game" or "children can wear lots of colors." In this way young people are supported in expressing themselves freely without being confined to limited societal restraints. (Goldman, 2010, p. 21)

GENDER STEREOTYPING AND LOSS

> LGB [lesbian, gay, bisexual] youth who come from highly rejecting families are more than 8 times as likely to have attempted suicide than LGB peers who reported no or low levels of family rejection. (Ryan, Huebner, Diaz, & Sanchez, 2009)

Gender stereotyping can be disturbing to a child of any age and can cause significant losses in childhood and adolescence. This stereotyping may begin at a young age, regardless of any predisposition to be gay or lesbian. Societal stereotyping can shape the way identity is internally and externally perceived by young people. One of the most enduring gender stereotypes is that girls are more emotional than boys. Another is that boys express more anger and girls more love, sadness, and fear. Children learn of gender traditional roles in society at a very young age as part of their socialization process.

Stereotyping might also be affected by cultural norms. Durik et al. (2006) cites an example of gender stereotypes within Hispanic American culture to theoretically center on the masculine ideal of machismo and the feminine ideal of marianismo. This research explains that according to these ideals, men are expected to be authoritative, aggressive, and dominant, whereas women are expected to be loving, passive, and subservient. Research by Ryan et al. (2009) concluded a clear link between specific parental and caregiver behaviors and negative health problems in LGBT adults, finding that in the Latino culture men reported the highest number of negative family reactions to their sexual orientation in adolescence.

For the young person that has self-identified as LGBT (lesbian, gay, bisexual, transgender), the fear of coming out to friends and family can be enormous. The constant bombardment of gender slurs, sexual harassment, and bullying in school, home, and community can instill terror of disclosure of sexual orientation or gender identify. Non-normative expressions of identity are too often correlated to the societal consequences: "Blaming the child for their failure to adapt to traditional gender norms is easy. . . . [These] behaviors are often taken as further evidence that something is wrong with the child, rather than a normal response to attempting to accommodate oneself to a hostile environment" (Mallon & DeCrescenzo, 2006, p. 219).

"Gender-atypical behavior provokes parents' concern that the youth might be lesbian or gay, and some parents react with efforts to diminish or suppress these behaviors to thwart homosexuality, especially in men" (D'Augelli et al., 2005, p. 658). Landolt, Bartholomew, Saffrey, Oram, and Perlman (2004) maintain factors in childhood, including gender nonconformity and rejection by parents and peers, are correlated with a gay orientation in males. Their research findings highlight "the role of gender nonconformity in contributing to childhood rejection and the importance of peer and relationships in the socialization of gay men, explaining peer and paternal rejection mediated the association between gender nonconformity and attachment anxiety" (Landolt et al., 2004, p. 117). This study emphasizes parental rejection of atypical gender behaviors before a child disclosed any sexual orientation. "Feminine behavior in young males, considerably less normative than masculine behavior in young females, is more negatively sanctioned" (D'Augelli et al., 2005, p. 658; Katz, 1986).

Alex was 8 when he realized he made gestures that family and friends found offensive and feminine. Alex's mother would often turn away from a conversation with disgust if he began to gesture with his hands or posture. His father seemed embarrassed by these gestures, chastising Alex, "Will you stop doing that?" His friends taunted him at school: "Why are you sitting like that? Are you a girl?" Alex worked hard to hide a part of himself, his natural movements. He explained they seemed natural to him but made others uncomfortable. "It takes so much energy to hide them. I am tired of having to sit on my hands."

By the time Alex turned 12, his grades dropped, and he said he had no friends. He told his sister he hated school, he hated life, and he didn't want to live. The gender atypical behaviors that emerged in childhood created stress so burdensome it manifested in depression and suicidal ideation. "More parental discouragement of childhood gender atypical behavior and more lifetime gay-related verbal abuse were characteristic of attempters. According to D'Augelli et al., "many were called 'sissy' or 'tomboy' by parents" (p. 657). They explain that "LGB youth who experienced more verbal abuse by parents as they were growing up . . . who were seen by parents as more gender-atypical during childhood, and whose parents made efforts to change gender-atypical behavior, were more likely to have made a suicide attempt" (p. 657).

Media has highlighted a rash of young people dying of suicide due to sexual harassment, hate crimes, social media disclosures, and cyber-bullying. At earlier and earlier ages young people may suffer, at the hands of their peers, harassment so horrendous in terms of gender stereotyping that suicide may feel like their only alternative. Two 11-year-olds were harassed constantly for being gay, even though they had never come out. One mother explained her little boy was constantly called gay until he could not take it anymore. She had complained to the school but felt they did not take action. The boy hung himself and was discovered by his mother. Two weeks later another suicide occurred of a young boy also harassed for being gay. Asher Brown was an eighth grader who shot himself in the head after enduring what his parents said "was constant harassment from four students in his school" (O'Hare, 2010). Tormentors relentlessly picked on him for his clothes, shoes, and size and accused him of being gay. Some mocked gay acts on him in physical education class. In the article, parents said bullies drove their son to take his life (O'Hare, 2010). Peggy O'Hare explains Asher's parents' advocacy against bullying: "[We] just want the harassment to stop so other students do not suffer. . . . Our son is just the extreme case of what happens when (someone is) just relentless" (2010).

Research findings indicate childhood gender nonconformity can be predictive of peer and parental rejection and can lead to attachment-related anxiety and avoidance as children grow into adolescence and adulthood. "Intervention efforts must be geared toward changing attitudes toward gender nonconforming behavior, reducing rejection often associated with that behavior, shifting the developmental pathway toward greater attachment security as an adult" (Landolt et al., 2004, p. 126).

WHAT IS ADOLESCENCE?

> Adolescence is life between childhood and adulthood. It starts with the physical beginnings of sexual maturity and ends with the social achievement of independent adult status. (Myers, 2005, p. 124)

The work of adolescence is that of forming an identity. Teenagers experiment with social, school, and home environments to learn firsthand what is comfortable and right for them. Ideas and feelings can be in constant change and flux as they begin to develop and strengthen the need for intimacy and forming close emotional ties to "synthesize past, present, and future possibilities into a clearer sense of self" (Erikson, as cited in Myers, 2005, p. 128). They may wonder "Who am I?" "What will I be?" and "What are my values and beliefs?"

Group support and approval is critical during the adolescent period; as separation from parents increases, attention turns to peers for acknowledgment. The following are important developmental tasks for young people (Goldman, 2008, p. 94):

- accepting one's body as it is and creating more mature relationships with peers;
- seeking to become responsible members of society and achieving their evolving values; and
- preparing for a future of economic success, marriage, and family life.

Adolescence can be extremely painful for those young people excluded or ostracized, especially in a school setting. High schools often contain a highly charged atmosphere of cliques and socially "in" groups, pushing those left behind to feelings of silent or unspoken depression and suicidal ideation or anger and hostility. Withdrawal, vulnerability, low self-esteem, and hopelessness can manifest in rejected teens.

LOSSES ASSOCIATED WITH BEING GAY AND ADOLESCENT

It is difficult to be a teenager. It is even more difficult to be a gay teenager. LGBT youth face more complex issues than their heterosexual peers. Significant losses occur due to the difficulty in achieving the developmental tasks of adolescence. While these young people experience the challenges commonly associated with adolescence development, additional complexities arise from exposure to stereotyping and rejection. Hidden agendas, sexual orientation, and gender identity conflicts often create larger problematic concerns in parenting, counseling, and teaching that must be recognized, overcome, and integrated into a healthy life outlook.

A new level of social awareness often marks the cognitive development of teenagers. Adolescents begin to refine their moral judgment, thinking a great deal about what others may think of them, especially peers. Relationships ride the tide of highs and lows and become all-important, sometimes creating great pleasure or stress. Common characteristics of impulsivity and egocentricity can be heightened for the LGBT youth. Young people commonly internalize misunderstood feelings, thinking adults, mostly parents, cannot ever imagine their experience.

Louise, age 16, was devastated after the breakup of a lesbian relationship. Her age-appropriate thinking that "no one can understand what I am going through" was magnified as a gay teen, since each relationship is extremely important under the barrage of gender stereotyping.

A LOOK AT LOSS FOR LGBT YOUTH IN TODAY'S WORLD

- According to the National School Climate Survey, 52.9% of LGBT students were harassed or threatened by their peers via electronic mediums, often known as cyberbullying. (GLSEN [Gay, Lesbian, Straight Educational Network], 2010).
- LGBT students who were more frequently harassed because of their sexual orientation or gender expression had grade point averages almost half a grade lower than for students who were less often harassed (GLSEN, 2009).
- Lesbian, gay, or bisexual youth who reported high levels of family rejection in adolescence were 8.4 times more likely to have attempted suicide (Ryan, 2009).
- Non-heterosexual youth suffer disproportionate educational and criminal-justice punishments that are not explained by greater engagement in illegal or transgressive behaviors (Himmelstein & Bruckner, 2011).
- Between 20-40% of all homeless youth identify as lesbian, gay, bisexual, or transgender (Ray, 2006).

By-products of societal judgment can become the inability to visualize a comfortable future and a much higher likelihood of rejection from family and peers. These can lead some youth that are sexually harassed into depression and suicidal ideation, becoming part of a high-risk subgroup. Healthy identity development and self-worth can substantially diminish for young people living in a culture where they are rejected, judged, and hated because of behaviors, sexual orientation, or gender identity.

AT-RISK FACTORS FOR LGBT YOUTH

> These kids shouldn't be called gay, they should be called gifted.
>
> —Kevin Jennings, Past Executive Director GLSEN

With the myriad of obstacles LGBT young people face, their natural attributes of resilience need to be supported. Too often rejection, anxiety, and depression can manifest. The prejudice or negativity experienced from their outer world from peers, family, and society may push them to find support in counseling, shelters, or mental health agencies. Many feel low self-esteem and isolation with nowhere to go and no one to turn to. They may form an at-risk group with suicidal feelings and actions. The following are risk factors more present for gay youth.

1. Psychological Distress Associated with Being LGBT

Gender nonconformity, lack of support, school dropout, family problems, victimization, homelessness, and substance abuse can be factors created by psychological distress. Comprehending the depth of these psychosocial stressors and their impact on suicide risk can be paramount in helping to improve the LGBT adolescent's quality of life.

> Gay and lesbian youth often turn to unsafe activities such as alcohol and drug use or high-risk sexual behaviors to cope with their sexual orientation. These high-risk behaviors place these young individuals at greater risk for addiction, unintended pregnancy, [and] sexually transmitted diseases, including HIV/AIDS. (Lindley & Reininger, 2001, p. 17)

2. Keeping the Secret of Being LGBT

"One study involving 350 gay adolescents between the ages of 14 and 21 reported that 54% made their first suicide attempt before coming out to others, 27% made the attempt during the same year they came out, and 19% made the attempt after coming out" (Kitts, 2005, p. 624).

Kitts maintains "important issues, such as suicide among gay [LGBT] adolescents, remain invisible not only to mainstream psychology, but to mainstream healthcare" (2005, p. 623). Mental and physical health professionals need to become aware that suicidal ideation is a danger for gay youth, especially those girls and boys that find life unbearable before or after revealing their sexuality orientation or gender identity.

3. Lack of Family Support

Lack of parental support can be a devastating loss. All too often parents' *initial* reaction can lead to the loss of the relationship. Sixteen-year-old Amelia had been extremely close with her mother. Growing up she inwardly knew she felt different but could never find the words to explain her feelings aloud. When Amelia finally was able to articulate her attraction to other females, she was excited to share this discovery with her mother. To her astonishment and devastation, Mom was enraged and angry. They became distant from that point on, and the loss of Amelia's idealized relationship with her mother created deep wounds and intense suffering. Counseling support for parents can help with processing new and complex feelings and free hidden prejudice and misconceptions.

This approach is underscored by findings of the Family Acceptance Project, a university-based research and education initiative, which shows that LGB young adults who report high levels of specific family rejecting behaviors during adolescence (such as blocking access to a gay friend or LGBT resources or telling a child that one is ashamed of them because of their gay or lesbian identity) have poorer health than peers from families that are not rejecting. Specifically, LGB young adults who reported high levels of family rejection during adolescence were 8.4 times more likely to report having attempted suicide, 5.9 times more likely to report high levels of depression, 3.4 times more likely to use illegal drugs, and 3.4 times more likely to report having engaged in unprotected sexual intercourse, compared with peers from families that reported no or low levels of family rejection (Ryan et al., 2009). Conversely, those whose parents support them show greater well-being, with lower rates of health and mental health problems (Ryan, Russell, Huebner, Diaz, & Sanchez, 2010).

The emotional isolation, rejection, and complete withdrawal from parents that many LGBT youth face can ultimately lead to depression, drugs, and alcohol and even homelessness. LGBT youth have a much greater incidence of being thrown out or opting to leave their homes than their straight peers. Goldfried (2001) reported that "1 out of 3 was verbally abused by family members; 1 out of 10 was physically assaulted by a family member" (as cited in Kitts, 2005, p. 625). The fear of potentially experiencing this rejection and abuse is a tremendous stressor.

Physicians, clergy, educators, and mental health professionals can become educated on LGBT issues and create strong support structures for gay youth. Being prepared and knowledgeable about information on resources can be life changing (see helpful organizations and references at the end of this chapter). Examples of useful available resources are PFLAG (Parents, Family, and Friends of Lesbians and Gays), COLAGE (people with a lesbian, gay, bisexual, transgender, or queer parent), GLSEN (Gay, Lesbian, Straight Educational Network), the Lesbian and Gay Child and Adolescent Psychiatric Association, the Association of Gay and Lesbian Psychiatrists, and the Gay and Lesbian Medical Association.

4. Discrimination and Victimization of LGBT Youth

The victimization of children and teens because of sexual orientation can present a real danger to today's youth. Coming out as gay can provoke serious hate crimes. Larry King was an openly gay eighth-grade boy murdered by his middle school classmate. Setoodeh (2008) reported Larry "was a troubled child who flaunted his sexuality" and speculates "kids are coming out younger, but are schools ready to handle the complex issues of identity and sexuality? For Larry King, the question had tragic implications" (p. 1). Toomey et al. (2010) underscores "victimization due to perceived or actual LGBT status fully mediates the association between adolescent gender nonconformity and young adult psychosocial adjustment" (p. 1580). Goldman (2008, p. 101) presents the following research.

Ploderl and Fartacek (2005, p. 661) indicate a higher incidence for most suicide-related risk factors with increased psychosocial stress and vulnerability and lack of family support for LGBT youth. LGBT youth who decide to come out risk rejection and abuse from parents, friends, family members, and society at large. "Goldfried (2001) reported that . . . one out of four [LGBT students] had experienced physical abuse at school" (Kitts, 2005, p. 625). "Research has demonstrated that adolescents struggling with issues surrounding their sexual orientation who do not receive appropriate health care services, accurate information, or support from family, school, and community, are in jeopardy of serious emotional, social, and physical difficulties" (Lindley & Reininger, 2001, p. 17).

PARENTS: COMMON REACTIONS

Parental acceptance is everything.
—Anonymous gay teen

The loss of acceptance by parents is all too common for LGBT youth. Accepting a child's sexual orientation can be life-affirming but rejecting a child's sexual orientation can sometimes be life-threatening. Parents of gay youth have a unique opportunity to "give birth" to a renewed embracing of their children as LGBT.

Bernstein (2003, p. 71) described stereotypical parental response to a daughter or son coming out as LGBT in a similar manner to the following:

- Disbelief: "I don't believe you. It's a phase. You will get through it."
- Self-blame: "It's my fault. What did I do wrong? I was too protective. I should have done more. It has to be my fault."
- Denial: "You are not gay. It is unacceptable. I will not have a gay son."
- Anger and depression: "That is ridiculous. Talk her out of it!"

Parental acceptance and approval is important to adolescents. Living a childhood of overt or covert parental disapproval as LGBT youth can manifest in strong emotions of depression, rejection, isolation, and suicidal ideation. These feelings are often compounded by peer rejection for atypical gender behavior, leaving the gay or lesbian youth feeling like they have nowhere to turn. Coupled with societal bias and mental, verbal, or physical abuse, mental health problems easily surface and fester. Resources for parents and professionals to normalize gender behaviors and reduce gender bias are available. They provide words to use on this subject that seemed so taboo only a few years ago.

Parents need to educate themselves on LGBT issues and create a family environment beginning in early childhood that dissolves gender stereotyping and anchors acceptance of all children, gay or straight. Mothers and fathers can provide words to use to talk to their children about LGBT issues and build a non-judgmental environment around gender issues. Parents can express advocacy, speaking out for any discrimination at home, in the school, or the community. Parents can become allies and role models for young people to visualize a successful future—economically, legally, and socially—and a present inclusive of love and acceptance.

Thomas's mother explained his coming out as gay in the following scenario: Thomas had disclosed his sexual orientation to his sister, Alice, while driving to dinner. "Will you tell Mom and Dad I'm gay?" he asked. "I will drive around the block a few times and wait for you to signal me. Put on the porch light if it is OK to come home." Thomas drove around for quite some time and finally called Alice. "What's happening?" he asked. "Mom and Dad are almost finished doing something," she responded. Thomas's parents were going to every room in the house, from the third floor to the basement, and lighting every light to show it was absolutely OK to come home.

Schools: Exposure to Bullying, Prejudice, and Anti-Gay Slurs

> I created GSAs to end the misery and isolation of being gay in high school.
> —Kelli Peterson, Founder of Gay–Straight Alliances in High School

Professionals in the field of mental health are realizing the implication of the effects of homophobia and sexual prejudice on the psyches of too many of our young people. Hearing and saying the phrase "You're so gay" as an insult, a slur, or an ignorant remark sends a message of verbal abuse to any young person, gay or straight. As one 15-year-old, Gavin, explained, "People think they can say 'You're so gay' or 'That's so gay' and add 'just joking.' It is not joke to me. I wish they would stop." Gavin was not gay, but he was harassed as gay nevertheless and confused by its implications.

GLSEN's 2009 School Climate Survey polled 7,261 students between the ages of 13 and 21. The report indicated that 9 out of 10 LGBT students experienced harassment at school, two-thirds felt unsafe at school because of their sexual orientation, and about a third skipped a day of school in the past month because of concern about safety.

Derogatory remarks such as "faggot" or "dyke" were often heard by 72.4% of students at school; 88.9% reportedly heard "gay" used in a negative way often or frequently at school; 40.1% reported being physically harassed at school because of their sexual orientation; and 18.8% were physically assaulted because of their sexual orientation (GLSEN, 2009, School Climate Survey, p. 3).

These hostile environments within schools are creating distress for our LGBT youth, often manifesting as depression and suicide ideation and attempts. Goldman and Livoti (2011) present the following indications of anxiety, depression, and suicide ideation which often followed awareness of same-sex feelings and disclosure of sexual orientation. Meyer's meta-analysis determined that the likelihood of mood and anxiety disorder was twice as high for lesbians and gays than their heterosexual counterparts (2003, p. 689).

The GLSEN School Climate presents positive outcomes as well. Students in schools with a gay-straight alliance report decreases in homophobic remarks, victimization, and increased safety (p. 11). Students with inclusive curriculum (including LGBT people, history, and events) relayed an increased sense of connectedness (p. 13). Although schools and social media have focused on bullying and bullying prevention, LGBT youth face potential prejudice not only in school, but also at home and in their communities.

Goldman and Livoti (in Neimeyer et al., 2011) emphasize that "adjustment problems for gay youth emerge from the interpersonal stressors associated with coping with sexual orientation in society, rather than being a characteristic of gay, lesbian, and bisexual identities" (Feldman, 2001, p. 1). These adjustment problems can also apply to straight youth experiencing sexual harassment, gender stereotyping, and an inability to feel safe at school.

- Two million U.S. teenagers were reported in 2001 as having serious problems in school because they were taunted with anti-gay slurs (Stepp, 2001, p. A1).
- Nearly two-thirds (61.1%) of students reported that they felt unsafe in school because of their sexual orientation, and more than a third (39.9%) felt unsafe because of their gender expression (GLSEN, 2009, p. 3).
- LGBT students missed a class at least once was 29.1% and 30.0% missed at least one day of school in the past month because of safety concerns, when compared to the general population of secondary school students (GLSEN, 2009, p. 5).

Dr. Vincent Livoti, a teacher trainer and youth media specialist at Lesley University, underscores the importance of having resources reflecting the reality of every child's experience, which includes materials depicting sexual minorities (see some suggestions in resource list). Livoti explains that American culture generally continues to deny that children have any sexual self-concept and that the politics of identity are a socially driven issue. "The universe of acceptable information for our youth should be enlarged to encourage basic notions of human sexuality earlier in life, before pervasive cultural prejudices become manifest" (Livoti, 2009, p. 110).

The 2009 National School Climate Survey conducted by GLSEN (2010) identifies the following positive interventions and supports for young people.

1. Having a Gay–Straight Alliance in school was related to more positive experiences for LGBT students, including fewer homophobic remarks, less victimization because of sexual orientation and gender expression, less absenteeism because of safety concerns, and a greater sense of belonging to the school community.

2. The presence of supportive staff contributed to a range of positive indicators, including fewer reports of missing school, fewer reports of feeling unsafe, greater academic achievement, higher educational aspirations, and a greater sense of school belonging.
3. Students attending schools with an anti-bullying policy that included protections based on sexual orientation and gender identity or expression heard fewer homophobic remarks, experienced lower levels of victimization related to their sexual orientation, were more likely to report that staff intervened when hearing homophobic remarks, and were more likely to report incidents of harassment and assault to school staff than students at schools with a general policy or no policy.

HOMELESSNESS AND GAY YOUTH

LGBTQ youth are frequently thrown out of their home, mistreated, or emotionally distanced after coming out or being discovered as gay. Too many of these young people find themselves homeless, again experiencing harassment in the shelter system.

Lesbian, Gay, Bisexual and Transgender Youth: An Epidemic of Homelessness explains "Our analysis of the available research suggests that between 20 percent and 40 percent of all homeless youth identify as lesbian, gay, bisexual, or transgender" (Ray, 2006, p. 1).

Matthew, age 14, came out to his dad as gay. His father threw him against the wall, screamed, "Get out of my house!" and never spoke to his son again. Homeless in an instant after parental rejection, he took to the streets without friends, shelter, or financial security. Matthew, as so many other LGBT youth, experienced abandonment and emotional and physical rejection, accompanied by harassment and victimization in his homeless environment.

The Center for American Progress report (Quintana, Rosenthal, & Krehely, 2010) on LGBT youth homelessness cites estimates from a national homelessness organization. This report presents consistent research that finds the following:

> Gay and transgender youth are strikingly over-represented among homeless youth. Although there are no nationally representative surveys that give an accurate count of the population of gay and transgender youth who are homeless, regional studies have been used to estimate that population size. Studies from various jurisdictions over the last decade (Table 1) have found that gay and transgender youth comprise between 7 and 39 percent of the homeless youth population. They are generally thought to make up 5–7 percent of the overall youth population. The National Alliance to End Homelessness estimates that gay and transgender youth make up about 20 percent of homeless youth nationwide. (2010, p. 6)

In a *Los Angeles Times* article, "Gay and Homeless: In Plain Sight, a Largely Hidden Population," Alexandra Zavis (2010) reported that "every year, hundreds of gay youths end up alone on the streets of Los Angeles County, where they make up a disproportionate share of the at least 4,200 people under 25 who are homeless on any given day." One homeless youth interviewed explained, "If I could be invisible, I would. I feel ashamed to admit that I'm homeless." He and his boyfriend hide their blankets and duffel bags in bushes and shower every morning at a drop-in center and choose a provided outfit to wear. The article explains that this boy's father told him at age 16 to get out of the house because he could not accept him being gay. The boy explained any effeminate gesture would drive his father to beat him. He moved from friend to friend, worked at a succession of jobs, and eventually got fired, leaving him with no place to go but the streets.

Another young person interviewed shared his background, saying "My cousins were gangbangers. . . . I knew in middle school that I liked boys and wanted to hold their hands." "At school, classmates would pelt him with food and milk cartons. To dull the hurt, he turned to alcohol and drugs. He stole money from his grandmother, swallowed his brother's medication, and cut himself with razors" (Zavis, 2010). His grandmother kicked him out of the house at 18 and filed a restraining order against him. He began selling his body on the street to support his methamphetamine habit.

Zavis emphasizes, "For some gay youths alienated from their families, the foster care system provides sanctuary. But too often, said Costello, the L.A. Gay and Lesbian Center's associate director for children, youth, and family services, they bounce between foster parents and group homes until they turn 18. Once emancipated, they have nowhere to go." Zavis (2010) reports that one 21-year-old explained he had more than 20 placements between the time he was removed from his parents' home at 5 and aged out of foster care (p. 2). Van Leeuwen, Boyle, Salomonsen-Sautel, and Baker (2006) strongly recommend child welfare provide services to LGB youth, recommending program funding, more training, technical support, and further research.

SUICIDAL IDEATION IN LGBT YOUTH

> According to research conducted in the past two decades, sexual minority youth (gay, lesbian, and bisexual) exhibit more suicidal ideation than do their heterosexual peers. (Rutter & Soucar, 2002, p. 290)

The internalization of homophobia and the sexual prejudice projected from the heterosexual world can too often culminate in great feelings of grief leading to despair. *Prayers for Bobby* (Mulcahy, 2010) is a film about a mother who could not accept her son being gay. After disclosing his sexual orientation,

Bobby pleaded with his mom to accept him for who he was. Her response was only "I will not have a gay son." Bobby could only reply, "Then you don't have a son." Bobby died of suicide. His mother realized and verbalized that Bobby's death was a direct result of her ignorance. Unfortunately, research validates that LGBT youth have a higher rate of suicide than straight young people. The Massachusetts Youth Risk Survey (2009) states that lesbian, gay, and bisexual youth are up to four times more likely to attempt suicide than their heterosexual peers.

David Crary (2010) explains in his article "Suicide Surge: Schools Confront Anti-gay Bullying" that "according to a 2009 GLSEN survey of 7,261 students, only 18 percent said their schools had a comprehensive program addressing anti-gay bullying, while gay students in schools that had such programs were less likely to be victimized and more likely to report problems to staff."

The article (Crary, 2010) explains that in 2010 at least four teens have killed themselves after being targeted by anti-gay bullying. Tyler Clementi was a gifted student at Rutgers who died of suicide after his college roommate streamed online, without permission, a sexual experience of Rutgers and another male. Tyler posted on Facebook his intention to jump off the George Washington Bridge, and he followed through with his plan. He was 18 years old. Another young person, Justin Aberg, 15, hung himself in his room. Crary reports that Aberg's friends told his mother that he was a "frequent target of bullies mocking his sexual orientation."

In 2011, the Trevor Project became one of the leading organizations focused on crisis and suicide prevention efforts for LGBT youth who have experienced so many losses in their life. This continuous effort to save lives includes a 24-hour confidential and free lifeline, in-school workshops, and online resources and advocacy. Their website (see helpful organizations) explains that often any suicidal youth may show signs of wanting to attempt suicide and describe the following modified warning signs to watch for:

- Isolation from friends and family
- Increased substance abuse
- Hopelessness and helplessness
- Change of behavior
- Loss of interest in normal activities
- Preoccupation with death
- Giving away possessions
- Inability to see a future
- Expressing a plan for suicide
- Signs of depression
- History of depression or suicide in family

The Trevor Project gives several suggestions for discussing suicide with young people: "When talking about suicide among LGBTQ youth, remember to stress that the increased risk is NOT a factor of identifying this way, but rather an outcome of the negative ways they are treated at home, in school, in their communities, and in their religious institutions" (2010, p. 8). The Trevor Project suggests a system of helpful responses to a suicidal young person, reminding them they are never alone, connecting them to resources and support, accepting and listening seriously to feelings, responding to a plan to attempt suicide, telling a trusted person, and empowering the person to get help.

In an article by Jane Brody (2011), "Gay or Straight, Youths Aren't So Different," there is an attempt to normalize the stress gay youth feel that leads to depression and suicidal ideation by presenting recent studies and research on this issue. Brody emphasizes that although "studies do suggest that severe emotional distress is somewhat more common among gay teenagers than straight ones." Young people are often targeted if they exhibit atypical behavior, and tend to be prey to bullying as well as LGBTQ youth.

Brody underscores the stressors on gay youth today, indicating clear signs of continued stress from a national study, *Criminal-Justice and School Sanctions Against Nonheterosexual Youth*, of 1,500 middle and high school students (Hillmelstein & Bruckner, 2011). This study found LGBT teens "more likely to be harshly punished by schools and courts than their straight peers" (Brody, 2011). Dr. Lisa Diamond, an associate professor on gender studies at University of Utah, explains that "gay teenagers most at risk for serious emotional distress are those whose families have rejected them" (Brody, 2011). For that reason Diamond advises parents: "Continue to express affection for your kids despite your own feelings about [their being gay]. Let them know they are loved and accepted. Hug them, spend time with them, watch movies together" (Brody, 2011). Diamond emphasizes that all young people, regardless of their sexual orientation, want to find a relationship and adults need to respond accordingly and with the assurance "I'm sure you'll find someone who will love and appreciate you" (Brody, 2011). This consolation would certainly be heightened with added assurance of love and appreciation by parents too.

Diamond found that although gay and straight young people may appear to have the same number of friends, "the composition of their friendships is somewhat different. . . . Gay teenagers tend to go out of their way to befriend youths of other races or those who are stigmatized for looks. But for gay and straight teenagers alike, Dr. Diamond said in an interview, the chief source of stress is the same: 'anxiety about being alone as an adult, about finding the kind of partner they want'" (Brody, 2011). Diamond summarized that being jilted by a romantic partner is a common factor contributing to suicide attempts in both gay and straight young people. Thus, the importance of listening, supporting, comforting, and reassuring them this is not their only chance of finding love (Brody, 2011).

CONCLUSION

Children and adolescents face losses throughout their life because of sexual stereotyping and societal confinement to prescribed norms. From a young girl loving to climb trees to a teenage boy coming out as gay, the gamut of loss of self-esteem and peer and parental approval can ultimately culminate in hate crimes, homelessness, and emotional and physical rejection. These challenges converge to form a fertile breeding ground for shame, substance abuse, anxiety, depression, suicidal ideation, and suicide. The interplay between shame and intimacy is profound. Losses of innocence, security, protection, self-esteem, relationships, identity, friends, family, and home are just a few of the many experienced on deep levels by these young people.

No child or youth should be discriminated against—girl or boy, gay or straight. No children or youth should be forced to leave their family for being uniquely themselves. No children or youth should be rejected from their spiritual community. Every young person has the right to be safe and feel self-respect, to form meaningful relationships, and to see a future with family, economic, and social success.

Our goal as caring adults is to provide empowerment for all young people by promoting self-esteem, encouraging self-acceptance, and building resilience. Establishing and perpetuating strategies for self-advocacy and intimate relationships are crucial in diminishing losses incurred during childhood and adolescence due to gender stereotyping, sexual orientation, and gender identity.

HELPFUL ORGANIZATIONS

AGLP: Association of Gay and Lesbian Psychiatrists: http://www.aglp.org

COLAGE: People with a lesbian, gay, bisexual, transgender, or queer parent: http://www.colage.org

Family Acceptance Project: http://familyproject.sfsu.edu

GLMA: Gay and Lesbian Medical Association: http://glma.org

GLSEN: Gay, Lesbian, and Straight Education Network: http://www.glsen.org

HRC: Human Rights Campaign: http://www.hrc.org

LAGCAPA: Lesbian and Gay Child and Adolescent Psychiatric Association: http://www.lagcapa.org

PFLAG: Parents, Family, and Friends of Lesbians and Gays: http://community.pflag.org

The Trevor Project: http://www.thetrevorproject.org; Trevor Lifeline: 866 4-U-TREVOR

RESOURCES

The following is a bibliography of helpful resources related to gender bias and LGBT issues for children and young adults.

Resources for Children on Gender Bias

Ewert, M. (2008). *10,000 dresses*. New York, NY: Seven Stories Press.
Fox, M. (1997). *The straight line wonder*. New York, NY: Mondo Publishing.
Howe, J. (1996). *Pinky and Rex and the bully*. New York, NY: Aladdin Paperbacks.
Johnson, A. (2004). *Just like Josh Gibson*. New York, NY: Aladdin.
Kilodavis, C. (2009). *My princess boy: A mom's story about a young boy who loves to dress up*. New York, NY: Aladdin.
Parr, T. (2009). *It's OK to be different*. New York, NY: Little Brown Books for Young Readers.
Zolotow, C. (1972). *William's doll*. New York, NY: HarperCollins.

Resources for Children on LGBT Issues

Brannen, S. (2008). *Uncle Bobby's wedding*. New York, NY: G. P. Putnam's Sons.
De Haan, L., & Stern, N. (2000). *King and king*. Berkeley, Toronto: Tricycle Press.
Elwin, R., & Paulse, M. (1990). *Asha's mums*. Toronto, Canada: Women's Press.
Ferro, U. (2007). *Mother's Day on Martha's Vineyard*. West Tisbury, MA: Marti Books.
Polacco, P. (2009). *In our mothers' house*. New York, NY: Penguin Young Readers Group.
Richardson, J., & Parnell, P. (2005). *And Tango makes three*. New York, NY: Simon & Schuster.
Snow, J. (2004). *How it feels to have a gay or lesbian parent: A book by kids for kids of all ages*. New York, NY: Harrington Park Press.

Resources for Adolescents on LGBT Issues

Garden, N. (1982). *Annie on my mind*. New York, NY: Farrar, Straus, and Girous Publishers.
Hartinger, B. (2003). *Geography club*. New York, NY: HarperCollins.
Konigsberg, B. (2008). *Out of the pocket*. New York, NY: Penguin Books.
Marcus, E. (2000). *What if someone I know is gay? Answers to questions about gay and lesbian people*. New York, NY: Price Stern Sloan.
Sanchez, A. (2003). *Rainbow high*. New York, NY: Simon Pulse.

REFERENCES

Bernstein, R. A. (2003). *Straight parents, gay children*. New York, NY: Thunder's Mouth Press.
Bontempo, D. E., & D'Augelli, A. R. (2002). Effects of at-school victimization and sexual orientation on lesbian, gay, or bisexual youths' health risk behavior. *Journal of Adolescent Health, 30*, 364-374.
Brody, J. (2011, January 3). Gay or straight, youths aren't so different. *The New York Times*. Retrieved from http://www.nytimes.com/2011/01/04/health/04brody.html
Brown, P. (2006, December 2). Supporting boys or girls when the line isn't clear. *The New York Times*. Retrieved from http://www.nytimes.com/2006/12/02/us/02child.html?-r&hp&ex=1165122000&en=4ba
Crary, D. (2010, October 8). Suicide surge: Schools confront anti-gay bullying. *MSNBC.com*. Retrieved from http://www.msnbc.msn.com/id/39593311/ns/us_news-life

D'Augelli, A. R., Hershberger, S., & Pilkintron, N. (2001). Suicidality patterns and sexual orientation-related factors among lesbian, gay, and bisexual youths. *Suicide and Life-Threatening Behavior, 31,* 250-264.

D'Augelli, A. R., Grossman, A., Salter, N., Vasey, J., Starks, M., & Sinclair, K. (2002). Predicting the suicide attempts of lesbian, gay, and bisexual youth. *Suicide and Life-Threatening Behavior, 35*(6), 646-659.

D'Augelli, A. R., Pilkington, N. W., & Hershberger, S. L. (2002). Incidence and mental health impact of sexual orientation victimization of lesbian, gay and bisexual youths in high school. *School Psychology Bulletin, 17*, 148-167.

Durik, A., Hyde, J., Marks, A., Roy, A., Anaya, D., & Schultz, G. (2006). Ethnicity and gender stereotypes of emotion. *Sex Roles: A Journal of Research, 54*(7/8), 429-445.

Earls, M. (2005). GLBTQ youth: The facts. Retrieved from http://advocatesforyouth.org/publications/factsheet/fsglbt.htm

Feldman, M. J. (2001). *Fact sheet on suicidal behavior in GLB youth.* San Francisco, CA: AGLP.

GLSEN (Gay, Lesbian, Straight Educational Network). (2007). *Executive summary: The 2007 National Climate Survey: Key findings on the experiences of lesbian, gay, bisexual and transgender youth in our nation's schools.* New York, NY: Author.

GLSEN (Gay, Lesbian, Straight Educational Network). (2010). 2009 National School Climate Survey. Retrieved from http://www.glsen.org/cgi-bin/iowa/all/news/record/2624.html

Goldfried, M. (2001). Integrating gay, lesbian, and bisexual issues into mainstream psychology. *American Psychologist, 56*, 977-988.

Goldman, L. (2008). *Coming out, coming in: Nurturing the well-being and inclusion of gay youth in mainstream society*. London, England: Taylor & Francis Group.

Goldman, L. (2010). *Great answers to difficult questions about sex: What children need to know.* London, England: Jessica Kingsley.

Herdt, G., & Boxer, A. (1993). *Children of horizons: How gay and lesbian teens are leading a new way out of the closet* (2nd ed.). Boston, MA: Beacon Press.

Himmelstein, K., & Bruckner, H. (2011). Criminal-justice and school sanctions against nonheterosexual youth: A national longitudinal study. *Pediatrics, 127*(1), 49-57.

Landolt, M., Bartholomew, K., Saffrey, C., Oram, D., & Perlman, D. (2004). Gender nonconformity, childhood rejection, and adult attachment: A study of gay men. *Archives of Sexual Behavior, 33*(2), 117-128.

Lindley, L., & Reininger, B. (2001). Support for instruction about homosexuality in South Carolina public schools. *The Journal of School Health, 71*(1), 17-22.

Livoti, V. M. (2009). *Forming a new generation: Constructing children's literature as a means for social action* (Doctoral dissertation). Retrieved from ProQuest Dissertations and Theses database. (AAT 3361944)

Johnson, C., & Johnson, K. (2000). High-risk behavior among gay adolescents: Implication for treatment and support. *Adolescence, 35*(140), 619-837.

Kitts, R. (2005). Gay adolescents and suicide: Understanding the association. *Adolescence, 40*(159), 621-628.

Mallon, G. P., & DeCrescenzo, T. (2006). Transgender children and youth: A child welfare practice perspective. *Child Welfare, 85*(2), 215-241.

Massachusetts Department of Education. (2009). *Massachusetts Youth Risk Behavior Survey*. Retrieved from http://www.mass.gov/clgy/publications.htm

Meyer, I. H. (2003). Prejudice, social stress, and mental health in lesbian, gay, and bisexual populations. Conceptual issues and research evidence. *Psychological Bulletin, 129*(5), 674-697.

Mufioz-Plaza, C., Quinn, S., & Rounds, K. (2002). Lesbian, gay, bisexual and transgender students: Perceived social support in the high school environment. *The High School Journal, 85*(4), 52-63.

Mulcahy, R. (Director). (2010). *Prayers for Bobby* [Motion picture]. New York, NY: A&E Home Video.

Myers, D. (2005). *Exploring psychology: Sixth edition in modules*. New York, NY: Worth.

Neimeyer, R., Harris, D., Winokuer, H., & Thornton, G. (Eds.). (2011). *Grief and bereavement in contemporary society: Bridging research and practice.* Contributing chapter, Linda Goldman & Vincent Livoti, "Grief in GLBT populations" (pp. 249-260). New York, NY: Routledge.

O'Hare, P. (2010, September 28). Parents say bullies drove their son to take his life. *Houston Chronicle*. Retrieved from http://www.chron.com/disp/story.mpl/metropolitan/7220896.html

Ploderl, M., & Fartacek, B. (2005). Suicidality and associated risk factors among lesbian, gay and bisexuals compared to heterosexual Austrian adults. *Suicide and Life-Threatening Behavior, 35*(6), 661-670.

Poteat, V. P., Aragon, S. R., Espelage, D. L., & Koenig, B. W. (2009). Psychological concerns of sexual minority youth. Complexity and caution in a group differences. *Journal of Consulting and Clinical Psychology, 77,* 196-201.

Quintana, N., Rosenthal, J., & Krehely, J. (2010). *On the streets: The federal response to gay and transgender homeless youth*. Washington, DC: Center for American Progress.

Ray, N. (2006). *Lesbian, gay, bisexual and transgender youth: An epidemic of homelessness*. New York, NY: National Gay and Lesbian Task Force Policy Institute and the National Coalition for the Homeless.

Rutter, P., & Soucar, E. (2002). Youth suicide risk and sexual orientation. *Adolescence, 37*(147), 289-299.

Ryan, C., Huebner, D., Diaz, R. M., & Sanchez, J. (2009). Family rejection as a predictor of negative health outcomes in white and Latino lesbian, gay and bisexual young adults. *Pediatrics, 123*(1), 346-352.

Ryan, C., Russell, S. T., Huebner, D. M., Diaz, R., & Sanchez, J. (2010). Family acceptance in adolescence and the health of LGBT young adults. *Journal of Child and Adolescent Psychiatric Nursing, 23*(4), 205-213.

Savage, T., Harley, D., & Nowak, T. (2005). Applying social empowerment strategies as tools for self-advocacy in counseling lesbian and gay male clients. *Journal of Counseling and Development, 83*, 131-137.

Setoodeh, R. (2008, July). Young, gay and murdered. *Newsweek Magazine*. Retrieved from http://www.thedailybeast.com/newsweek/2008/07/18/young-gay-and-murdered.html

Stepp, L. (2001, June 19). A lesson in cruelty: Anti-gay slurs common in school. *The Washington Post*. Retrieved from http://highbeam.com/doc/1P2-446825.hgml

Toomey, R. B., Ryan, C., Diaz, R. M., Card, N. A., & Russell, S. T. (2010, September 6). Gender-nonconforming lesbian, gay, bisexual, and transgender youth: School victimization and young adult psychosocial adjustment. *Developmental Psychology, 46,* 1580-1589.

The Trevor Project. (2010). Suicide prevention: Warning signs of suicide. Retrieved from http://www.thetrevorproject.org/suicide-resources/warning-signs

The Trevor Project. (2010). *The Trevor Project lifeguard workshop guide.* West Hollywood, CA: Author.

Van Leeuwen, J., Boyle, S., Salomonsen-Sautel, S., & Baker, D. (2006). Lesbian, gay and bisexual homeless youth: An eight-city public health perspective. *Child Welfare, 85*(2), 151-171.

Zavis, A. (2010, December 12). Gay and homeless: In plain sight, a largely hidden population. *The Los Angeles Times.* Retrieved from http://articles.latimes.com/2010/dec/12/local/la-me-gay-homeless-20101212

SECTION 2

Loss of Relationship and the Restoration of Intimacy in Families

Families are the primary social nexus in which we learn about intimacy and sexuality. With family members we share our most basic experiences of loss. This section introduces us to specific kinds of family relationships, perhaps those whose contemporary complications make them especially interesting. The authors of each chapter observe the impact to intimacy and sexuality that loss has upon family relationships: when the mourning of a father is affected by the use of erectile dysfunction drugs; when a parent dies and the survivors' emotions are complicated by their histories with that parent, even to the point that the parent's death may be "welcomed"; when the transition from "couple" into "family" takes determination, intentionality, and technology (losses that accompany the decision to attempt in vitro fertilization); and when there are "unseen" losses in the lives of soldiers and their families because intimacy becomes collateral damage in wartime.

The issue in this chapter is not just our awareness of the impact of loss but also the many hurdles that can accompany the effort to regain firmer footing in life and in new relationships.

Harold Ivan Smith, DMin, FT, is a grief specialist on the faculty at Saint Luke's Hospital in Kansas City, Missouri, and the Carondlet Medical Institute in Eau Claire, Wisconsin. An active member of ADEC, he is recognized as a Fellow in Thanatology. He earned a doctorate in spiritual formation from Asbury Theological Seminary and an EdS from Vanderbilt University. His forthcoming books are *Borrowed Narratives* and the second edition of *A Decembered Grief*. Smith's current research focuses on the grief of U.S. presidents and first ladies. As a storyteller, he uses innovative and creative techniques to support grieving persons. Here he discusses how the use of medications for erectile dysfunction, or what many adjudge as a performance or quality issue, affect both the intimacy/sexuality options of grieving widowers and the responses to their choices of family members and friends.

Richard B. Gilbert, PhD, DMin, CT, speaks to the loss of love and meaning between parents and adult children because of earlier "deaths" that destroyed the family long before its destruction by death itself. Looking at family life this way often involves the discarding of what we *believe* to be the proper definition of marriage, on the one hand, and the parent–child relationship on the other. Some factors, such as culture or ethnicity, particularly redefine the role of the father and his absence from parenting. Other factors can include addictions, abuse, incest, imprisonment, leaving because of a job, or financial ruin. Dick teaches on several campuses and resides in Galesburg, Illinois.

Darcy L. Harris, PhD, FT, is an associate professor in the Department of Interdisciplinary Programs and coordinates the thanatology program at King's University College at the University of Western Ontario in London, Ontario, Canada. Dr. Harris also maintains a private clinical practice specializing in issues related to change, loss, and transition. She also serves on the board of directors of ADEC and is a consultant for community agencies who work with individuals that are facing different types of loss and grief. She has written many articles and book chapters. She has edited a book, *Counting our Losses: Reflecting on Change, Loss, and Transition in Everyday Life* (2010), that explores grief after non-death losses in addition to coediting another book entitled *Grief and Bereavement in Contemporary Society: Bridging Research and Practice* (2011), and she recently coauthored a book entitled *Principles and Practice of Grief Counseling* (2012). In our book, she explores losses related to the impasses of infertility and the effects that the choices that couples make have upon their intimacy.

Doug Harvey, MDiv, CT, Chaplain (Captain), USAR, is a veteran of OEF/OIF (our war in Iraq) and an on-site counselor of soldiers in the war zone as well as of veterans. He is a former board-certified chaplain with experience in hospice care, older adult services, and military chaplaincy. While he does have congregational experience, he has spent the majority of his years in ministry as a health care chaplain working in hospice programs both in Louisville and Lexington, Kentucky, and has also taken that expertise into the long-term care setting. Doug is certified in thanatology with ADEC. He is well acquainted with the systemic reality for veterans and how that can both help and hinder the healing of our veterans and our responses to them.

CHAPTER 3

Momma's Dead and Daddy's on Viagra! Elder Widowers, ED Drugs, and New Romantic Relationships

Harold Ivan Smith

> At 82 I thought my sex life was pretty much over, but not so!
> I'm back in the saddle again!
> —Satisfied customer ("Supersize Your Male Sex Drive!" 2004, p. D12)

> I feel like a kid again—"a 25-year-old."
> —Arnold Palmer, 75, moments after remarrying ("Arnie Remarries," 2005, p. D2)

> Sexed-up seniors do it more than you think.
> —Headline on website, *NBC News* (Marshall, 2008, p. 21)

Levine (1992) identifies four psychological factors that influence erectile dysfunction in elderly widowers: (a) guilt about impulses to have multiple partners, (b) a sense of "still" being married, (c) confusion about the new freedom, and/or (d) discomfort about reactions of children and friends. In a study of 1,112 males with prostate cancer, 62% of white males and 65% of African-American males agreed with the statement "I do not think that I could find a new relationship if I had an erection problem," while 43% of whites and 55% of African-Americans concurred with the statement "My partner would lose desire for me if I could not perform" (Jenkins et al., 2004, p. 88).

In the late 1990s, scientists halted clinical trials on a new drug for treating heart disease after concluding that it was ineffective. Many male participants, however, were reluctant to give up the medications because of the effect of hardening their penises and, subsequently, improving their intimate relationships *and* self-identities. Sildenafil citrate, commercially marketed as Viagra since 1998—and competitor phosphodiesterase type 5 (PDE5) inhibitors such as

Cialis (tadalafil) and Levitra (vardenafil)—enhance erection, sexual performance, and sexual satisfaction by relaxing the smooth muscle in the penis and increasing blood flow to accommodate penetration. Within six months of the U.S. Food and Drug Administration's approval, more than six million prescriptions for Viagra had been written (Broderick & Lue, 2002; Lamberg, 1998). In the first year of marketing, Pfizer Pharmaceuticals sold more than one billion dollars' worth of "blue magic" (Loe, 2001, p. 120); 2004 sales reached $1.7 billion (Bufalino, 2004; Schmidt, 2005). As subsequent American sales have diminished, the drug's manufacturers have marketed globally. Viagra—and its competitors and counterfeits—is everywhere. By the time Viagra was aggressively marketed in China in 2004, more than 170 million prescriptions had been written worldwide (Zhang, 2007). Pharmaceutical producers are seeking to expand the current $17 billion market for "men's health," primarily erectile dysfunction, or ED (Marshall, 2008, p. 22).

In our sexual-centric society, many aging adults are unwilling to accept declining sexual impulse in aging as "nature's wisdom." Barnett, Robleda Gomez, and Pachana (2012) bemoan that psychological aspects and social implications of the drug use are clearly absent from the research that has pathologized "sexual capacities once linked with normal aging" as sexual dysfunction (p. 84). ED is a problem to be solved if one believes one is entitled to "sex for life," a "new sexual imperative" according to Potts, Grace, Vares, and Gavey (2006, p. 313), an idea not discordant from "the right to the pursuit of happiness" in the minds of some. Indeed, Gullette notes that many males use memories of *adolescent* sex experiences as a reference point, which fuels "sexual nostalgia" (1998, p. 17). Potts, Grace, Vares, and Gavey (2006) report that the numbers of men "suffering" from ED has increased dramatically *since* the introduction of Viagra in 1998. What once was considered "a natural component of aging" is becoming a "medical disorder" requiring treatment (p. 312), perhaps aggressively. Marshall contends that sexual health has become "equated with sexual function" and specifically, "the desire and ability to have intercourse" (2008, p. 22). Thus, in the "Age of Better Sex through Pharmaceuticals," Gross and Blundo (2005, p. 23) suggest that ED is a medical "problem" to be solved. Simply, "the penis becomes a much regarded part of a man's body over the man's lifetime and remains a central construct for aging men's masculinity" (Gross & Blundo, 2005, p. 89). The "sexual self-narrative" of many widowers, especially elders, is defined by genital functioning and a comparison to "what I used to be able to do." Polkinghorn (1988) warns that, while "life is not over," the sexual component of the narrative is presumed over. Viagra may give an individual a chance to "reauthor" life, or at least his sexual narratives (Neimeyer, 2001).

Given the 2.168 million widowers 65 and older in the United States (United States Bureau of the Census, 2008, p. 52), in a youth-oriented society, what effect does male erectile dysfunction have on grief narratives or on what Gullette (1998) identified as "midlife decline narratives"? The pivotal concern for those who study mourning and its patterns is that the use of Viagra, or other drugs for erectile dysfunction and "sexual health," can distract from grief work by triggering "replacement" relational choices. Does Viagra and the subsequent intimate relationships facilitated by an ED drug have an impact upon grief or even disrupt the reintegration of family and support networks? Levine observes that men commonly "use dating [and sex] as a distraction from . . . inevitably difficult aspects of grief" (1992, p. 204). Consider the lament of George, age 62, widowed after 39 years of marriage, who went through an aborted "encounter" with a potential sex partner:

> I said, "I can't even make a fist." She said, "With me you don't have to." So I said, "Well, thank you very much. That's the best offer I have had in I don't know how long." And then I walked on my way. But it was very demoralizing, a very sad experience. Because it put me in touch with the fact that part of my life seems light years away. . . . I know enough about my body to know that at this moment I would be of no use to anyone, that I would be impotent. I know that this is a likely response, and an appropriate one, and that even this shall pass, but it doesn't make it less agonizing. (Campbell & Silverman, 1996, p. 34)

WHAT IS ERECTILE DYSFUNCTION?

Erectile dysfunction, commonly abbreviated in medical research and in this chapter as ED, is "a persistent or recurrent inability to attain, or to maintain until completion of the sexual activity, an adequate erection" (American Psychiatric Association, 2004, p. 545). ED is the most common chronic medical disorder in males over 40 (Carson, 2002). It affects one out of every four men over age 40 and one in every two men over age 75 (Golden, 2004; MacReady, 2003). Globally, between 15 and 30 million men "suffer from some degree of this condition" (Wentzell, 2008, p. 888) and *suffer* may not be too severe a word. Seventy percent (Shabsign, 2002) or 80 percent (Carson, 2002) of ED goes undiagnosed. A study examining the sexual behaviors of more than 33,000 subjects, found that although 44% of males in their sixties, 66% of males in their seventies, and 69% of males in their eighties acknowledged experiencing ED in the previous 90 days, only 11% of those in their sixties, 13% of those in their seventies, and 8% of those in their eighties sought medical or psychological help (Schover et al., 2004, p. 444). Is ED its own grief that is disenfranchised?

The issue is not new. Zhang (2007) notes that Chinese traditional medicine has offered cures for impotence for 2000 years, primarily herbs and acupuncture. Moreover, this was a cultural barrier to Viagra sales in China. In many areas of the world, ED is understood as a "curse" or an intervention of malevolent spirits. Some argue that stress on an immune system significantly increases susceptibility to illness (Campbell & Silverman, 1996). An estimated 80% of individuals over age 65 have one or more chronic diseases that impact sexual functioning, performance, and satisfaction (MacReady, 2003). Examples of such are diabetes (Giuliano, Leriche, Jaudinot, & de Gendre, 2004; Sun, Seftel, & Swindle, 2004); alcoholism and alcohol abuse (McCarthy, 1992); recreational drugs (Venes, 2009); hypertension, peripheral vascular disease, and severe cardiac disease (Carson, 2002; Zipes, Libby, Bonow, & Braunwald, 2005); prostate cancer or treatments for enlarged prostate (Jenkins et al., 2004; Schover et al., 2004); Parkinson's disease (Bronner, Royter, Korczyn, & Giladi, 2004); cancer of the bladder (Zippe et al., 2004); and HIV/AIDS (Jacobson, 2007). Additionally, medications taken for blood pressure or heart ailments, anti-depressants, or inappropriate dosage of medications (Perelman, 2001) may lead to impotence.

SEXUALITY, AGING, AND THE QUALITY OF LIFE

Some elderly widowers paraphrase Descartes, "I can have sex, therefore I am." Leaver, Perreault, and Demetrakopoulos insist that "a healthy sexual desire, after all, is a marker of well-being" (2008, p. 49). Erectile difficulties, however, challenge male perceptions of masculinity, intimacy, sexuality, and personal self-confidence (Bokhour, Clark, Inui, Silliman, & Talcott, 2001; Graham, 2003; Marshall, 2008; Siegel & Schrimshaw, 2003;) and alter sexual and social narratives. Americans are obsessed with "penetrative sex" and discount "alternate modes of relating sexually" that many elders come to identify as "'normal,' 'healthy,' and 'enjoyable'" and that some widowers *and their partners* report as satisfying (Potts et al., 2006, p. 306). Forty-three percent of males agreed with the statement "Having a sexual problem makes me feel less of a man," while 46% concurred with the statement "Women gossip about a new lover who cannot get an erection" (Jenkins et al., 2004, p. 88). Loe concludes, "If the penis is in trouble, so is the man" (2001, p. 109).

Aging has its own impact upon sexual performance (Hillman & Stricker, 1996; Marshall, 2008). Elder males commonly have difficulty achieving and maintaining an erection capable of penetration (Laumann, Paik, & Rosen, 1999). "There is no question that the human male's sexual responsiveness wanes as he ages" (Masters & Johnson, 1966, p. 262).

Although Marsiglio and Donnelley report that 56.2% of males ages 66 and over had not had sex in the past month (1991, p. S341), ED was not the only factor accounting for their sexual frequency. In fact, several factors curtail sexual expression among older men. One is the already named health issues, but others include the lack of an available and *interested* partner as well as negative attitudes toward elder sexual expression (Floyd & Weiss, 2001). Marsiglio and Donnelley contend that clinical practice and research on sexual behaviors of elders are biased by "youth-oriented definitions of sexuality as coitus" (1991, p. S338), that is to say, penetration equals sex or "real" sex. "Sexual ageism"

(Floyd & Weiss, 2001; Waitzkin, 1989) challenges acknowledgment of sexual response in elders. Commonly, elders are perceived to be sexually undesirable, disinterested in sex, and unable to perform (Levy, 1994)—as captured in a common cliché, "too old to cut the mustard."

Sexual ageism also affects elders' attitudes toward themselves and contributes to their failure to seek medical or psychological attention, particularly from younger physicians. Consequently, elderly widowers may be ashamed of their sexual desires, fantasies, capacities, interests, and behaviors to the point they may *self*-disenfranchise, ignore their sexual desires, "opt out," or hide their relationships from family and friends.

VIAGRA TO THE RESCUE!

The copy line in a full-page ad in *The Wall Street Journal* featuring a smiling elder teases, "Get back to mischief. Ask your doctor if VIAGRA is right for you" (Viagra, 2004, p. A7). Some widowers cannot imagine getting "back to mischief," initiating and maintaining new intimate relationships, or ever initiating a conversation with a physician about erection difficulties.

Many males have experienced, or fear experiencing, widowers' syndrome, a post-marital anxiety resulting in ED that "typically involves complex interactions of dating, new partners, and unresolved mourning/guilt" (Broderick & Lue, 2002, p. 1632)—as well as objections from or ridicule by family members. Some elder widowers have had little or no sexual experience outside of marriage (Levy, 1994). Others have been married celibates. Morgenthaler, a urologist with extensive experience prescribing Viagra, finds heightened anxiety in males not yet in a committed, long-term relationship, especially if they "equate their attractiveness and self-confidence with their bedroom abilities" (2003, p. 159). McCarthy counsels: "A widower needs to realize that he probably will not have easy, automatic erections with the new partner. It will take time, communication, and the partner's cooperation to develop a comfortable and functional sexual relationship" (1992, p. 321).

Elder widowers must navigate what Rohr (2004) labels the "hierarchy of age" and the "hierarchy of attraction." A wife's death may escalate a widower's fears of his own death, particularly if he has had or expects to have significant health issues, and motivates attempts to validate and enhance self-esteem and hope through sexual intimacy.

The timing of remarriage—or acknowledging a new intimate relationship, which may not initially be premarital—is critical to avoid censure from family and the social support network (Neimeyer, 2005), particularly in fundamental Christian communities of faith that reject *all* nonmarital sexual behavior.

Society, desirous of some measure of social order in sexual expression and marital relationships, has traditionally expected a period of transition between marital statuses (Timmerman, 2001) or between "what was" and "what will yet be." This "time out," or imposed abstinence, functions for the widower "as a bridge between one identity status and another" (Neimeyer, 2005). Initial grief support within a social network bestows a new, although perhaps unspoken, communally sanctioned "reinscription of identity" upon widowers (Romanoff & Terenzio, 1998). By complying with community-defined norms of social propriety and resisting new romantic involvements "for an explicit or implicit period of time" (Neimeyer, 2005, p. 13) widowers gain—or retain—social support and avoid social condemnation. In some condolences males hear "We'll keep an eye out *for* you" and "We'll be keeping an eye *on* you!"

Though support keeps widowers socially connected in a predominately coupled social orbit (Caserta, Lund, & Obray, 2004), discomfort may fuel an urgency to remarry in order to get back to "a marital normal." "Everywhere I look," one elder widower told me, "I am reminded of what I *once* had." Moreover, the support network may collude to help "behaving" widowers meet "acceptable" potential spouses, particularly in retirement communities or activities or groups focused on senior adults.

CLASSIFICATIONS OF VIAGRA-USING ELDER WIDOWERS

I classify Viagra-using elder widowers into three generalized categories: traditionalists, transitionalists, and transformationalists.

Traditionalists

The traditionalist widower objects—at least publicly—to *any* sexual behavior outside of marriage, including, for some, masturbation. This widower may defend his choice: "I am old-fashioned about some things." This widower may remarry to have sanctioned sexual experience, sometimes before integrating the death, sometimes to avoid thorough grief. "A man's got needs and I do not believe in shackin' up!" one elder snapped at his children, defending his immediate remarriage following their mother's death. Some families expect an elder or patriarch to model a high moral standard for younger generations (Marsiglio & Donnelley, 1991).

Religious fundamentalists hold socially conservative views forbidding all nonmarital sexual behaviors. "Religion and sexuality are inextricably intertwined for many" widowers because most religions regulate sexual behavior to some degree (Worthington, 2004, p. 741). Thus, the "cultural or religious indoctrination" of a widower (Broderick & Lue, 2002) has to be considered in any Viagra dialogue or therapeutic conversation. Conservative religious belief coupled with the belief "a man *has* to have sex" may encourage not only rapid remarriage but also clandestine sexual experiences with prostitutes, escorts, and publicly unacknowledged "just sex" relationships.

Children of traditionalists may question the timing of the initiation of a romantic relationship, particularly when following a mother's long illness, dementia, or Alzheimer's. Did the new relationship *predate* the death of the mother or stepmother? The real issue—although unspoken—may be fears about the new relationship's impact on the estate or potential inheritance.

How does the widower, or partner, receive and relieve what is perceived as intrusive questions from adult children? Does this seem a role reversal in that the child assumes the role of parent? One son told me, "My father's life has always been an open book *until now*. He will not tell me when he met this woman. He's hiding something." One widower defensively dismissed his children's concerns: "I grieved before their mother died. I watched her die in increments. I grieved *before* she died!" Tensions are heightened if fathers dismiss concerns with blunt remarks like "It is none of your business!"

Transitionalists

The transitionalist widower may be awed, or intimidated, by the potential for sexual partners and experiences, but he perceives this time in his life as a period "between marriages." Most transitionalists are not in a rush to marry again. He is trying to adjust to sexual mores and current circumstances. "Boy, has the world changed since I was a teenager!" one widower remarked. Many transitionalists seek "freedom" from predictable sexual responses and sexual boredom experienced in marriage (Masters & Johnson, 1966). Some goal-centered, traditionalist-leaning transitionalists do find themselves wanting to "fast forward" to marriage, perhaps not being entirely comfortable with being "in between." Most, however, after a while, settle in and befriend the transition, particularly if experiencing sex with multiple partners—given the imbalance of unmarried females to unmarried males. Some perceive widowerhood as an opportunity to "make up" for lost sexual opportunities while married or to sample sexual repertoire that had been off-limits in marriage, such as oral sex. As one widower said, "I've got a whole lot of living to do . . . while I *still* can!" As one transitionalist informed me, "She makes me feel alive from the top of my head to the soles of my feet—and *everywhere* in between!"

The relocation of widowers into age-segregated retirement communities, a significant transition for some widowers, may facilitate sexual relationships and experiences beyond the awareness, and interference, of adult children—especially children who live some distance away. Among residents in selected high-rise senior adult retirement complexes in Chicago, Illinois, and West Hartford, Connecticut, researchers documented "exchanges of sex and drugs for cash with male and female commercial sex workers, group sex, and drug use" (Radda, Schensul, Disch, Levy, & Reyes, 2003, p. 6), as well as subsequent high-risk sexual behaviors among residents, such as failing to use a condom. Elderly residents who had engaged in risky sex practices or illegal drug use before becoming residents continued these behaviors. Some regularly sought the company of commercial sexual workers and chose unprotected vaginal intercourse over other penetrative sex (Schensul, Levy, & Disch, 2003), facilitated, in some instances, by Viagra use. Some female commercial workers disclosed regular use of injected heroin or crack cocaine—behaviors that place them, their partners, *and* their partners' future partners at risk for HIV and other sexually transmitted diseases.

Some transitionalists are responding spontaneously to sexual opportunities without serious reflection on consequences. Many sexually active widowers, because of their age, do not consider themselves at risk for HIV and STDs and engage in unprotected behaviors they are reluctant to acknowledge (Karlosvsky, Lebed, & Mydio, 2004) to adult children, friends, or clinicians (Meris, 2002; Whipple & Scura, 1996). HIV prevalence estimates for seniors range from 10% to 17% (Ory & Mack, 1998; Radda et al., 2003). The myth that HIV/AIDS warnings apply only to "those other kinds of people" may place the senior widower at elevated levels of risk.

Transformationalists

The transformationalist elder widower experiences a sexual reawakening with a new interest in and enthusiasm for sexuality and intimacy. Rather than being weighed down by mourning, he experiences it as a personal transformation. His enhanced self-image is sometimes buoyed by perceptions of the effectiveness of Viagra. For example, one widower told me, with a large grin, that he'd found his "new lease on life." Bonanno, Nesse, and Wortman note that some widowers "involved in an unrewarding marriage" may feel relieved "from a challenging set of circumstances and demands," particularly as a caregiver (2004, p. 261). In their sample, almost half showed little or no depression following the death of a spouse "and approximately 10 percent showed improved mental health following the loss" (2004, pp. 269–270). Transformational sexual experiences and expectations redefine a widower's perception of self as a sexual person and a potentially attractive romantic or marital partner. Moreover, this transformation may redefine the way the widower is perceived by potential suitors since ED also has an impact upon the partner (Chevret, Jaudinot, Sullivan, Marrel, & De Gendre, 2004). One widow explained bluntly, "I want a man who is *reliable* in bed." Viagra's ads promise, in the perception of many, reliability. Moreover, some widows whose previous partners experienced ED are not interested in "dealing with it" again.

A widower's sexual transformation may be unwelcomed within the social support network because vitality challenges the sexual status quo of peer marriages. "Don't go getting any ideas!" more than one wife has cautioned a husband after observing a widowed friend's "new lease on life." Some friends cannot acknowledge, or encourage, a new relationship without feeling they are being disloyal to the deceased; some feel the same way after a divorce. Thus, the widower may grieve for changes in his support system even as he embraces his new sense of self.

SEXUAL DISENFRANCHISEMENT

Sexual expression may be a key threat in the disenfranchisement of elderly widowers by certain peers. When survivors' losses cannot be openly acknowledged, publicly mourned, or socially supported or when their right to grieve is unrecognized or under-recognized, that loss is disenfranchised (Doka, 1989). Attig (2004) contends that Doka does not "explicitly articulate" what is included in a "right" to grieve. If, as Attig suggests, "Holders of rights are entitled to non-interference from others in the free exercise of their rights" (2004, p. 198), are they not equally entitled to non-interference in their sexual choices and relationships? Moreover, might a statement such as "I am so lonely" be a "safe" way to express the mourning of loss of sexual intimacy? Attig notes:

> The right to grieve entitles a bereaved person to grieve in a manner and on a timetable . . . free of interference from others. No one is obligated to grieve in a particular way. In response, others are obligated to honor the right and refrain from interfering in the experiences and efforts of others. Disenfranchisement of grief or the disenfranchisement of sexual longing "violates the griever's right to grieve." (2004, p. 198)

Clinicians may be prejudiced by their own perceptions of "appropriate" elder sexual expression and thus be reluctant to recognize fully the impact of the loss of a sexual partner, or predictable patterns of sexual intimacy, as significant secondary losses. I ask grieving widowers, "Who are you without sexual intimacy?"

Historically, elder widowers remarried primarily for sexual access and secondarily for caregiving, financial resources, or security and to avoid scandal and sanction within the community. Many elders feel helplessness and loneliness, particularly if the wife was the magnet in social relationships. Widowers may explain the desire for remarriage, or sexual relationships, in phrases such as "I want companionship" or "because I'm so lonely." Often the widower's adjustment is threatened by intrafamily estrangement that intensifies the loneliness. These days, "keeping each other company" may imply more than family members imagine or would acknowledge.

Some family members want a predictable father or widower who lives by the basic tenets that have previously guided his life. Some family members perceive any emerging sexual interests as a challenge to tradition and the psychological equilibrium of the family system.

In reality, within some marriages, extramarital sexual experiences or relationships were tolerated by spouses but were unknown, even unsuspected, by adult children. Thus, an unknown or unsuspected extramarital partner may emerge as front-runner candidate for marriage so that the remarriage may not be as *premature* as initially assumed. For religious fundamentalists, as well as representatives of certain cultures or family functioning, the pre-death romantic or sexual conduct is adjudged adultery.

VIAGRA AND "SHOW ME THE MONEY!"

Contemporary economic policies discourage remarriage of elders with low incomes (Moore & de Costa, 2003). To protect pensions, Social Security benefits, family unity, or loss of independence, some elders relationally invest in non-marital sexualized relationships. Given the 4:1 ratio imbalance of widows to widowers (United States Bureau of the Census, 2008, p. 52), some widowers enjoy their marketability and maintain multiple relationships. Some ration disclosure to adult children or friends; some prefer clandestine sexual experiences with escorts, prostitutes, strangers, or cyber contacts to avoid emotional commitment and potential sanction by family and community.

While the comments of adult children reflect their grief issues, the difference in roles and responsibilities as spouses vs. children is not the only motivation. There are sibling wars over who did the most to help Mom and Dad and other conflicts. In some families, "it all boils down to the money," and that can be a strong fuel for family stress. Protecting Dad from a "gold digger" or making sure that Dad can protect his resources for future security often becomes contentious.

Peisah, Brodaty, and Bridger (2008) point to another hurdle: a widower may be vulnerable to romantic manipulation and abuse. The Healthy Aging Taskforce (2000) defines elder abuse as, "any act occurring within a relationship where there is an implication of trust, which results in harm to an older person" (as cited in Peisah, Brodaty, and Bridger, 2008, p. 883). What is the widower's mental "capacity to marry"? Moreover, who has the right to challenge—or sabotage—an elder's decision to marry or become involved in a romantic/sexual relationship? This is troubling if the romantic partner is unknown to the family or has recently met the widower and if the widower has significant financial assets.

Identifying, acknowledging, and owning real motivations for opposition to a new relationship are critical for an authentic relationship. The greed and expectations of adult children may be disguised as "concern" for the widowed parent's well-being. Some adult children, believing "their" future inheritance to be an entitlement, challenge anyone who threatens "the loot." They may support, or perhaps prefer, a live-in relationship that does not evolve into a marriage and, thereby, legally threaten an anticipated inheritance or threaten their ability to "manage" (or manipulate) the widower. This becomes complex if the widower has, even during the previous marriage, acted as a "banker" to an adult child, loaning or giving money. Will the new spouse challenge that role? Clinicians may find it useful to ask: "Does your objection to your father's new relationship have anything to do with money or a potential inheritance?"

Butler and Lewis (2002) counsel elders, "Your estate is your own to disperse (or amend) as you see fit." Thus, they suggest, it is important to be "decisive and remain unintimidated by veiled or open threats, pressures, and pleadings focused upon your property" (2002, p. 304)—or sexual choices.

IMPLICATIONS FOR CLINICIANS

Thanatologists may find the navigating of these issues—which may function as a "landmine" to new romance—to be complicated and stressful. The following suggestions may be of value when counseling elderly widowers or "concerned" family members.

Guidance 1: Caring professionals must audit their own attitudes on aging, grief, and sexuality. These beliefs fuel the lingering taboo in the field of thanatology: grief *and* sex. Thanatologists must ponder in what ways they project discomfort on this issue. Shaw, advising clinicians how to confront issues of aging and sexuality, challenges societal bias: "Most of us have been socially conditioned to think that old people are—or should be—non-sexual, and old demented people receive not an afterthought" (2001, p. 142). Thanatologists must exhibit "an accepting, nonjudgmental attitude toward *all* clients" that recognizes the individual's right to ascribe to particular beliefs (Brusich, 1990, author's emphasis added) and recognizes the widower's right to choose how he experiences and expresses sexual behaviors even with a significantly younger partner. Chin urges professionals to reexamine the classic definition of prejudice by Allport (1954) as "a preformed opinion, usually an unfavorable one, based on insufficient knowledge, irrational feelings, or inaccurate stereotypes" (2010, p. vii). If not in themselves, thanatologists might often observe such negative, "preformed opinions" in the clients they serve.

My experience with John, a 75-year-old retired minister, widowed 12 months, living in a small town, was instructive. John was involved in a self-described "platonic" relationship with a 55-year-old woman. "I have needs," he explained, "*Strong* needs." I assured John that such needs were normal for 75-year-old males, including retired clergy. John replied:

> Well, my son does not think so and he's a physician! He told me that I was behaving like an "old-goat in heat." That's his *exact* words. He said that I was an embarrassment to him and his children and the church. He claims the whole community is making fun of me behind my back. "Dad, you are too old for these kinds of feelings. It's not natural." And he called me "a dirty old man!"

Through questioning, I learned that although John's daughters supported their father, the son, as the oldest child *and* as a physician, expected his opinions to trump his siblings' opinions. I asked the father to consider the possibility that his son had skipped classes in medical school when elder adult sexual behavior was discussed. Eventually, John married the woman and they had, seemingly, two "wonderful" years together, although family gatherings were tense when the son was present.

Bonanno, Neese, and Wortman (2004) caution about "the importance of maintaining a healthy skepticism toward traditional assumptions" in grief. In fact, therapists "still have much to learn about the variety of ways [widowers] cope with loss" (Bonanno et al., 2004, p. 270), particularly those who "clinicalize" bereavement.

A widower will not be candid or committed to counseling until convinced that the thanatologist will respect his right to express sexual behaviors.

Guidance 2: Ask about this widower's "sex life." Males experiencing ED want their physicians to initiate conversations on the issue (Ward et al., 2001). In the Mirone et al. study of 12,761 males with ED, however, only 50.3% had discussed their condition with their physicians, and only 56.9% had discussed with a partner (2002, p. 256). Thanatologists should remember Griebling's advice to physicians: "If you wait for the patient to initiate the discussion, they won't do it" (as cited in MacReady, 2003). *Taber's Encyclopedic Medical Dictionary* suggests "primary practitioners should make questions about sexual function a routine part of history-taking" (Venes, 2009, p. 704). Thus, a thanatologist might initiate a "door-opening" conversation by noting, "Some grieving widowers tell me they are surprised by their sexual feelings." Thanatologists may understand the physiology of erectile dysfunction and the psychological and pharmacological interaction of Viagra on sexual confidence but *under*appreciate the emotional distress captured in a widower's lament, "I felt empty, as if I was no longer a man" (Simons, 2003, p. 110).

Obtaining a thorough, honest sexual narrative with an elder widower can be challenging (Shives, 2005) because of sexual euphemisms. One elderly widower told a counselor, "I may be old but I can *still* shoot bullets!" Some might have missed the use of *shoot bullets* as a synonym for *ejaculate*. Moreover, "silent stories" embedded in autobiographical narratives are commonly "denied acknowledgment in the presence of others, or perhaps even to the self" (Neimeyer, 2005). For some widowers this may evoke religious issues or concerns (Timmerman, 2001). I asked, given one widower's religiosity, "Have you talked to your minister?" "I can't," he replied. "He's my best friend and golfing partner. I could *never* bring it up with him."

A thanatologist must "lean in" to understand jumbled jargon in order to catch the intentionality of seniors who are uncomfortable verbalizing sexual desires for fear of reprimand by an authority figure, particularly a younger person. The thanatologist might ponder how to respectfully solicit and "receive" *this* widower's sexual narrative. This can lead to discussion with a simple observation, "*Some* widowers have shared with me sexual anxieties about initiating a new relationship." The client may respond or not or may wait another session to respond.

Zilbergeld advises clinicians: "We helping professionals need to remind ourselves continually that the problems we deal with are human problems *not penis problems*, and that the men with whom we apply our methods are frightened and fragile" (1992, p. 50, author's emphasis added). Such conversations may trigger anxiety or concern in the clinician who is older or who has an older widowed father or father-in-law.

Guidance 3: Particular support must be offered to elderly widowers and their choice to re-enter a highly sexualized dating world that has changed radically since the widower last dated. Elder widowers may immediately face a challenge: "how to be sexually active outside of marriage" (Levy, 1994, p. 303). Imagining a sexual "future" is challenging. Letting go of "the memory of things past and the metamorphosis of letting go of who you were, in order to become who you will be," note Leaver et al. (2008, p. 47), is a "difficult process," no doubt with right turns, left turns, and u-turns. It can be a difficult process for widowers, their partners, and their family members. Rudavsky (2010) comments on a study of 5,865 American adults, ages 14–95, that sexual behavior has become very complex. Even defining *sex* can be a challenge for researchers and individuals. Thus, "having sex" "can encompass a variety of acts other than intercourse" (Rudavsky, 2010, p. 4D). Some widowers may wish to explore ways in which sexuality can be more meaningful.

There may be the need to examine sexual regrets. One elder widower, after a sexual relationship "imploded," lamented: "Everyone is going to say that I am an old fool!" I received his comment, then responded, "Those who care about you—and there are a great many who do—will only be sorry for the incredible pain this has caused you."

Initiating new sexual relationships can be so threatening that elders may repress their sexual desires (Eliopoulos, 2005). An elderly widower may doubt his ability to attract a good partner or spouse given the particular contours of his sexual narratives. Indeed, some males may be surprised to experience the female as sexual initiator or that she has sexual expectations.

Many elders, particularly those using anti-depressants, need sustained genital stimulation to achieve and maintain erection (Koenig & Herman, 1994). Thanatologists must "be attentive to a surprising interplay of the care-seeker's religious heritage in the context of sexual self-discovery" (Graham, 2003, p. 38). Koenig and Weaver found "that persons from more conservative, fundamentalist religious traditions were less likely to experiment with different sexual practices that might help facilitate arousal and increase pleasure" (1999, p. 205), such as oral sex. Koenig and Herman are clear: "Religiously oriented older adults . . . may need special encouragement and permission to widen their array of sexual behaviors" (1994, p. 84), or to redefine their meaning of "making love" or "having sex." Oral sex—or mutual oral sex—may not have been part of the widower's marital sexual repertoire. Walt, a retired minister, initially informed me that oral sex was "a filthy abomination practiced by homosexuals that deserves the severest judgment of God!" In preparing for remarriage, a few years later, Walt discovered that his fiancée—and the clinician leading their premarital counseling—did not share that assessment. Walt later grinned as he informed me, "Who says an old dog cannot learn new tricks?"

Anxieties may intensify if or as a relationship evolves to "the test" of sexual performance (Campbell & Silverman, 1996) before a commitment to marriage. Some widowers—and their partners—perceive sexual episodes, especially with significantly younger partners, as "something to prove" auditions. Butler and Lewis caution:

> When men or women doubt their sexual performance, or fear that the person with whom they are involved may be measuring them against the behavior of a previous partner [or other current partners], it will affect their sexual ability. It takes an active effort by both you and your current partner to make the present moment satisfying. (2002, p. 278)

Guidance 4: Thanatologists must be aware that Viagra and other ED drugs do not work "magic" for all widowers. Viagra does not "work" to the level of expectation for 30% to 40% of males (Broderick & Lue, 2002; Klotz, Mathers, Klotz, & Sommer, 2005); 50% do not seek refills of the initial prescription (Parker-Pope, 2002, p. R3). "Good sex" requires more than a firm, erect penis. Pharmaceuticals do not make anyone "more appealing as a human being or as a potential partner" (Morgenthaler, 2003, p. 159). Moreover, not all sexual partners welcome Viagra (Cayan, Bozlu, Canpolat, & Akbay, 2004; Morgenthaler, 2003). Some partners resent arousal via "the little blue pill" rather than by romantic attraction and foreplay and reject the emphasis on "penetrative sexuality" (Wentzell, 2008, p. 889). Lamberg (1998) labels this annoyance as "Viagravation."

Some individuals stop taking the medications. Rarely, Barnett and Pachana (2007) note, are sexual partners included in the medical consultation. It must be remembered that ED also has an impact upon partners (Chevret et al., 2004). Some elderly widowers may be resuming taking Viagra without their physicians' awareness that they are widowed. Some may obtain Viagra on the black market or the Internet (Bufalino, 2004; "Viagra's License," 1998), where few, if any, medical questions are asked. Viagra cannot take a history of "bad" sex and suddenly redeem it.

Guidance 5: Thanatologists must be aware that sexual dysfunction affects between 30% and 50% of patients on selective and nonselective NRSs for depression. The Family Physician Inquiries Network (2008) reports that in some studies ED ranges from 70% to 80%. A significant number of patients stop taking the antidepressant because of sexual side effects or the fear of side effects (Family Physician Inquiries Network, 2008, p. 793). This can have significant consequences on the widower's mental state.

Guidance 6: Thanatologists must be aware that ED may have been a factor in the marriage. Some males experience ED with selected partners rather than *all* partners. At this point in life, the widower may be unwilling to do significant psychological work to explore the condition. In essence, in a new approach, the sexual grief may be "rebooted."

IMPLICATIONS FOR FUTURE RESEARCH

Further research is needed to expand thanatological awareness of the sexual influence on grief integration among elder widowers. Thanatologists must explore new ways to navigate the narrative landscape of widowers and anticipate and reduce communication barriers around sexuality. This may become significant as the first boomers hit "older age" in 2011. Thanatologists can expect a growing pharmaceutical response to female sexual dysfunction (Family Physicians Inquiries Network, 2008), which can be its own significant grief. Moreover, there are significant implications for gay or bisexual men in an age-focused gay community. This is also true for heterosexually married gay men, now widowed, who must redefine their sexual landscape.

REFERENCES

Allport, G. (1954). *The nature of prejudice*. Cambridge, MA: Addison-Wesley.

American Psychiatric Association. (2004). *Diagnostisc and statistical manual* (4th ed.). Washington, DC: American Psychiatric Association.

Arnie remarries in private ceremony. (2005, January 28). *The Kansas City Star*, p. D2.

Attig, T. (2004). Disenfranchised grief revisited: Discounting hope and love. *Omega: Journal of Death and Dying, 49*(3), 197–215.

Barnett, Z., & Pachana, N. (2007). Viagra: The little blue pill with big repercussions. In S. McLaren (Ed.), The abstracts of the 2nd APS psychology and interest group conference (2007, November), Geelong, Victoria, Australia (pp. 366). *Combined Abstracts of 2007 Australian Psychology Conferences*.

Barnett, Z., Robleda Gomez, S., & Pachana, N. A. (2012). *Aging & Mental Health, 16*(1), 84-88.

Bartlett, J. (2002). *Bartlett's familiar quotations* (17th ed.). Boston, MA: Little, Brown.

Boerner, K., Schulz, R., & Horowitz, A. (2004). Positive aspects of caregiving and adaptation to bereavement. *Psychology and Aging, 19*(1), 668–675.

Bokhour, B. G., Clark, J. A., Inui, T. S., Silliman, R. A., & Talcott, J. A. (2001). Sexuality after treatment for early prostate cancer. *Journal of General Internal Medicine, 16*(10), 649-655.

Bonanno, G. A., Nesse, R. M., & Wortman, C. B. (2004). Prospective patterns of resilience and maladjustment during widowhood. *Psychology and Aging, 19*(2), 200–271.

Broderick, G. A., & Lue, T. F. (2002). Evaluation and nonsurgical management of erectile dysfunction and priapism. In P. C. Walsh (Ed.), *Campbell's urology* (8th ed., pp. 1619–1671). Philadelphia, PA: Saunders.

Bronner, G., Royter, V., Korczyn, A. D., & Giladi, N. (2004). Sexual dysfunction in Parkinson's disease. *Journal of Sex & Marital Therapy, 30*, 95–105.

Brusich, J. (1990). Religious influence and sexuality. In C. I. Fogel & D. Lauver (Eds.), *Sexual health promotion* (pp. 160–177). Philadelphia, PA: W. B. Saunders.

Bufalino, J. (2004, February). Boning up: Viagra's challengers are finally on the market. How stiff is the competition? *GQ*, 68–70.

Butler, R. N., & Lewis, M. I. (2002). *The new love and sex after 60* (Rev. ed.). New York, NY: Ballentine Books.

Campbell, S., & Silverman, P. R. (1996). *Widower: When men are left alone*. Amityville, NY: Baywood.

Carson, C. C. (2002). Erectile dysfunction in the 21st century: Whom we can treat, whom we cannot treat and patient education. *International Journal on Impotence Research, 14*(Supplement 1), S29–S34.

Caserta, M. S., Lund, D. A., & Obray, S. J. (2004). Promoting self-care and daily living skills among older widows and widowers: Evidence from the Pathfinders demonstration project. *Omega: Journal of Death and Dying, 49*(3), 217–236.

Cayan, S., Bozlu, M., Canpolat, B., & Akbay, E. (2004). The assessment of sexual functions in women with male partners complaining of erectile dysfunction: Does treatment of male sexual dysfunction improve female partner's sexual functions? *Journal of Sex & Marital Therapy, 30*, 333–341.

Chevret, M., Jaudinot, E., Sullivan, K., Marrel, A., & De Gendre, A. S. (2004). Impact of erectile dysfunction (ED) on sexual life of female partners: Assessment with the Index of Sexual Life (ISL) questionnaire. *Journal of Sex & Marital Therapy, 30*, 157–172.

Chin, J. L. (2010). Introduction. In J. L. Chin (Ed.), *The psychology of prejudice and discrimination. A revised and condensed edition* (pp. vii–xiii). Santa Barbara, CA: ABC CLIO.

Doka, K. (1989). Disenfranchised grief. In K. Doka (Ed.), *Disenfranchised grief: Recognizing hidden sorrow* (pp. 3–11). Lexington, MA: Lexington Books.

Eliopoulos, C. (2005). *Gerontological nursing* (6th ed.). Philadelphia, PA: Lippincott, Williams & Wilkins.

Floyd, M., & Weiss, L. (2001). Sex and aging: A survey of young adults. *Journal of Sex Education and Therapy, 26*(2), 133–139.

Giuliano, F. A., Leriche, A., Jaudinot, E. O., & de Gendre, A. S. (2004). Prevalence of erectile dysfunction among 7689 patients with diabetes or hypertension, or both. *Urology, 64*(4), 1196–1201.

Golden, F. (with Klarreich, K., & Maloloy, W.). (2004, January 19). Still sexy after 60. *Time, 163*(3), 110–115.

Graham, L. K. (2003). *Discovering images of God: Narratives of care among lesbians and gays*. Louisville, KY: Westminster.

Gross, G., & Blundo, R. (2005). Viagra: Medical technology: Constructing aging masculinity. *Journal of Social Welfare, 32*(1), 85-97.

Gullette, M. M. (1998). Midlife discourses in the twentieth century United States: An essay on the sexuality, ideology, and politics of middle-ageism. In R. A. Shweder

(Ed.), *Welcome to the middle age! (and other culture fictions)* (pp. 3-44). Chicago, IL: University of Chicago Press.

Healthy Aging Taskforce. (2000). Cited in Elder Abuse Prevention Unit website: http://www.Eapu.com.au/ElderAbuse.aspx

Hillman, J. L., & Stricker, H. (1996). Predicators of college students' knowledge of and attitudes toward elderly sexuality: The relevance of grandparental contact. *Educational Gerontology, 22*, 539–555.

Jacobson, J. (2007). Informing our psychosexual practice for treating erectile dysfunction in gay and bisexual men living with HIV: A response to the 2006 National Health Service Greater Glasgow HIV needs assessment report. *Sexual and Relationship Therapy, 22*(4), 397–414.

Jenkins, R., Schover, L. R., Fouladi, R. T., Warneke, C., Neese, L., Klein, et al. (2004). Sexuality and health-related quality of life after prostate cancer in African-American and white men treated for localized disease. *Journal of Sex & Marital History, 30*, 79–93.

Karlosvsky, M., Lebed, B., & Mydio, J. (2004). Increasing incidence and importance of HIV/AIDS and gonorrhea among men aged >50 years in the US in the era of erectile dysfunction therapy. *Scandinavian Journal of Urology and Nephrology, 38*(3), 247–252.

Klotz, T., Mathers, M., Klotz, R., & Sommer, F. (2005). Why do patients with erectile dysfunction abandon effective therapy with sildenafil (Viagra)? *International Journal of Impotence Research, 17*(1), 2–4.

Koenig, H. G., & Herman, S. (1994). Religion and coping with sexual impotence in later life. *Journal of Religious Gerontology, 9*(1), 73–87.

Koenig, H. G., & Weaver, A. J. (1999). *Counseling troubled older adults: A handbook for pastors and religious caregivers*. Nashville, TN: Abingdon.

Lamberg, L. (1998). New drug for erectile dysfunction boon for many, "Viagravation" for some. *Journal of the American Medical Association, 280*(10), 867–869.

Laumann, E. O., Paik, A., & Rosen, R. C. (1999). Sexual dysfunction in the United States: Prevalence and predictors. *The Journal of the American Medical Association, 281*(6), 537–544.

Leaver, C. A., Perreault, Y., Demetrakopoulos, A., & the AIDS Bereavement Project of Ontario's Survive & Thrive Working Group. (2008). Understanding AIDS-related bereavement and multiple loss among long-term survivors of HIVB in Ontario. *The Canadian Journal of Human Sexuality, 17*(1–2), 37–52.

Levine, S. B. (1992). Intrapsychic and interpersonal aspects of impotence: Psychogenic erectile dysfunction. In R. C. Rosen & A. R. Leiblum (Eds.), *Erectile disorders: Assessment and treatment* (pp. 198–225). New York, NY: Guilford Press.

Levy, J. A. (1994). Sex and sexuality in late life stages. In A. S. Rossi (Ed.), *Sexuality across the life course* (pp. 287–309). Chicago, IL: University of Chicago Press.

Loe, M. (2001). Fixing broken masculinity: Viagra as a technology for the production of gender and sexuality. *Sexuality and Culture, 5*(3), 97–125.

MacReady, N. (2003, May 15). Routine questions about sex important to elderly: Initiate the conversation. *Family Practice News, 33*(10), 19.

Marshall, B. L. (2008, Spring). Older men and sexual health: Post-Viagra views of changes in function. *Generations*, 21–27.

Marsiglio, W., & Donnelley, D. (1991). Sexual relations in later life: A national study of married persons. *Journal of Gerontology: Social Sciences, 46*(6), S338–S344.

Masters, W. H., & Johnson, V. E. (1966). *Human sexual response*. Boston, MA: Little and Brown.

McCarthy, B. W. (1992). Treatment of erectile dysfunction with single men. In R. C. Rosen & S. R. Leiblum (Eds.), *Erectile disorders: Assessment and treatment* (pp. 313–340). New York, NY: Guilford Press.

Meris, D. (2002). Beyond the threat of AIDS: Focusing on other deaths within the LGBT community. Poster session presented at the annual conference of the Association for Death Education and Counseling, Portland, OR.

Mirone, V., Gentile, V., Zizzo, G., Terry M., Longo, N., Fusco, F., et al. (2002). Did men with erectile dysfunction discuss their condition with partner and physicians? A survey of men attending a free call service. *International Journal of Impotence Research, 14*(4), 256–258.

Moore, M., & de Costa, C. (2003). *Dick: A user's guide*. New York, NY: Marlow & Company.

Morgenthaler, A. (2003). *The Viagra myth: The surprising impact on love and relationships*. San Francisco, CA: Jossey-Bass.

Neimeyer, R. A. (2001). Reauthorizing life narratives: Grief therapy as meaning reconstruction. *Israeli Journal of Psychiatry and Related Sciences, 38*, 171–183.

Neimeyer, R. A. (2005). Widowhood, grief and the quest for meaning: A narrative perspective on resilience. In D. Carr, R. M. Neese, & C. B. Wortman (Eds.), *Spousal bereavement in late life*. New York, NY: Springer.

Ory, M. G., & Mack, K. A. (1998). Middle-aged and older people with AIDS: Trends in national surveillance rates, transmission routes, and risk factors. *Research on Aging, 20*, 653–664.

Parker-Pope, T. (2002, November 11). So many jokes, so many misconceptions: What the Viagra experience is really like. *The Wall Street Journal*, p. R3.

Peisah, C., Brodaty, H., & Bridger, M. (2008). Abuse by marriage: The exploitation of mentally ill older people. *International Journal of Geriatric Psychiatry, 23*, 883–888.

Perelman, M. A. (2001). Integrating Sildenafil and sex therapy: Unconsummated marriage secondary to erectile dysfunction and retarded ejaculation. *Journal of Sex Education & Therapy, 26*(1), 13–22.

Polkinghorn, D. E. (1988). *Narrative knowing and the human sciences*. Albany, NY: State University of New York Press.

Potts, A., Grace, V. M., Vares, T., & Gavey, N. (2006). "Sex for life"? Men's counter-stories on "erectile dysfunction," male sexuality and aging. *Sociology of Health & Illness, 3*, 306–319.

Radda, K. E., Schensul, J. J., Disch, W. B., Levy, J. A., & Reyes, C. Y. (2003). Assessing Human Immunodeficiency Virus (HIV) risk among older urban adults: A model for community-based research partnership. *Family and Community Health, 26*(13), 203–213.

Rohr, R. (2004). *Adam's return: The five promises of male initiation*. New York, NY: Crossroad.

Romanoff, B. D., & Terenzio, M. (1998). Rituals and the grieving process. *Death Studies, 22*, 697–711.

Rudavsky, S. (2010, October 4). Survey engages in "having sex." *USA Today*, p. 4D.

Schensul, J. J., Levy, J. A., & Disch, W. (2003). Individual, contextual, and social network factors affecting exposure to HIV/AIDS risk among older adults in low-income housing complexes. *Journal of Acquired Immune Deficiency Syndrome,* 33(Supplement 2), S138–S152.

Schmidt, J. (2005, February 3). Impotence drugs selling slowly: Sales below expectations as ads increase. *USA Today*, p. 3B.

Schover, L. R., Fouladi, R. T., Warneke, C. L., Neese, L., Klein, E. A., Zippe, C., et al. (2004). Seeking help for erectile dysfunction after treatment for prostate cancer. *Archives of Sexual Behavior, 33*(5), 443–454.

Seftel, A. D., Sun, P., & Swindle, R. (2004). The prevalence of hypertension, hyperlipidemia, diabetes mellitus and depression in men with erectile dysfunction. *Journal of Urology, 171*, 2341–2345.

Shabsign, R. (2002). *Back to great sex: Overcome ED and reclaim lost intimacy.* Atlanta, GA: Kensington Books.

Shaw, J. (2001). When you're asked to speak about sex, intimacy, and Alzheimer's. *Journal of Sex Education and Therapy, 26*, 140–145.

Shives, L. R. (2005). *Basic concepts of psychiatric-mental health nursing*. Philadelphia, PA: Lippincott, Williams & Wilkins.

Siegel, K., & Schrimshaw, E. W. (2003). Reasons for the adoption of celibacy among older men and women living with HIV/AIDS. *Journal of Sex Research, 40*(2), 189–200.

Simons, J. (2003, June 9). Taking on Viagra. *Fortune*, 102–112.

Smith, H. I. (2004). *Griefkeeping: Learning how long grief lasts*. New York, NY: Crossroad.

Stulberg, D., Ewigman, B., & Hicker, J. (2008, December). Family Physicians Inquiries Network. Antidepressants causing sexual problems? Give her Viagra. *The Journal of Family Practice, 57*(12), 793–796.

Sun, P., Seftel, A. D., & Swindle, R. (2004, May). *The prevalence of four diagnosed concurrent conditions among male health plan members with erectile dysfunction.* Poster session presented at the annual meeting of the American Urology Association, San Francisco, CA.

Taubman-Ben-Ari, O. (2004). Intimacy and risky sexual behavior—What does it have to do with death? *Death Studies, 28*, 865–887.

Timmerman, J. H. (2001). When religion is its own worst enemy: How therapists can help people shed hurtful notions that masquerade as good theology. *Journal of Sex Education and Therapy, 26*(4), 259–266.

United States Bureau of the Census. (2008). *The statistical abstract of the United States.* Washington, DC: U.S. Government Printing Office.

Venes, D. (Ed.). (2009). *Taber's encyclopedic medical dictionary* (21st ed.). Philadelphia, PA: F. A. Davis.

Viagra. (2004, August 20). [Ad]. *The Wall Street Journal*, p. A7.

Viagra's license and the internet. (1998, September 5). *The Lancet*, p. 751.

Waitzkin, H. (1989). A critical theory of medical discourse: Ideology, social control, and the processing of social context in medical encounters. *Journal of Health and Social Behavior, 30*, 220–239.

Ward, R., Fidler, H., Lockyer, J. M., Basson, R. J., Elliott, S., & Toews, J. (2001). Physical outcomes following an intensive educational program on erectile dysfunction. *Journal of Sex Education & Therapy, 26*(4), 358–362.

Wentzell, E. (2008). Impotence. In Y. Zhang (Ed.), *The encyclopedia of global health* (Vol. 2, pp. 888–890). Los Angeles, CA: Sage.

Whipple, B., & Scura, K. W. (1996). The overlooked epidemic: HIV in older adults. *American Journal of Nursing, 96*(2), 23–29.

Worthington, R. L. (2004). Sexual identity, sexual orientation, religious identity, and change: Is it possible to depolarize the debate? *The Counseling Psychologist, 32*(5), 741–749.

Zilbergeld, B. (1992). The man behind the broken penis: Social and psychological determinants of erectile failure. In R. C. Rosen & S. R. Lieblum (Eds.), *Erectile disorders: Assessment and treatment* (pp. 27–50). New York, NY: Guilford Press.

Zipes, D. P., Libby, P., Bonow, R. O., & Braunwald, E. (Eds.). (2005). *Braunwald's heart disease: A textbook of cardiovascular medicine* (7th ed.). New York, NY: Elsevier Saunders.

Zippe, C. D., Raina, R., Massanyi, E. Z., Agarwal, A., Jones, J. S., Ulchaker, J., et al. (2004). Sexual function after radical cystectomy in a sexually active population. *Urology, 64*(4), 682–686.

Zhang, C. Y. (2007). Switching between traditional Chinese medicine and Viagra: Cosmopolitanism and medical pluralism today. *Medical Anthropology, 26*, 53–96.

CHAPTER 4

Grieving a Not-So-Loved Parent: Sinking in the Mud of Hurtful Memories

Richard B. Gilbert

Yesterday was Mother's Day. Flowers everywhere. Empty greeting card racks. Packed restaurants. Churches looking extra busy. Sermon titles listed in the paper showed that many churches honored mothers as a liturgical event. Others seemed to ignore it all together. Some congregations recognized the larger picture: when the mother has died, when mothers grieve, when problematic family dynamics arise after a divorce or another family tragedy.

An article about mothers in a local shoppers' guide was a feature story about two television shows, *Leave It to Beaver* and *Father Knows Best*, shows that continue to run on our local nostalgia channels. Is that our image of parents? Of mothers? Breakfast served by a mother in a proper dress and those ever-present pearls? A mother who seems to hide in the background while following her husband's directives? The movie *My Big Fat Greek Wedding* (Zwick, 2002) captured a different perspective. When the stubborn Greek father, clinging to past traditions about marrying out of the family (Greek), reminded his family that he is the "head of the household," the bride's world fell apart. The daughter, crying as she joined her mother and aunt in a corner booth in their restaurant, strongly criticized her father. Respecting the "company line" while not caving in to it, the mother said, "Yes, dear, your father is the head of the household, but your mother is the neck, and I control which way the head moves!"

Before we move to the discussion of troubled families, angry adults, and the lack of memorial stories or relationships worthy of grief, we first need to understand the parent/adult–child relationship and the grief that comes when that relationship is disrupted.

CLAIMING YOUR PLACE ON THE STAGE OF THE BEREAVED

Parents seem to get a spot center stage. We stood there at one time. Children are not supposed to die. Children are the fulfillment of all the dreams and ambitions of a family and the parents. Our family not only celebrates our adult daughter, but we now relive many of the stories while carving out new ones with our grandsons.

Parents grieve. Infertility. Ectopic pregnancies. Miscarriages. Stillbirths. Death of an infant, including SIDS; death of a school-age child; death of a teen child; death of an adult child. These not only carry a terrifying level of pain but also violate our standards, values, and beliefs. Children (of any age) die from disease as well as experience the fast deaths from heart attacks, strokes, trauma, violence, and addictive disorders. We often feel a misplaced rage for a child killed in the war. They are center stage.

Nearby are those grieving the death of a spouse or the "death" of the spouse now a stranger. They are on the stage too. So are the grieving siblings, neighbors, and friends who have died and certainly the countless deaths, many still unknown, due to war, tsunami, earthquakes, and disasters. The description from a friend in Tuscaloosa, Alabama, communicates the pain and shock of the horror he continues to feel and see all around his city after nature's devastation there. Progress and growth, now in rubble.

Is there room on the crowded mourning stage for adults grieving the death of a parent? It is a death, a loss, a significant change that can redefine the family and leave the family without a wall or post to lean against. We deserve our spot on the stage!

SHOULD WE DEMAND A BETTER SPOT ON THE STAGE?

The bereaved commonly feel overwhelmed, numb, and without any sense of direction or purpose. It takes a lot of work, reflecting and feeling, to *begin* acknowledging the reality of the loss and its impact.

Under "normal" circumstances the bereaved want and deserve caring listeners, people with a few gentle words and, when requested, information and counsel. Like the person standing alone and invisible in a thick forest, so it is for the bereaved. The stage of mourning is that forest, and to be with others "on the journey" is its own measure of comfort.

Though people often avoid grieving parents, children, families of veterans, the traumatized, and those grieving after a suicide, at least there is a general sentiment or awareness of the significance of their loss and, for them, a better chance at finding people who care. It means dismissing the notion that people should stay away because they don't know what to say or do. It is when they realize it is about general presence, affirmation, and acceptance, often at the encouragement of other grievers, that there is a recognized loss in need of support.

Adult children grieving the death of a parent often find it harder to feel part of this "family" of grievers. It's not that people were indifferent to my sorrow when my father died in 1989, my mother in 1995, and my mother-in-law in 2010. Quite the contrary. There were outpourings of sympathy and support. Yet it was different. *There was a sense of completion or closure that was both affirming and derailing.* My father died when he was 84, after an extended struggle with health issues, surgery, and dementia. My mother essentially died when my father died but took 6 years to be released. My mother-in-law, at age 89, died after numerous surgeries and ongoing respiratory problems. The message from my comforters was "I know this comes with sadness and grief, but you also should feel good about the great lives they lived." True. Some even reminded us that the last gift parents give is "to go ahead and prepare a place for their children."

Grieving adult children need the same space, safety, and affirmation. Words of comfort can be wonderful, but not if they diminish our right and need to grieve. You can grieve and celebrate at the same time, but for some mourners their sense of "celebration" may be jolting.

The numbers are stacked in favor of grieving adult children. We are a large group. The Center for Disease Control (CDC), in summarizing the death statistics for 2006, found the total deaths in the United States of those 50 years old or older were 2,426,264 (CDC, 2009). That leaves a lot of adult children grieving!

Grieving adult children share many of the common experiences of loss that are felt by others. We also need support of a different kind. Many adult children have to regroup as a family and as parents. They have been in the middle between the older generation and the younger generation. Many children, especially teens, make significant sacrifices. Some lose a bedroom because it was needed for the hospital bed. Others feel overlooked or forgotten when they needed help with homework, supplies for school, or someone to talk to. There may be very difficult pathways for teens to navigate, but they also are milestones that warrant the participation and affirmation of their parents.

In addition to being in the middle, adult children might be experiencing alterations in their roles with their parents. Often adult children speak of this as "role reversal." This way of speaking might be telling in itself. John Bowlby recognizes that "caregiving specifies the complementary behaviour directed towards someone conceives as less able to do so" (1982, p. 377). Because in illness as in life, as Bowlby puts it, "continuity of role is not inevitable" (1982, p. 377), adult children can find themselves needing to provide care for their parent. Bowlby makes this distinction:

> Role *change* can occur also when a grown-up son or daughter care for a parent in old age. By contrast, the *reversal* of roles between child, or

> adolescent, and parent unless very temporary, is almost always not only a sign of pathology in the parent but a cause of it in the child. (1982, p. 377, author's emphasis added)

Adult children who have experienced abusive parents might be more likely to speak of role reversal than role change.

Previously independent parents become more dependent. Adult children have their sense of independence challenged, perhaps even weighed down by their increasingly more dependent parents. Yet adult children may resist all of this change because supporting their parents' independence may be the last thread of affirmation of them as parents. It is too much to ask of the adult children.

Other aspects of parent loss include the madness of all the medical bills, the decisions to be made, and the need to help parents adjust to necessary alterations in responsibility, prompted by their changing mental or physical health. Adult children, not wishing to increase their parents' sense of dependence, now face with them (or often alone) unpaid bills, Social Security issues, funeral expenses, and decisions about the house or living arrangements. Adult children find themselves trying to give support when they still need some back. It probably would help if the surviving parent remembered that they have adult children rather than shunning them because "they are 'the children.'"

We must also consider the death of the surviving parent. On the one hand, I did feel at the time of my mother's death that I had learned some things from my father's funeral that enabled me to focus more on my sorrow than the arrangements. On the other hand, there are feelings about being "orphaned," that strange sense of feeling alone in the world after both of one's parents have died:

> The death of a surviving parent is the final reminder that neither Mom nor Dad will be here for us, that we are now the elder of the family, and that, on some level, we are now on our own. Saying goodbye was tough once, and we wanted it to be a one-time thing. On some level, we never believed that a second round of goodbyes would be ahead for us. (Gilbert, 1999, p. 84)

This all comes together when we face the reality that the adult children are now the "old ones" in the family. Parents may have shielded their children from death's reality. After all, we were "safe." Everybody "knows" that your parents are supposed to die before the adult children. It has biblical precedence, is the "traditional" ritual, and fits neatly into our comfort zone of denying and defying our own mortality. After both parents die, everything changes! No one is safe.

The issues of intimacy and loss have not been discussed particularly in the literature. There is a strong connection between them that cannot and should not be silenced if we value both our capacities for intimacy and the ways loss cuts through it. In this regard, it is helpful to revisit the teachings of Erik Erikson and the discussion of intimacy (Erikson, 1963, p. 311) and discussed in Santrock (2006, p. 472). Santrock introduces his thoughts with a reflection on Erikson's definition of intimacy, noting the importance of "the role of intimacy in relationship maturity, and how people juggle for intimacy and the motivation for independence" (2006, p. 472). Erikson's discussion of intimacy occurs in the context of what he says about "identity v. identity confusion" (as cited in Santrock, 2006, p. 472), the point here is how Santrock reconnected the comments triggered by Erikson in (1963, p. 311). For the *adult* grieving the death of a parent, intimacy may be less about sexual and emotional expression and more about exhaustion, the challenge of rebuilding, sorting out the new relationship with the surviving parent, and reconstructing one's own family.

Some have an ongoing problem with relationships that can be compounded by a parental loss. This is particularly true if the deceased was actively involved in the adult child's social life, including the state of the child's marriage or partnership. If the parent, adult child, or both seem nested in a codependent relationship or were bound in a relationship that could be described as "strong parent and childlike adult child," then the adult child's capacity for intimacy could at least be interrupted for some time. On the other hand, how parent–child relationships are handled between them as adults could also redefine them, even freeing them from previous traditions. We are what we love. That speaks volumes in loving families, even when grieving. But it also raises questions for adults stuck in the mud of wounded lives and painful memories.

It also needs to be said that some intimacy issues may relate more to the spouse/partner and family than to the deceased parent. If it has been a long journey to death for a parent, coupled with all of the stress put on the family that now needs to be released, they may find that embracing denial is the safer and more comfortable alternative.

No matter what choices have led up to the event of a parent's death, Dale Lund and M. Caserta (*Death Studies*, 1996) and referenced in Hooyman and Kramer (2006, p. 332) insist on its significance as benchmark: "No matter how well adult children may have prepared emotionally for a parent's death and engaged in participatory mourning, it can be a life-changing event" (Hooyman & Kramer, 2006, p. 268). Similarly, J. H. Harvey (2000) comments:

> A parent's death may shake up an adult child's life in such a way that the child feels that he or she no longer has an anchor. Our beliefs about parents' invincibility and immortality are shattered. In addition, when both our parents die and we become orphans, we become aware of our own mortality and may lose our primary source of unconditional love. We are no longer somebody's child, and our primary connection with the past is gone. (Hooyman & Kramer, 2006, p. 268)

Another grieving adult son shared this story with me when I was his mother's hospital chaplain. He prefaced his comments by saying, "I have had a religious crisis since my mom died and I don't know what to do." It wasn't a profound theological disruption but truly expressive of his feelings after the death of his mother. His lack of church attendance was because every Saturday night his mother would call and say, "I know I will see you at church tomorrow. The service is at 8:30." She died at age 84; the son was 62! So many alternative plans came to mind, but this was about a spiritual tradition that was interrupted because his mother was no longer there to parent him to church. A piece of his sense of intimacy (with God, with his mother, and with his family) had, for a time, been shaken.

In the dying process, routines, traditions, even language can be interrupted. Harold Ivan Smith shared this personal testimony about his experience of the death of his father:

> There were many times, especially as the weeks went on, when drugs and pain rendered him inert and silent, I'd sit beside his bed, trying to find something to say to reassure him and myself, yearning to leave so I would not have to see his veins, swollen and purple along his wrists, the pulse that wiggled like a small dark worm in his forehead. Worst of all was the smell of decay like a rank mist from his body. I couldn't understand how my mother endured the endless hours she spent with him. After sitting with him for a while, I'd lie to him about an appointment or an errand that prevented my staying longer. He never complained about my departures, never tried to detain me, but urged me to go and meet my obligations. (Smith, 1994, p. 36)

Again from Smith:

> Sometimes we forget because our memories are like under-exercised muscles. Blessed are those who have siblings or friends who can "jump start" the memories. "Don't you remember when Mom . . . ?" "How could you forget the time your mom . . . ?" Mothers are not dead until we stop telling stories about them or repeating, often to a new generation, "My mother always said. . . ." (Smith, 2003, p. 116)

Smith is right to comment on how a parent's memories are kept alive in the stories that their children tell about them. And this is indeed a heartwarming experience when those stories are positive. But our focus here is on the underbelly of children's grief for their parents. When adult children are stuck in bad memories, telling stories about them takes on a different emotional tone and meaning. This circumstance too is an important addition to the discussion of intimacy and loss.

This chapter started with descriptive statements of a "normal" experience of adults grieving the death of a parent because, rightly or not, it is how we gauge the grief journey of "the stuck." By comparing the free and the stuck we can gain a deeper appreciation for those parent–child relationships that "died" before the physical death of either of them. It is also significant because it is the standard around which "the stuck" often judge themselves and their parent(s) and how others discern whether it is purposeful, even safe, for them to approach those who grieve a long-dead relationship.

BACK TO THE NUMBERS

The same statistics quoted earlier also apply to this need to take into account the other side of parental relationships. Earlier I made an observation about the likelihood of the presence of grieving adult children in your circle of friends, neighbors, and coworkers based on the number of deaths of adults over the age of 50. Some statistics for the same age group, the same year, give these startling numbers of deaths by their causes (Centers for Disease Control [CDC], 2009, Table 5, p. 32):

- Drug-induced deaths: 38,396
- Alcohol-induced deaths: about 75,000
- Homicides: 18,573
- Suicides: 33,300
- Legal interventions: 434
- Women murdered by intimate partners: 1,181 (3 a day)
- Intimate partner-related physical assaults and rapes: 4.8 million

THE STORIES I HAVE READ: A SAMPLING

The second story of the life-long effects of growing up in an abusive family is from an historical novel. The setting is Staten Island, New York. It was a nostalgic stroll down many familiar streets and a raw look at the violence in the author's world. His father was an abusive, drunk cop. Often he abused his son, wife, and daughter. He was a bully cop who stretched the laws and policies to "make a collar." He had no use for his son. His father was gunned down on a sidewalk near his house. It was an alleged mob hit. Drunk. A cop. A bad husband. A worse parent. His son took on the role of the policeman trying to heal the wounds caused by his father. It didn't take long. He now looked, talked, and smelled like his father. His life, especially after leaving the force, was about drinking and abusing.

His story, told at length here in a quote from Loehfelm's novel, *Fresh Kills* (2008), is an example of long-buried rage and grief, buried under broken relationships; a life spent "living" on beer and cigarettes; and the growing realization that he was just like his father. His "vitamins" were doses of a fiery hate that lived in constant tension with the little boy still hoping to shed this bad dream and "restore" the family with a loving and nurturing father, mother, and sister. That would never come.

> I got another beer and headed out into the backyard. I dragged an old, rusty lawn chair into a spot of sun and settled into it, slouching. I pulled off my shirt and slid on my shades. The beer sat untouched at my side. I lit a cigarette.

> There had to be a way to get through these next few days [after his father was shot down] without losing my grip. Outside Joyce's and the Staten Island mall and then in the kitchen. I'd come too close. That wasn't the way it should be. Hadn't I, in some way, won? My father was gone. My lifelong battle with him had ended the only way it could, with one of us dead.
>
> I'd always figured that when he died I'd feel some satisfaction, or at least some relief. I thought I'd feel a thousand pounds lighter. I'd grow six inches taller, walk differently, breathe differently. All this space would open up in the world just from knowing he wasn't in it anyone. It'd feel like letting go of that breath you hold when you pull open the closet door looking for monsters. Like when you wake from a nightmare and not only realize that it wasn't true, but you can feel yourself forgetting it with every breath.
>
> Sitting there in the yard, I didn't feel any of that. All I felt was the same things I'd felt for twenty years when I thought of him, like there was something hard inside me, pushing up against my lungs. Like a fist clutched the muscles in my back. Like I was loading a weapon, waiting for my enemies.
>
> But the enemies had passed me by and left me in the dust of their horses, their gun smoke in my nose and their bullets in my father. They'd left me standing with a jagged rock in my hand and no one to throw it at. With a body to bury and a family to console, a family of one.
>
> Why wasn't there any relief? Was it that the war had ended a couple of decades before I'd ever thought it would? That someone else had ended it for us? That my war had ended it for us? That my war had ended without me? Before I was ready? Ready for what? (Loehfelm, 2008, pp. 118–119)

This was Staten Island, not Hollywood. It doesn't come with a guaranteed redemption and healing as only Hollywood can produce. It is anger turned to hate, a life thus far wasted by a son whose choices left him a copycat. Anger, even rage, can be both healthy and helpful. But hate? Where is this love? Forgiveness? The courage to start over? The little boy has been crushed underfoot like one of his endless cigarette butts shaping into a mountain beside his rusted lawn chair or squeezed to an unrecognizable shape that blended in with the other crushed beer cans stacking up beside that same chair. He was his father's son!

This police officer, shoved aside from the workplace until he "gets healthy," still didn't get it. There was no rainbow, no pot of gold, no quick fixes. He was victimized by his father's quick fixes, which became his death bullet (Loehfelm, 2008). His "treasure" was a pile of cigarette butts and a pyramid of crushed beer cans. What he inherited from his father was "his father." His father robbed him, at least by his logic, of his ability and right to love in a meaningful, nurturing relationship, including with his sister. His father robbed him of his childhood, teen years, adulthood, and even the option to be a good cop because it was his own choice. The only "love" that bound brother and sister was their common enemy.

Abuse of children has many triggers, but it is always wrong. Physical abuse. Sexual abuse. The son could have won the Nobel Prize and it wouldn't have mattered. There is nothing that fixes the smashed events of yesterday. It means that we need to find the willingness, the encouragement, and the vision to begin all new stories and new events. Some children may escape, at least for a time, as the changes with puberty give them a taste of a different lifestyle and self-image. Maybe it was the other parent, often victimized in similar ways, who finds that the path to wholeness takes him or her through the present hell and to a different shore, a brighter light, a new start.

Loehfelm's book identified the family as one of the many ethnic white families on Staten Island. These adult children are, at least until they close the door on any kind of religious community, every kind of Christian, Jew, Hindu, Muslim, and so on. Many have been abused by religious leaders and members and some by parents who know only a god who is merciless and judgmental and dragging us deeper into unhealthy, codependent relationships with their god pulling the strings. Some groups seem very predisposed to this angry god. As one struggling along this same path once said to me, "God would have more fun zapping us with a plague of locusts rather than drawing us closer through forgiveness and hope."

Religions and cults, economic factors, educational levels, age, race—none are free of angry victims torn apart by an abusive parent. The Rev. Al Miles, an African American who has done a great deal of work in hospices and also with victims of domestic violence, describes his own racial experience and how it sinks people into the same mud:

> Historically, the African American community and the faith community have not had easy access to the resources available for abused women and their children. "The Rev. Cherrye Cunnigan and I presented a few events together during Domestic Violence Month [October]," recalls Mary Walton a pioneer in the domestic violence assistance movement and long time Christian "We wanted to reach the underserved group of African Americans and the underserved group of church folk. So we put together a worship service." (2002, p. 59)

Located in Long Beach, California, their joint project is called Creating A Safe Environment (CASE). One of CASE's primary goals is to promote knowledge of domestic violence resources among the faith communities, "The African American community is very patriarchal," Cheryl Cunningan, in an interview with the author of the book (Miles, 2002, p. 160), shared:

> In this patriarchal community, women who are committed Christians who are living in marriages where they are subjected to violence and abuse many times find that violence reinforced by their male pastors. For instance, the pastor will often say such things as "God will not give you more than you can bear." A female [or a male] who has just been abused, maybe even the night before, and who is now sitting in the congregation hearing her [or his] pastor say that will not feel supported. (Miles, 2002, p. 160)

Cunnigan also discussed how the patriarchal system in the African American community can prevent male clergy members from holding Christian men accountable for their abusive behavior. "Many times the abuser has a high profile and is well-respected by leaders in the congregation," she says (Miles, 2002, p. 52). "And the leaders are so invested in the male parishioner that they choose not to see, and they don't want to hear, that this man may be abusing his wife. The faith leaders don't want to even enter that possibility into their equation" (Miles, 2002, pp. 159–160).

Every group of people, however defined, does not have to look far to see this and other forms of abuse, as do the various groups of professionals. Although the character in Loehfelm's story was a police officer, it could have been someone from any professional group, including the retired. However, continued studies would suggest that there are even greater risks among police officers, their coworkers, and their families (Kirschman, 2007, p. 69). "Cops expect crooks to try to hurt them. But when they feel as if their own organizations are turning on them, it is like being stabbed in the back by a member of the family" (Kirschman, 2007, p. 69). In law enforcement circles, a "thin blue line" provides its own shield and cover for what are often histories of abuse and violence over generations in families. Since such histories are not unique to police officers, one might wonder what analogous "line" runs around and through the families of other professionals. All histories of abuse and violence complicate adults grieving the deaths of their parents.

THE STORIES I HAVE HEARD: A SAMPLING

Harriet was in her late thirties when I met her, though, thanks to her camouflage, I could only guess at her age. We met as she was knocking on my office door. She was dressed all in black, including a hat and veil. My first thought was that the pranksters in Social Services were trying to pull off a prank on the chaplain. There was precedent. Fortunately I was not too distracted by the possibility that a surprise was coming my way—until the real surprise arrived.

She asked, "Are you the chaplain who 'understands' grief?" I started to reply when she cut me off, "Do you know that bastard minister, Rev. M—" "Yes, I know him quite well," I said with caution and curiosity. She quickly went on:

> Let me tell what *I* know about him. He's a son of a bitch, just like my father. He had the nerve to say nice things about my father at the funeral. He sang my Dad's praises. He lied, but I know about the truth, and God knows the truth. My mother knows too but is too ashamed to talk about him. He still is controlling her. He spoke of his generosity to the city in encouraging economic development. At church he sang in the choir, served on the vestry and even helped in Sunday school. He also helped youth baseball.

There was a time of silence that seemed to last forever. She reached for her purse. I thought she was ready to leave. I stood up as a courtesy and she said, rather sharply, "Sit down! We aren't done here!" I sat, I listened, and I tried to stay calm and focused as she told me her story about her father:

> One night—I was around four—he was babysitting while my mom was at a meeting. He carried me to bed. He would fuss with my hair, pat my cheek, and tell me how much he loved his little girl. That continued, off and on, until the next time my mom had a meeting. He then gently touched me in many places. I didn't know what the "places" were called. I was nervous but trusted my daddy. Sometimes he would poke at me with his finger. It sometimes hurt, especially when he began to stick his fingers in places I learned were off limits to him. He then had me touch him and do things that made me feel so naughty. But he's my daddy? By the time I got to junior high school and the kids started talking and bragging about what they called "sex," I knew all of that—from my dad.

I will say more about Harriet's story later, in speaking about her grief journey from victim to survivor.

CHOOSING SURVIVORSHIP GRIEVING

No one chooses to sink deeper into the abyss of mud. People are put there and the putting most frequently is done *to* them by people who were expected to love them. Sometimes they are so terrified of the abuser (as Loehfelm's character was of his father) that they stay "where they are put" because they don't have a vote. They are the victims, the disenfranchised. Some may slip into the victim role because it appears to be the more familiar role. Most who were shoved, kicked, or thrown into that mud hole seldom blame the ones who put them there. They have been preconditioned to assume responsibility for all that happens to them or is done to them. Victims seldom realize that by bearing the burden of blame they can further victimize themselves. Nor do they seem to be aware that, when that burden is placed on those responsible it becomes a first step toward their healing and living.

When victims of abuse and violence find themselves grieving the deaths of the parents who perpetrated that abuse (or tolerated its perpetration), they find themselves grieving their victimization as well. They grieve their lost childhood, their lost innocence, their lost sense of security in this world. But they also grieve that they could not prevent themselves from becoming victims. They may even grieve the fact that "victim" has become their identity, in whole or in part. All of this mourning for circumstances in their own lives overwhelms them, and overshadows whatever grief they might otherwise have felt for their parents. This is what happens when mourning begins in "the mud."

People don't choose the victim route. It is decided for them. They can choose the survivor route, however. The bigger tragedy is when they feel that victimhood is their destiny, their only option. It has been said that "abused children are isolated from other family members as well as the wider social world. They have discovered that not only is the most powerful adult in their world dangerous but that other adults who are responsible for their care have not protected them" (Hooyman & Kramer, 2006, p. 212). Still, their whole grief cycle is locked into victimization and the ways it complicates mourning. This makes choosing to be a "survivor" an essential first step in mourning one's way out of the muck of one's past.

Victims may never understand what they did that was so wrong, so horrible, that they were punished with a mud hole. That's the danger, the supreme expression of power and control imposed upon another person. How is a child, or even an adult, able to discern power and control and that it is not their doing? When the victim is blamed, it is much like inparting a guilty verdict from this court with no lawyer and no rights. Survivorship is a choice. It is there, awaiting the victims. More than that, it becomes them. The special difference is that they get to choose. They can choose the mud, which is familiar and perceptively judgmental. The hold is powerful. The first step toward survivorship, healing, and wholeness seems to be the toughest step. It can be terrifying. They may re-experience the power of punishment and the despair of loneliness. There may be some stumbling. Mud flies everywhere and there are those slippery spots. But there are people eager to walk with them.

Survivorship is a choice. It is there, awaiting the victims. More than that, it beckons them. The special difference is that they get to choose. They can choose the mud, which is familiar and perceptively judgmental. The hold is powerful. The first step toward survivorship, healing, and wholeness seems to be the toughest step. It can be terrifying. They may re-experience the power of punishment and the despair of loneliness. There may be some stumbling. Mud flies everywhere and there are those slippery spots. But there are people eager to walk with them.

They may search for ages, seeking the right person, the right replacement parent. Their views will soon change because others will see the difference in them—the determination, the reaching out—and they will find others are ready to reach out to them, the victims. Victims are often worn down trying to educate doctors, lawyers, counselors, and even family members so that these professionals can be sensitized to their journey.

Memories can be freeing and they can be controlling. They can be "uppers" and they can be "downers." For some it can be a little of each. Here are some comparisons.

> My father's blessing was especially important to me because I was concerned that I'd disappointed him. He'd put me through college, and now, five years into my career, I'd quit a good job with no plan for what I would do next. When my father told me he was proud of the choices I'd made, I took it to mean that he supported me in my decision to stop and reevaluate my career direction. I felt the pressure lift and began to trust myself to make the right next steps. (Chethik, 2001, p. 259)

Benny, an angry ex-police officer, offers his assessment and explanation:

> You may feel a childlike need to cry out to your dead parent, to alert her, just as an infant cries out to alert a sleeping parent. Some people cry in their sleep, or wake up to find their father's name on their lips, sometimes years after the death. Dreaming of the dead person is common. One dream that has been reported a few times is of the dead mother or father trying to make a phone call to their child but having trouble speaking when the receiver is picked up, the voice becoming a squeak or a whisper. Others have told of even more disturbing dreams or nightmares. (Marshall, 2000, p. 63)

Harriet, the mysterious woman in black discussed earlier, was controlled by her father and, more so, by the anger and rage that became her way of life. Her father took away her childhood and messed up those formative years we call adolescence, and the collar and leash lasted into her adult years. Everything that is considered "normal" for families never happened. The mud.

Then the mud became the script and the cycle spun out of control. Harriet found herself leaping from husband to husband, to say nothing about the many men in between while telling herself she was looking for a meaningful relationship. Her choices defied the label "a meaningful relationship." A lot of sex, much of it rather distasteful, and empty of love. Such a life does discover a meaningful relationship, but destroys it. She became a feminine expression of her father—abuse, drugs, alcohol. Here is how she described her life:

> I just kept marrying or sleeping with my father. My mother lived in her denial and fear. My siblings knew of this, and, of course, I knew of what they had to put up with. I have three children, now entering adulthood, two by different husbands and the third, well, it was someone who was ready and willing. I never knew what a family Christmas was. I never taught it to my children. We never embraced boundaries or discipline that could lead them to a better story. We only knew physical abuse and its meaning was found in a judgment that was based on nothing else but fear and control. We managed to get the kids through college, and one went on to military service. It seems his only happy memories are from service in the Army. I cringe when I think that what was done to me and passed on to my children will become the lifestyle for my grandchildren.

"I couldn't love myself, so I certainly could not feel or give love and could not respect my right to say no," she told me.

Survivors will not "get over" the abuse. They know it is in their story and may keep them safe from future intrusions. They get shallow advice, often from people who ought to know better, that the best step is to "forgive and forget."

It takes a lot of love, courage, and dedication to befriend someone in the mud. Your expensive shoes will be beyond cleaning and polishing. At some point the shoes no longer matter. You step into the hole, the valley of another person, not because you know all of the answers, not like *Father Knows Best*, but because, even with knees trembling, you are willing to hear and live through "the rest of the story" with those who would confide in you.

REFERENCES

Bowlby, J. (1982). *Attachment*. New York, NY: Basic Books.

Caserta, M. S., & Lund, D. A. (1996). Beyond bereavement support group meetings: Exploring outside social contacts among the members. *Death Studies, 20*(6), 537-556.

Centers for Disease Control (CDC). (2009, April). *National Vital Statistics Reports, 57*(14), Table 5, p. 32.

Chethik, N. (2001). *FatherLoss: How sons of all ages come to terms with the deaths of their dads*. New York, NY: Hyperion.

Cunningan, C. (2002). (A quote from a personal interview) in Miles, A. *Violence in families: What every Christian needs to know*. Minneapolis: Augsburg.

Erickson, E. (1963). *Childhood & society* (2nd ed.). New York, NY: W. W. Norton.

Gilbert, R. (1999). *Finding your way after your parent dies*. Notre Dame, IN: Ave Maria.

Harvey, J. H. (2000). *Give sorrow words: Perspectives on loss and trauma*. Philadelphia, PA: Taylor & Francis.

Hooyman, N., & Kramer, B. (2006). *Living through loss: Interventions across the life span*. New York, NY: Columbia University Press.

Kirschman, E. (2007). *I love a cop: What police families need to know* (Rev. ed.). New York, NY: Guilford.

Loehfelm, B. (2008). *Fresh kills: A novel*. New York, NY: Berkeley Prime Crime.

Marshall, F. (2000). *Losing a parent: Practical help for you and other family members*. Tucson, AZ: Fisher.

Miles, A. (2002). *Violence in families: What every Christian needs to know*. Minneapolis, MN: Augsburg Fortress.

Santrock, J. (2006). *Life span development* (10th ed.). Boston, MA: McGraw-Hill.

Smith, H. I. (1994). *On grieving the death of a father*. Minneapolis, MN: Augsburg.

Smith, H. I. (2003). *Grieving the death of a mother*. Minneapolis, MN: Augsburg.

Zwick, J. (director) & Hanks, T. (producer). (2002). *My big fat Greek wedding*. Canada/ USA: Playtone Films.

were pregnant even before she put on the hospital gown. She felt like screaming back to her, but she calmed herself in realizing that this question was just part of the generic hospital protocol before a procedure was being performed in the radiographic suite. The doctor had two residents with him, and she was not asked if she minded them being present while the technician placed her feet in the stirrups and draped her for the procedure. The procedure was like a pelvic examination, except that a metal instrument was inserted through her cervix, which was very uncomfortable. When the dye was injected, it hurt, and she had an intense, painful cramping sensation. The doctor spoke to her and to the residents that were with him from behind a drape, and she closed her eyes and clenched her hands together due to the discomfort.

Two weeks later, Rob and Susan met with the specialist to review their results. All of them were normal. The specialist suggested oral medication to try to induce ovulation in Susan as a start. Susan took the medication for 3 months. It caused her to feel bloated and irritable much of the time. She felt frustrated. It had now been 6 months since she had spoken with her family doctor, and nothing had happened. Over the next 2 years, Susan and Rob gradually went from one medication to another, with Susan being switched from pills to injectable medications (Rob had to learn to give the injections to Susan) and then proceeding to intrauterine insemination (IUI), which involved having to go to the clinic early in the mornings for daily blood work and then returning for several vaginal ultrasounds every month and finally having Rob's sperm directly injected into her uterus when it was determined that she was ovulating. Susan had to cancel several out-of-town meetings because she couldn't leave town when she was in the midst of a treatment cycle, and she was often late getting into work because she had to wait at the clinic for her blood to be drawn in the mornings. And every month Rob had to go to the clinic and try to produce a specimen to be used for the treatments.

They decided not to go on vacation in the summer months so that they could continue with the treatments, both due to the need to remain close to the clinic during the time when Susan would be ovulating and because the costs were beginning to accumulate. When Rob needed a new car, he purchased a used Toyota to replace his Lexus sedan because their medical insurance was no longer covering the costs of the medications and procedures. They finally decided to pursue a cycle of in vitro fertilization (IVF), hoping that this procedure would help them to have the child of their dreams. The cost of one cycle of IVF was almost $10,000. They decided to take out a second mortgage on their home. Susan had to receive hormonal injections several times a day, and she had to go to the clinic daily for blood work and ultrasounds. When the eggs were finally retrieved from her body, she spent the day in the outpatient surgical suite of the hospital. They were told that three of the eggs had been fertilized and placed in a petri dish to grow and mature for a few days while they waited. Rob and Susan were so hopeful—they felt like they were actually parents at that time.

The embryologist took pictures of their "children" under the microscope—three little embryos, a few cells in each one. The embryos were then transferred back into Susan's uterus, and Rob and Susan had to wait for 2 weeks for Susan to have a pregnancy test to see if they "took."

The day before Susan was to go for her pregnancy test, she began cramping and spotting. She lay in bed, hoping that if she didn't move, the cramping would stop. Later that night, when she got up to use the bathroom, she began to bleed. Susan crumbled to the floor, sobbing. Rob came running to the bathroom when he heard her, and when he saw her crying on the floor, he felt paralyzed because he knew he couldn't help her and couldn't make it better for her. He slowly walked back to bed and lay awake, listening helplessly to Susan crying.

Over the past 3 years, their lives had been dictated by their quest for a baby. They had spent almost $30,000 in their attempts to get pregnant. Their sexual intimacy had become a rote, prescribed act to be completed on certain days of Susan's cycle. They no longer initiated sexual contact at other times because there was no chance of a pregnancy and every aspect of their lives was now focused on this goal. Their circle of friends became smaller and smaller, as other couples had children or traveled more, and Susan had become quiet, moody, and sullen. She could not be around women who were pregnant or who had young children. She could not attend baby showers for her friends and Rob's sister, which caused a strain with his family. Susan decided to take stress leave from work, so their income was even lower while their bills were getting higher. Rob was often afraid to approach Susan about plans that needed to be made because she was so reactive and angry. He tried to stay busy with work and with video games and the computer when he was home. They met with the infertility specialist to discuss their situation after the failed IVF cycle. They were told that they could try another IVF cycle (which would cost another $10,000); that they could consider trying to find a younger woman to donate her eggs, since Susan was now close to 40 and her chances of becoming pregnant were diminishing; or that they could go back to trying medication and monitoring, as they had done before the IVF cycle. It was at this time that Susan asked about the possibility of seeing a counselor who was familiar with infertility.

THE IMPACT OF INFERTILITY

Infertility is defined as the inability to conceive after one year of unprotected intercourse or the inability to carry a pregnancy to term. For women over 35, the definition of infertility changes to the inability to conceive after six months (Keye, 2006). *Primary infertility* is defined as the failure to conceive in a couple that has never conceived, and *secondary infertility* refers to the inability to conceive by a couple that had previously conceived (Keye, 2006). The incidence of infertility in North America is approximately one in five couples, or 10%–15%

of the reproductive-age population (Keye, 2006). Infertility rates are increasing, and the cause of the increase is thought to be due to the changing roles of women and delayed childbearing, a higher incidence of sperm abnormalities, and the long-term effects of sexually-transmitted diseases (STDs) on the reproductive system. Infertility is viewed as a type of reproductive loss (Burns & Covington, 2006; McShane, 1997).

Rob and Susan's story is not unique. Many couples go through repeated cycles of medications and procedures like IUI and IVF, attempting to become pregnant, depleting their financial resources, becoming emotionally and physically exhausted, and living with loss after loss each month (Collins, Feeny, & Gunby, 1997). Almost every form of infertility treatment requires the woman, especially, to become very focused upon her monthly cycle and to make frequent adjustments in her personal and professional life in order to accommodate the medication side effects and the time required to have the various procedures performed (Bateman-Cass, 2000; McShane, 1997). Many women report that the intensity of the monitoring of their body, the invasiveness of the treatments themselves, and the loss of control over their body and daily life add a tremendous amount of stress and anxiety to their unwanted childless state (Bateman-Cass, 2000; Daniluk, 1997; Domar, 1997; Eriksen, 2001; Watson, 2005). Women can go through infertility treatment for years and thus live in a chronic cycle of anticipation, attachment, and then loss that repeats itself over and over again (Bateman-Cass, 2000; Becker & Nachtigall, 1994; Leiblum & Greenfeld, 1997).

Most couples who enter infertility treatment are unaware of the high levels of physical, financial, and psychological investment and stress that they will encounter while undergoing treatment. They often have very unrealistic expectations about the success rates of these treatments. Many have heard media accounts of sensational or near-miraculous conception and birth through the use of medical technology and believe that it will only be a "matter of time" before they will become pregnant with their efforts (Bateman-Cass, 2000; Daniluk, 2001; Greil, 1991). There are myriad references to the life-altering impact of infertility and infertility treatment upon women in the literature published on the psychological effects of infertility treatment. Many of the participants in these studies describe the "emotional roller coaster" effect of treatment (Bateman-Cass, 2000; Daniluk, 1991). Several authors describe the diagnosis and treatment of infertility as a life crisis (Applegarth, 2006; Daniluk, 1997; Dupuis, 1997; Gerrity, 2001; Hart, 2002; Johansson & Berg, 2005; Leiblum & Greenfeld, 1997). Many women speak of their awareness of their infertility and going through the treatments as "devastating" and as "the worst experience of their lives" (Bateman-Cass, 2000; Domar, 1997). Burns (2005) refers to the entrance into infertility treatment as "paradise lost," as the couple loses the view of themselves as healthy, procreative, and in control of their lives and future. Domar, Zuttermeister, and Friedman (1993) described anxiety and depression scores in infertile women as similar to women who were suffering from cancer, hypertension, and cardiac rehabilitation.

Of great importance are the descriptions of grief in couples who have undergone extensive infertility treatments. The losses in infertility are both tangible (i.e., no baby after the ending of the treatment) and intangible (i.e., loss of the dreams of parenthood and loss of the view of oneself as capable and successful). The losses associated with infertility have been described in literature pertaining to nonfinite loss (Schultz & Harris, 2011), chronic sorrow (Casale, 2009; Harris, 2009), and ambiguous loss (Boss, Roos, & Harris, 2011). The loss is ongoing, as the hopes and dreams of having a child are repeatedly dashed through failed medical treatments. There is also evidence to support that even if a couple eventually achieves parenthood through adoption, there is always a residual sense of loss and grief that remains present from the couple's experiences in infertility treatment (Daniluk & Hurtig-Mitchell, 2003; Leiblum, Aviv, & Hamer, 1998).

In failed infertility treatments, women experience a loss of their dream of motherhood at the same time that the intensity of these same treatments strengthens their focus, investment, and resolve to be a mother. Most of the infertility treatments are enacted upon their bodies and require a significant sacrifice of time, endurance of embarrassment and loss of privacy, and a tolerance of discomfort. These women also experience loss of control over their bodies and their everyday life. For many, the losses are not only a chronic loss of a sense of themselves as fertile and the ongoing loss of the identification with or dream of being a mother but also the loss of the "children" that were conceived in the petri dish that "disappeared" after they were transferred into the would-be mother's body. For some women, this loss includes the potential life in the follicles they saw on an ultrasound screen (Salzer, 1993; Seibel & Levin, 1987). The close monitoring, imagery, and medical procedures in much infertility treatment allow a woman the opportunity to be highly involved and invested in a pregnancy at preconception levels, and all of her time and energy is devoted to continuing through the rigors of the treatment cycle (Sandelowski, Harris, & Holditch-Davis, 1990). Kluger-Bell (1998) noted that the high level of involvement by the woman during the treatment cycles and the technology that allows visualization of the entire process can contribute to attachment and emotional bonding to a *potential* pregnancy during the ultrasound monitoring of the woman's follicles. However, there were no studies found that examined women's feelings of bonding or attachment during infertility cycle monitoring prior to fertilization of retrieved eggs.

It was noted by Glazer (1997) that after a failed IVF cycle, the majority of women described feelings similar to women who have experienced the loss of a confirmed pregnancy (miscarriage), and she termed this loss as a "technical miscarriage." Covington (2006) used the term "preimplantation miscarriage" to describe the loss experience after failed IVF. Sandelowski et al. (1990) use the term "pregnant moments" to describe some women's feelings of loss after a failed IVF cycle, as many feel they were pregnant, if only for a brief period of time. These same researchers concluded that for women in infertility treatment, pregnancy is often experienced as a series of steps whereby the woman begins to feel more and more pregnant as the process unfolds. There are no studies of men's perceptions of loss after a failed treatment cycle. However, it is important to note that the woman's experience is very intense and focused during the treatment cycles, while many of the male partners feel they are relegated to a single function and are typically not the focus of the treatments or the attention of the medical care providers during this time. It is difficult to feel like an expectant father when the process reduces one to being a "sperm donor."

According to Seibel and Levin (1987), most women feel that their embryos are living human beings—their *children*. Greenfeld, Diamond, and DeCherney (1988) administered a semi-structured psychosocial screening interview to women and their husbands entering an IVF program. These same couples were interviewed again after a failed treatment cycle. In these interviews, 25% of the women experienced intense grief reactions with a significant amount of anxiety, depression, irritability, and guilt. These reactions were not paralleled by the husbands in the study—perhaps itself an indication of the marginalization of men by this process. These researchers suggested that the demands of IVF and the technology involved can intensify and foster an attachment to the embryo(s) that is similar to women who experience quickening, hear their baby's heartbeat, or see ultrasound pictures of their fetus.

Hurwitz (1989) describes a failed IVF cycle as more than the loss of a fantasized child and compares it more closely to the loss of a real child due to the awareness of the woman that there was an embryo or embryos. In an earlier study, Greenfeld and Haseltine (1986) reported that women who felt they were pregnant at the time of the embryo transfer experienced grief reactions similar to women who have experienced a miscarriage. Garner, Arnold, and Gray (1984) reported that many women viewed embryo transfer in IVF to be the time of conception; when the pregnancy tests were negative, these women grieved the loss of their child(ren).

There is reinforcement of this position from various social forces. For instance, the Roman Catholic Church views an embryo as a form of human life from the moment of conception, and there have been legal battles between couples in the United States over the disposition of frozen embryos, which are viewed as the viable offspring of the couple with rights as human beings (Cooper & Glazer, 1998). Certainly, seeing fertilization occur in the laboratory setting after a very involved monitoring process in a woman who has an intense desire to be a mother will have a profound impact upon the women who undergo this form of treatment. For many of these women, the loss is real and the attachment to these "children" is also very real. To take this discussion a step further, many women indicate that the follicles that they see during the ultrasound monitoring of their cycles are their potential children, so the possibility of very early attachment exists within this context (Bateman-Cass, 2000; Glazer, 1997; Pretorius et al., 2005; Salzer, 1993; Seibel & Levin, 1987).

Thus, women who enter infertility treatment often meet the criteria for forming an attachment bond to another living being, even at times earlier than conception, and their investment in the pregnancy (or potential pregnancy) is extremely high (Bateman-Cass, 2000; Cooper & Glazer, 1998; Johansson & Berg, 2005). The grief of these women is real, even though there is no apparent "death." There is very little research on the effects of failed infertility treatment on the male partner. Most men describe their feelings of grief associated with the loss of their partner as she once used to be, and the loss of their relationship as it once was, as well as painful feelings of powerlessness and helplessness through the treatment process (Daniluk, 1991, 1997; Daniluk & Tench, 2007).

Infertile couples mourn losses that are often invisible and unrecognized by others (Bateman-Cass, 2000; Kirkman, 2003). In infertility, there is no baby to hold and no person with whom experiences have been shared, and yet there is a significant loss with often debilitating grief. The experience of infertility is disenfranchised as a result of its invisibility, and infertile couples rarely receive the social recognition and support that other losses might engender (Doka, 1989, 2002). Many individuals keep their infertility treatment private; thus, family and friends may not even know about their difficulties. However, even if family members and friends are informed of the infertility treatments, they often do not understand the complexities involved in these treatments or the intense and invasive nature of the procedures (Klock, 1997). These couples are still told by well-meaning others that they will conceive if they relax (which is unproven) or that they can always adopt a child, which is often not the case (Dupuis, 1997; Grant, 1994). Involuntarily childless couples are often lectured about the advantages of not being encumbered by children's demands by others who think this information will somehow assuage the pain of their inability to conceive a much-desired baby. The experience of many couples who endure ongoing unsuccessful infertility treatment is similar to that of bereaved parents. However, because there is a lack of understanding regarding their losses, and because of the fact that there is no visible child that has been lost, these couples often remain isolated in their grief and do not receive the support that they need from those who are closest to them.

CONSIDERING ADOPTION

Rob and Susan found themselves at a fork in the road. They could continue trying to conceive with more treatments or with an egg donor. These options did not provide a guarantee that they would eventually have a child and could potentially devastate them financially. The next option was the possibility of choosing to remain childless and to focus on each other, their careers, and the freedom to travel and do things that might not be possible if they had a child. Susan felt that she had already spent most of her life doing what she wanted, and she did not see how she could ever embrace a life without having a family of her own. The third option was to consider adoption. Susan had researched the possibility of adoption a while back, and she found the process to be confusing and overwhelming. She resented having to undergo a home study and endure the scrutiny and potential criticism of an outsider sent to evaluate their home, finances, and relationship. She also worried that they would not be chosen as parents by someone trying to place a baby privately for adoption. Even worse, she worried that they would be chosen and be excited and ready for a baby and then the birth mother would change her mind and dash their hopes. She was already exhausted enough without entertaining this possibility. International adoptions looked complicated and expensive, and the children were usually older and had been placed in orphanages. She felt concern about not knowing anything about a child's background, and she wondered what it would be like to raise a child that did not physically look like her. And to add insult to injury, when she brought up the idea of adoption to Rob, he wasn't very supportive of adopting someone else's child and was afraid that he would not feel a connection to a child that was not biologically his.

The point at which Susan and Rob were faced with these choices is a common point for couples who have endured long-term infertility treatment. They are approaching a major decision at a time when they are often physically, emotionally, and socially depleted—and often when their relationship has suffered under a tremendous amount of pressure and stress. The decision to explore adoption always involves some form of approval process of the couple either through a governmentally sanctioned reviewer or through an agency review, most often referred to as a "home study." This review process can be highly intimidating to couples who have become exhausted emotionally and depleted financially through the infertility treatments. In addition, the decision to adopt doesn't necessarily guarantee that there will be a child appearing in their home in a short period of time.

Another common issue that was exemplified in the example of Rob and Susan is that partners often begin to consider adoption at different points in the treatment process, and they may not necessarily agree with each other about the decision to adopt or which path toward adoption they should take. Having a disagreement or hitting an impasse at this time adds further stress to the couple, and often seeking assistance with a counselor may be of benefit for each of the partners to hear the other and to obtain accurate information about the adoption process and expectations for parenting after adoption.

Many couples believe that once they have decided to pursue adoption, their stress and anxiety will begin to abate as they journey down a path to parenthood that is hopefully more promising than the medical treatments were. However, the adoption process can be time-consuming, highly bureaucratic, and fraught with disappointment as well. As discussed previously, inaccurate and unrealistic expectations about infertility treatments are readily present in the media and public perception. The same is true of adoption, where the public perception is based upon the media coverage of high-profile individuals who have no difficulties adopting children from various sources. Thus, the expectation is that couples can easily adopt babies that are readily available and in need of loving homes. The reality is that there are very few babies that are available for adoption domestically, and for most couples wishing to adopt a baby in their locale, the waiting time is long and there are just not enough babies available for adoption to meet this need. With the advent of birth control, the lessened stigma of being a single mother, and the availability of abortion to women who do not carry their unwanted pregnancies to term, there are fewer babies in need of adoption than a generation ago (Salzer, 2006). In addition, courts now attempt to honor the attachment needs of children by keeping family units together. Decisions concerning the final placement will now often allow time for young children to be fostered while the circumstances surrounding a birth parent's incapacity are addressed, for example through psychiatric treatment or rehabilitation, and there are now greater attempts to place young children with relatives and extended family members than with individuals who are not related to the children.

Domestic adoption involves a child and adoptive parents who reside in the same country. There are many agencies that assist with domestic adoptions, and these agencies may be government-based or private social services agencies, such as those affiliated with specific religious communities. In traditional agency adoptions, the birth mother places the child with an agency, which then will select the adoptive parents from the agency's list of prospective parents who have gone through a prescreening and approval process. In most agency adoptions, the birth mother and the adoptive parents remain anonymous to each other, although nonidentifying information is generally exchanged (Salzer, 2006). More recently, there have been greater variations in the sharing of information between birth mothers and adoptive parents, with some situations allowing for an actual meeting between the parties and a greater exchange of historical and personal information. Many couples who have already undergone years of infertility treatment are discouraged by long waits in this process and little guarantee of a child within a specific timeframe. In addition, many agencies try to promote fostering a child who is not currently available for adoption but may become available at a later date, and this option can be stressful for couples who have already experienced deep losses associated with the repeated pattern of hope followed by devastation from the failed infertility treatment.

Some couples will pursue *domestic independent adoption*, which is also referred to as *private adoption*. In this situation, the couple locates a birth mother and makes an independent arrangement for placement of the baby without the use of an agency as an intermediary. Most adoptive parents in this situation will assist the birth mother with costs associated with the pregnancy and delivery of the baby. However, these costs can also include living costs, transportation costs, and medical and legal fees, which can become significant. It is illegal in most countries to pay specifically for a baby, and most industrialized countries participate in the tenets set out by the Hague Convention, which includes a prohibition about direct payment for babies (Salzer, 2006).

International adoption is increasingly seen as an option by couples who decide to adopt. International adoption wait times are generally less than those of domestic adoption, and when a child is available for adoption through an international agency, there is very little chance that the adoption would not be completed due to a change in circumstance of the birth parents (Salzer, 2006). Fees for international adoption can be steep, as there are significant costs incurred by the adoption agency for translation, court costs, care of the child, transportation, travel documents, immigration paperwork, and lodging for when the couple must travel to the country where the child is located. Some countries have specific restrictions for adoptive parents regarding age, marital status, whether there are other children at home, and other factors such as the presence of obesity, work status, income (even though the costs of such adoptions already limit this option to those of a certain class), and if there is any criminal history. The children most often available for international adoption are usually 6 months of age and older and are often living in institutions where the care provided might be very poor. In most cases, knowledge regarding the child's history and information about the parents is scant. These factors may have an impact upon the future health of the child and the ability of the child to attach to a parental figure (Shapiro, Shapiro, & Paret, 2001).

Initially, couples often experience a sense of powerlessness and frustration at having every aspect of their lives placed under scrutiny as part of the home study approval process. This sense of powerlessness dovetails with the feelings of powerlessness and futility that were often experienced in the medical treatment setting. Couples often experience feelings of being persecuted or of being singled out for difficulty as they watch others couples start their families without any apparent difficulties at all or as they hear of someone who becomes pregnant by accident or who has a baby without the means or lifestyle to adequately care for a child (Harris, 2009). The loss of privacy over their sexual intimacy and history in infertility treatment gives way to loss of privacy in their relationship and personal space in the home study assessment and the bureaucratic maze of adoption.

The experience of adoption for infertile couples represents a shift in focus that has usually occurred as a process over time. Studies of adoption after infertility treatment have demonstrated that there is generally a very good adjustment to parenthood once the adoption process is completed and a child has been placed with the couple (Daniluk & Hurtig-Mitchell, 2003; Leiblum et al., 1998; Sandelowski et al., 1990; Sydsjo, Ekholm, Wadsby, Kjellberg, & Sydjo, 2005). It is typical for concerns about the ability to attach to a child that is not genetically related to oneself to gradually dissipate as the attachment bond strengthens with ongoing engagement with the child. It is important to recognize that adoption is not a "cure" for infertility but a choice that the couple has made to pursue parenthood. After adoption, many couples who underwent unsuccessful infertility treatment will state that their focus changed from *getting pregnant* to *becoming parents* (Daniluk & Hurtig-Mitchell, 2003).

A LEGACY OF LOSS

Both infertility and adoption are loss-related experiences. Both can be considered wounds to the attachment system for all of the parties involved. As stated previously, infertility treatment activates attachment behaviors and increases investment in the mother role for women. Daniluk describes infertility as being "like a death for which there are no rituals and little public acknowledgment" (1991, p. 318). In failed infertility treatments, couples lose their hopes and dreams of having a child from their union. In addition, women experience many other losses, such as loss of their health due to side effects from medication, loss of normalcy in their lives, loss of income from having to take time off work for treatments (or job loss as a result of inability to fulfill work commitments during treatments), loss of friends who have children or who cannot understand the intensity of the infertility experience, loss of self-identity and self-esteem, and loss of equilibrium in their lives (Bateman-Cass, 2000; Burns, 2005; Daniluk, 1997; Domar, 1997; Johansson & Berg, 2005; Pavone, 2005).

Unsuccessful treatment cycles can feel like the loss of a baby over and over again, with significant damage to the ability to attach to others and to enter into regular life throughout this process. This damage to the attachment system also affects the couple's ongoing sexual relationship. It is important for couples to have the opportunity to recognize the significance of this experience to their relationship and to explore how they now view themselves after they decide to discontinue the treatments. Salzer (2006) describes areas of concern for infertile couples who are considering adoption to be (a) serious disagreements regarding future steps, (b) the focus on a baby as a means to repair a marriage or to provide distraction in a marriage that is fraught with high conflict, (c) serious mental health problems that have not been treated, and (d) a refusal to engage in a process of exploration about the unique issues that surround adoptive families. If these issues are present in a couple presenting for adoption, counseling should be sought to work through the issues before considering the start of the home study process. Although professional helpers may have a strong desire to help the infertile couple who has already been through so much pain and expense, the focus of the adoption process is upon protection of the child who may be adopted. Thus, there must not be any possibility of compromising a child's well-being in order to assuage the pain of an infertile couple that has not worked through issues that could interfere with the ability to provide a child with a safe and secure home environment.

Adoption has been described as a triad of grief (Schacter & Schacter, 2010). For an adoption to occur, the birth parent or parents relinquish a child for adoption, the child that is adopted loses his or her birth parent(s), and the adoptive parents have typically grieved the loss of their ability to produce a biological child of their own. There is often stigma surrounding both infertility and adoption, as infertility is seen as "completely curable" in the public perception, so the couple that is involuntarily childless may be stigmatized as selfish or as not a complete family because of the absence of children. In families where adoption has occurred, the stigma focuses on adoption as a "second choice," and there is a tendency to view adoptive children as the compromise choice in the absence of a biological child. In addition, families are defined as "normative" in Western society based upon a model of a heterosexual married couple with their own biological children; variations from this standard view are often seen as anomalies rather than representations of a diverse range of possibilities for family systems (Johnson, 2002). Language often reinforces this view of the family and can be very difficult for adoptive parents and their children (e.g., referring to birth parents as an adopted child's "natural" parents or "real" parents).

CLINICAL IMPLICATIONS

Name and Validate the Losses

Clinicians who work with infertile couples must be prepared for the layers of loss that accompany this experience, and each aspect of loss needs to be named, validated, and grieved for what it represents. Most couples who go through infertility treatment will share that their losses are often invisible to others and that their experience is either minimized or dismissed by others who do not understand what they have endured. Support to these couples includes the ability to normalize the intensity of the treatment process and to explore how that process affected them individually and as a couple. The use of ritual may be of value in this process to help validate the losses and to point a way toward finding meaning in the experience. The validation of the many losses helps to name and give credence to the experiences of couples who have endured the layers of loss described in this study. Validation of the losses is cited by Doka (1989, 2002) as the first step in offering support to individuals who have experienced disenfranchised grief.

Encourage the Practice of Presence

Studies of couples who did not become pregnant through infertility treatments discuss the importance for support to be offered that is more about a sense of "being there" instead of giving advice, trying to make them feel better, and encouraging unrealistic expectations about the future. Most couples find it hard to handle well-intentioned but painful advice and platitudes, and attempts at trying to make them feel better often seem simplistic and condescending (Daniluk, 1991; Harris, 2009). Some couples may find it helpful to talk with others who have been through similar experiences, and for those couples who are considering adoption, the ability to have open discussion with other couples who have adopted might be very beneficial. However, the most important form of support is to simply listen, to be present, and to not try to give advice or "fix" things.

Be an Informed Supporter

Individuals who offer professional support to infertile couples must understand the ins and outs of infertility treatment, including what is involved in specific types of treatment, typical medications and their side effects, what the various procedures involve, and a general understanding of the terminology that accompanies the treatments. Clinicians who work with individuals in infertility treatment need to be informed about the specific medical and technical aspects of this experience in order to follow their clients' stories and to understand their experiences more deeply. A list of qualification guidelines for mental health professionals in reproductive medicine can be found in Covington and Burns (2006). These guidelines specify that understanding the medical aspects of infertility treatment is essential to provide informed support to individuals in infertility treatment. Having an understanding of the adoption protocols in your local area is also very important, in addition to knowing the different adoption agencies and home study procedures so that couples can obtain this information in advance and feel prepared if they choose to explore the possibility of adoption.

Recognize the Different Forms of Grief That May Be Present

As stated previously, both infertility and adoption are experiences that are rooted in loss and grief. However, these losses and the grief may not be readily apparent and may not "fit" into a category or expression that is recognized. Keep in mind that even after adoption is completed, the experience of infertility treatment has etched a wound in the assumptive world for those who had to face the realization that their bodies did not work as they should have, that their lives took a sharp turn in a direction that was never anticipated, and that the ongoing financial, emotional, and social hardships that occurred from the infertility treatment that will take a long time to heal, both individually and as a couple.

CONCLUSION

The experience of infertility and the adoption of a child both carry some of the most painful and potentially transformative experiences in human relationships. Both experiences are interwoven with feelings of frustration and powerlessness and a sense of injustice at life for all of the parties involved. Infertility affects the view of oneself, the perception of others, and coming to terms with the disparity between how the world *should* work versus how life events *actually occur* in reality. As in many situations where there is the possibility of great pain and upheaval, there is also the potential for the couple's relationship to become closer and more resilient after this experience. Support to these couples needs to be proactive, informed, and compassionate.

REFERENCES

Applegarth, L. D. (2006). Individual counseling and psychotherapy. In S. N. Covington & L. H. Burns (Eds.), *Infertility counseling: A comprehensive handbook for clinicians* (2nd ed., pp. 129–142). New York, NY: Cambridge University Press.

Bateman-Cass, C. (2000). The loss within a loss: Understanding the psychological implications of assisted reproductive technologies for the treatment of infertility. *Dissertation Abstracts International, 61*(03), 1624B. (UMI No. 9965385)

Becker, G., & Nachtigall, R. D. (1994). Born to be a mother: The cultural construction of risk in infertility treatment in the U.S. *Social Science Medicine, 39*(4), 507–518.

Boss, P., Roos, S., & Harris, D. (2011). Grief in the midst of ambiguity and uncertainty: An exploration of ambiguous loss and chronic sorrow. In R. Neimeyer, D. Harris, H. Winokuer, & G. Thornton (Eds.), *Grief and bereavement in contemporary society: Bridging research and practice* (pp. 163–175). New York, NY: Routledge.

Burns, L. H. (2005). Psychological changes in infertility patients. In A. Rosen & J. Rosen (Eds.), *Frozen dreams: Psychodynamic dimensions of infertility and assisted reproduction* (pp. 3–29). Hillsdale, NJ: Analytic Press.

Burns, L. H., & Covington, S. N. (2006). Psychology of infertility. In S. N. Covington & L. H. Burns (Eds.), *Infertility counseling: A comprehensive handbook for clinicians* (2nd ed., pp. 1–19). New York, NY: Cambridge University Press.

Casale, A. (2009). *Distinguishing the concept of chronic sorrow from standard grief: An empirical study of infertile couples.* Doctoral dissertation, New York University, Silver School of Social Work. (UMI No. 3353016)

Collins, J. A., Feeny, D., & Gunby, J. (1997). The cost of infertility diagnosis and treatment in Canada in 1995. *Human Reproduction, 12*(5), 951–958.

Cooper, S. L., & Glazer, E. S. (1998). *Choosing assisted reproduction: Social, emotional, and ethical considerations*. Indianapolis, IN: Perspectives Press.

Covington, S. N. (2006). Pregnancy loss. In S. N. Covington & L. H. Burns (Eds.), *Infertility counseling: A comprehensive handbook for clinicians* (2nd ed., pp. 290–304). New York, NY: Cambridge University Press.

Covington, S. N., & Burns, L. H. (Eds.). (2006). *Infertility counseling: A comprehensive handbook for clinicians* (2nd ed.). New York, NY: Cambridge University Press.

Daniluk, J. C. (1991). Strategies for counseling infertile couples. *Journal of Counseling & Development, 69,* 317–320.

Daniluk, J. C. (1997). Gender and infertility. In S. R. Leiblum (Ed.), *Infertility: Psychological issues and counseling strategies* (pp. 103–125). New York, NY: Wiley.

Daniluk, J. C. (2001). "If we had it to do over again . . .": Couples' reflections of their experiences of infertility treatments. *Family Journal: Counseling and Therapy for Couples and Families, 9*(2), 122–133.

Daniluk, J. C., & Hurtig-Mitchell, J. (2003). Themes of hope and healing: Infertile couples' experiences of adoption. *Journal of Counseling & Development, 81*, 389–399.

Daniluk, J. C., & Tench, E. (2007). Long-term adjustment of infertile couples following unsuccessful medical intervention. *Journal of Counseling & Development, 85*, 89–100.

Doka, K. J. (1989). *Disenfranchised grief: Recognizing hidden sorrow.* Lexington, MA: Lexington Books.

Doka, K. J. (2002). *Disenfranchised grief: New directions, challenges, and strategies for practice*. Champaign, IL: Research Press.

Domar, A. D. (1997). Stress and infertility in women. In S. R. Leiblum (Ed.), *Infertility: Psychological issues and counseling strategies* (pp. 67–82). New York, NY: Wiley.

Domar, A. D., Zuttermeister, P., & Friedman, R. (1993). The psychological impact of infertility: A comparison with patients with other medical conditions. *Journal of Psychosomatic Obstetrics and Gynecology, 14*, 45–52.

Dupuis, S. R. (1997). Understanding reproductive loss. *Dissertation Abstracts International, 58*(01), 414B. (UMI No. 9717693)

Eriksen, K. (2001). Infertility and the search for family. *Family Journal: Counseling and Therapy for Couples and Families, 9*(1), 55–61.

Garner, C. H., Arnold, E. W., & Gray, H. (1984). The psychological impact of in vitro fertilization. *Fertility and Sterility, 41*(2), 13.

Gerrity, D. (2001). Five medical treatment stages of infertility: Implications for counselors. *Family Journal: Counseling and Therapy for Couples and Families, 9*(2), 140–150.

Glazer, E. S. (1997). Miscarriage and its aftermath. In S. R. Leiblum (Ed.), *Infertility: Psychological issues and counseling strategies* (pp. 230–245). New York, NY: Wiley.

Grant, K. R. (1994). The new reproductive technologies: Boon or bane? In B. S. Bolaria & H. D. Dickinson (Eds.), *Health, illness, and health care in Canada* (2nd ed., pp. 362–383). Toronto, Ontario, Canada: Harcourt Brace.

Greenfeld, D. A., Diamond, M. P., & DeCherney, A. H. (1988). Grief reactions following in vitro fertilization treatment. *Journal of Psychosomatic Obstetrics and Gynecology, 8*, 169–174.

Greenfeld, D. A., & Haseltine, F. (1986). Candidate selection and psychosocial considerations of in-vitro fertilization procedures. *Clinical Obstetrics and Gynecology, 26*(1), 119–126.

Greil, A. L. (1991). *Not yet pregnant: Infertile couples in contemporary America.* New Brunswick, NJ: Rutgers University Press.

Harris, D. (2009). *The experience of spontaneous pregnancy loss in infertile women who have conceived with the assistance of medical intervention*. Available from ProQuest Dissertations and Theses database. (UMI No. 3351170)

Hart, V. A. (2002). Infertility and the role of psychotherapy. *Issues in Mental Health Nursing, 23*(1), 31–41.

Hurwitz, N. (1989). The psychological effects of in vitro fertilization. *Pre- & Peri-Natal Psychology Journal, 4*(1), 43–50.

Johansson, M., & Berg, M. (2005). Women's experiences of childlessness 2 years after the end of in vitro fertilization treatment. *Scandinavian Journal of Caring Sciences, 19*(1), 58–63.

Johnson, D. E. (2002). Adoption and the effect on children's development. *Early Human Development, 68*, 39–54.

Keye, W. R. (2006). Medical aspects of infertility for the counselor. In S. N. Covington & L. H. Burns (Eds.), *Infertility counseling: A comprehensive handbook for clinicians* (2nd ed., pp. 20–36). New York, NY: Cambridge University Press.

Kirkman, M. (2003). Infertile women and the narrative work of mourning: Barriers to the revision of autobiographical narratives of motherhood. *Narrative Inquiry, 13*(1), 243–262.

Klock, S. C. (1997). To tell or not to tell: The issue of privacy and disclosure in infertility treatment. In S. R. Leiblum (Ed.), *Infertility: Psychological issues and counseling strategies* (pp. 167–188). New York, NY: Wiley.

Kluger-Bell, K. (1998). *Unspeakable losses: Understanding the experience of pregnancy loss, miscarriage, and abortion*. New York, NY: W. W. Norton.

Leiblum, S. R., Aviv, A., & Hamer, R. (1998). Life after infertility treatment: A long-term investigation of marital and sexual function. *Human Reproduction, 13*(12), 3569–3574.

Leiblum, S. R., & Greenfeld, D. A. (1997). The course of infertility: Immediate and long-term reactions. In S. R. Leiblum (Ed.), *Infertility: Psychological issues and counseling strategies* (pp. 83–102). New York, NY: Wiley.

McShane, P. M. (1997). Infertility diagnosis and reproductive options: A primer. In S. R. Leiblum (Ed.), *Infertility: Psychological issues and counseling strategies* (pp. 20–40). New York, NY: Wiley.

Pavone, T. (2005). A phenomenological heuristic study of the emotional impact of infertility on the working woman. *Dissertation Abstracts International, 66*(06), 3453B. (UMI No. 3178455)

Pretorius, E. K., Newton, R., Uyans, K., Hull, A. D., Hollenbach, K., & Nelson, T. R. (2005). Effects of ultrasound on maternal-fetal bonding: A comparison of two- and three-dimensional imaging. *Ultrasound in Obstetrics and Gynecology, 25*(5), 473–477.

Salzer, L. (1993, August). The emotional experience of IVF. *RESOLVE: Emotional Aspects of Infertility*, 6–7.

Salzer, L. (2006). Adoption after infertility. In S. N. Covington & L. H. Burns (Eds.), *Infertility counseling: A comprehensive handbook for clinicians* (2nd ed., pp. 387–410). New York, NY: Cambridge University Press.

Sandelowski, M., Harris, B. G., & Holditch-Davis, D. (1990). Pregnant moments: The process of conception in infertile couples. *Research in Nursing & Health, 13*, 273–282.

Schacter, S. R., & Schacter, J. R. (2010). Adoption: A life begun with loss. In D. Harris (Ed.), *Counting our losses: Reflecting on change, loss, and transition in everyday life* (pp. 75–92). New York, NY: Routledge.

Schultz, C., & Harris, D. (2011). Giving voice to nonfinite loss and bereavement. In R. Neimeyer, D. Harris, H. Winokuer, & G. Thornton (Eds.), *Grief and bereavement in contemporary society: Bridging research and practice* (pp. 235–245). New York, NY: Routledge.

Seibel, M. M., & Levin, S. (1987). A new era in reproductive technologies: The emotional stages of in vitro fertilization. *Journal of In Vitro Fertilization and Embryo Transfer, 4*(3), 135–140.

Shapiro, V., Shapiro, J., & Paret, I. (2001). *Complex adoption and assisted reproductive technologies*. New York, NY: Guilford.

Sydsjo, G., Ekholm, K, Wadsby, M., Kjellberg, S., & Sydjo, A. (2005). Relationships in couples after failed IVF treatment: A prospective follow-up study. *Human Reproduction, 20*(7), 1952–1957.

Watson, R. I. (2005). When the patient has experienced severe trauma. In A. R. Rosen & J. Rosen (Eds.), *Frozen dreams: Psychodynamic dimensions of infertility and assisted reproduction* (pp. 219–235). Hillsdale, NJ: Analytic Press.

CHAPTER 6

The Tolls of War: Intimacy and Sexuality Challenges for Soldiers and Their Families

M. Douglas Harvey

One never loses memories of a significant relationship.
—J. William Worden

Outside of participating in unit training missions, leading chapel services, attending and leading various briefings, staff meetings and formations, my early reserve weekends as an Army Reserve Chaplain included only a few soldiers entering my office seeking counseling, usually for the communication challenges they were experiencing in their marital or dating relationships. There was the occasional religious debate or fun philosophical challenge, but most soldiers understood the chaplain to be for when you needed prayer or needed to talk about your marriage.

Reserve soldiers, however, place a great deal of stock in your past military experience, especially any active duty time, as well as your civilian profession. My past military experience was as a fulltime enlisted Marine without any time in a combat zone, and my civilian job was as a hospice chaplain. From the perspective of the reserve soldiers, I work with old dying people. Having been enlisted before, I could be someone to chat with, but not at a high level of trust with intimate issues since I was lacking that military bonding experience of war.

This was all before I deployed to the Middle East in the War on Terror. I returned from that tour of duty as a combat veteran, having seen and experienced the lives of soldiers traumatized by the effects of war and walked, though not in their shoes, at their sides. As a result, my office was being frequented more often by soldiers and their family members expressing more intimate concerns than I knew existed before. They were not new issues to them, yet the person to whom they now chose to speak had had new experiences. Their new assessment of me told them I could now understand and be trusted. They saw me as a new person.

There were also new additions to our unit. We had been joined by several former active duty soldiers from a high-profile, elite, combat-experienced division. Our brigade in this training command was now one-third combat-experienced vets, with the numbers increasing each month as soldiers returned stateside, leaving active duty and joining reserve units. At that point, I had to request of my commander to participate in fewer training briefings due to the sheer volume of counseling sessions and the training I needed to help address the issues that were being brought to the table. This went on for over a year. The concerns expressed included depression, anxiety, adjustment disorders, addictions, chronic pain (physical and spiritual), emotional trauma, insomnia, sexual dysfunctions, lack of intimacy, and physical and psychological abuse. The majority of the complaints were related to experiences of combat and loss. I realized I was pushing the envelope of my professional expertise and chose to make many referrals.

This experience prompted me to come to a greater understanding of the traumas of war, particularly as they related to personal loss from the spiritual and mental health perspectives. While I was serving with a command chaplain team in Kuwait during the early years of the war, one of my many and varied responsibilities was to participate in redeployment briefings for soldiers returning home. Medical professionals, chaplains, and, when available, mental health professionals, spoke with troops about adjustment challenges and the consequences of long-term separation combined with the intense emotional, psychological, and physical trauma they might have experienced while in the war zone. Many things were discussed in those briefings that are now also listed in such documents as the U.S. Army Center for Health Promotion and Preventive Medicine brochure "Soldier Combat Stress Reaction: A pocket guide for spouse and loved ones" (USACHPPM, 2007). However, as in the brochure, difficulty with sexual and nonsexual intimacy was only mentioned at those early briefings before leaving the desert without adequately preparing soldiers for what might truly await them upon their return. Resources and contact numbers were offered, yet it was on the individual soldier to remember (after 6 months to a year, or sometimes more, of war and separation) those resources and take full responsibility for finding his or her own help.

Later, as a stateside reserve chaplain working with returning soldiers in the reserve system without full access to active duty resources, I experienced the professional pain of the lack of what we offered soldiers before leaving the desert. Since my return in 2005, there are many more mental health professionals in uniform in the war zone; such resources stateside have also increased. The intimacy concerns and challenges in the sex lives of couples as well as dating single soldiers are many, yet this remains a topic from which even professionals tend to shy away. Even to me as a chaplain, it seemed too personal, yet it arose prolifically. It was as if soldiers were insisting that we professionals deal with their intimacy and sexuality concerns.

It must be mentioned that any participation in sexual activity or possession of sexually related material is considered inappropriate behavior for service members while deployed to a war zone. Never mind that this is a strong physical desire for the largest age group of deployable soldiers (60% of active military are 18–30 years old) and never mind that deployment meant separation from this regular activity with their significant other for a long period of time (Department of Defense, 2008). Like it or not, humans are created as sexual beings. Not having a healthy sexual outlet is a loss, and human beings will attempt to satisfy or address this loss in a myriad of ways. The same is a concern for the significant other left stateside. Most of these soldiers and their partners work diligently at remaining celibate during this separation, with admirable fidelity. At issue here is maintaining physical health and healthy relationships. To this point there is much written about the effects of the long-term absence of sexual activity and intimacy on military couples as well as how the military addresses those concerns.

Unfortunately, many soldiers return from war zones with major emotional and physical trauma, which exacerbate those concerns. Trauma adds to the challenges that soldiers and their partners experience in sexual activity and intimacy. In addition to amputations, paralysis, burns, or other evidence of obvious physical wounds a soldier may come home struggling with, there are other less visible wounds, such as symptoms of poly-trauma or other traumatic brain injury (TBI). Returning soldiers also fight with such possibly debilitating diagnoses as post-traumatic stress disorder (PTSD), depression, chronic emotional and spiritual pain, anxiety, insomnia, and a host of other psychosocial disorders. Of the latter, I heard one uniformed mental health specialist say that these problems live and breed like cockroaches; if you have one, you probably have others. I would add to that analogy the fact that these psychological and spiritual diagnoses usually aren't evident in the daylight of a soldier's life but rather in the dark moments of living when life is most intimate.

When being welcomed home by their significant others, soldiers do not view sex and intimacy as a nice *part* of the return. After a year or more of abstinence, it *is* life! For the returning married or committed service member with a strong sense of fidelity, that relationship and the love shared within it are often the only salve for the wounds that disfigure their bodies and distort their souls. One does not look forward to coming home after such a long separation, coupled with the trauma of war, only to have to admit to a partner that one is no longer the same—not even as a lover.

It appears to be a common understanding that veterans experiencing PTSD primarily demonstrate symptoms that are related to aggression management. This is precisely why good psycho-education is important for soldiers and their family members as well as commanders and employers of returning soldiers

(Wilson, 2001). This line of thinking would direct a focus on anger management and a diagnosis related primarily to anxiety when these could be secondary to feelings of inadequacy and inappropriate self-image brought on by the impact of the trauma itself. Remember too that the trauma here is not "an event" so much as it is a collection of events coupled with physical traumas that take place over time. While there likely will be verbal aggression and quite possibly violence against spouses and partners, these are usually due to the inability to communicate feelings, the inability to trust, and the fact that veterans with PTSD are less self-disclosing and expressive with their partners, leading to an inappropriate or nonhealthy expression of emotional needs (Price & Stevens, 2009). There is much more going on than just being angry!

My own return home from the desert after a year had me hyper-vigilant and aware of my surroundings to the point that some friends would jokingly say I was "shell-shocked." As a chaplain, I was not even a part of any direct-fire operations. Yet like most clergy, I was easily swept into the depths of the tragedies for which I was the professional listening ear, while claiming no care for myself—only the constant and vigilant presence for my soldiers. After a year of my hearing the stories and being with the soldiers and their intense emotional responses, it was as if I too were experiencing the hyper-arousal symptoms of PTSD—my own PTSD emerging from my personal and professional self. For traumatized soldiers, however, such hyper-arousal could seriously impact their sense of safety and their ability to trust people, even their most intimate partners. If a soldier also avoids dealing with the experienced trauma or begins to numb the effects, what results is an impact on his or her ability to identify and express feelings. A breach in a trusting bond coupled with the effects of avoidance symptoms can certainly impact what happens in the dark moments of soldier's life at home—whether those dark moments are emotional downs (i.e., depression) or the dark bedroom, the place of intimate and sexual activity.

In addition to my hyperaroused return stateside, I also came home with a more direct and blunt expression of my sexuality and experiences of intimacy. I admit there may be an argument here to explain some of my own aggressive behavior such as experiences of guilt and shame as well as some symptoms of threatened safety and trust. I also felt that the expectations on me as clergy were different from those on other returning soldiers. It was as if clergy returning from war would *not* have any sexuality and intimacy challenges. Nevertheless, I found I had much in common with others returning from war.

Returning soldiers with traumatic experiences often return with major emotional detachment, pervasive enough that it affects their interpersonal relationships. Ripping away at the pleasurable moments with a significant other are such things as numbing emotional responses to the trauma, which anesthetizes the ability to express other emotional responses, or being preoccupied with the trauma. This in turn leaves one emotionally detached from the sexual experience.

Wrapped up in intimate and sexual experiences are now guilt and grief—be they related to the course of events defined as the trauma of war or to the inability to perform or even relate in the intimate experience. Guilt and grief are both emotionally and spiritually powerful experiences. A prolonged focus on these may also lead to a vicious circle of shame: a feeling of worthlessness, poor self-image, inadequacy, and low self-esteem. This shamecycle can catapult the soldier into a downward spiral of self-hate and depression.

These things could certainly be devastating to a soldier's capacity for intimacy and, ultimately, sexual performance. Aside from being emotionally crippled, returning soldiers may experience complete intimate disability. Most often intimate disability is treated as a sexual impairment. For instance, prescriptions are given for erectile dysfunction, but a differential diagnosis is not made to determine whether functional challenges are arising from the trauma of war or may be a result of the common side effects of the antidepression and/or antianxiety medications already prescribed.

The tolls of war are many, and clearly some concern the sexuality and intimacy challenges of soldiers and their significant others. There are multitudes of physical challenges that can impair sexual relations and hamper the intimate moments between couples. Principle among these are the more obvious amputations, burns, physical scarring, and traumatic brain injury. However, just as debilitating are the possibility of poly-trauma, the exposure to high-pressure waves, and explosive fragments and falling debris from explosions that result in a wide range of clinical symptoms typically associated with post-concussive syndrome. Poly-trauma results in profound neurological issues but also severe psychological distress, communication challenges (emotional and physical), altered sexual drive, and sometimes poor erectile function and inability to experience orgasm (Ducharme, 2008).

On these previously mentioned diagnoses and challenges, much as been researched and written; more still needs to be done. PTSD is a pervasive diagnosis of returning soldiers today, sometimes appropriately and sometimes as an inappropriate stereotype. An accurate assessment of PTSD takes into account a plethora of symptoms, many of which might stand as a diagnosis of their own. This is an indication that the trauma of war is replete with psychological and emotional penalties. Wounded soldiers continually find themselves making adjustments to the impact of these varied symptoms on their intimate relationships. Intimacy and sexual closeness can be daunting and physical performance sometimes unpredictable—so much so that some soldiers would rather avoid sex than to experience failure.

With the number of news articles related to the mental health of returning soldiers and the work of the Veteran's Administration and Department of Defense to deal with these concerns, there is increasing awareness of the need to research and address the issues of battlefield trauma. There also seems to be some continued apprehension with direct conversation related to issues of intimacy and sexuality for returning soldiers. While it is recognized to be necessary, within private rehabilitation centers, relationship and sexuality issues are still not being addressed: "sexual concerns are simply not perceived as a priority" (Ducharme, 2008, p. 3).

Appropriate and healthy disclosure for the soldier and psycho-education for the significant other have been key ingredients for me in offering help to returning soldiers and their families. These are classical components in PTSD treatment and near the limit of my expertise in pastoral care and counseling as a chaplain without a background in psychotherapy. Critical to my working with both soldier and partner has been two factors: not forgetting the teaching related to the context of the traumatic event itself and not stopping at just teaching about the symptoms of PTSD or any of the related diagnoses. The disconnect couples experience in communication often concerns the reality of the originating event—or, in the case of war, the compilation of events and experiences. These can be terrifying to conjure up and relive for the soldier or to have a first taste of for the family member. In the words of Laurie Harkness and Noka Zador, "an important aspect of the psycho-educational process is that it helps to 'detoxify' the traumatic material" (Wilson, 2001, p. 348). Again, it is important to remember that the traumatic material here may be experiences that span months or even a year.

When returning soldiers confide in me their concerns about sexual dysfunction and problems with intimacy, they often think of themselves as "freaks" or "odd characters." They are helped when I share with them what I know from researched resources and what other soldiers have given me permission to share anonymously. The goal is to "normalize" or at least to "contextualize" soldiers' experiences, to mitigate their shame, confusion, and fear. Not only are they dealing with legitimate mental health diagnoses, returning soldiers are facing extreme emotional and existential challenges, all of which affect personal relationships. Combat experiences are riddled with challenges. Included in them is significant grief and loss—not just in the experience of death but also with regard to nonfinite and ambiguous losses, such as happen when combat changes a soldier's identity or sense of self. Losses faced by some returning soldiers can be significant and frequently are unrecognized or not acknowledged by both the military and the community back home. Lack of clarity, by all concerned, about how to mourn these losses creates a sense of ongoing uncertainty regarding what will happen next in life (Bruce, 2001).

The lack of intimacy or the fear of aggressive outbursts during intimacy challenge a soldier's self-worth and self-image as an adequate partner in a loving relationship. Erectile dysfunction, inability to ejaculate, or absolute avoidance of sexual intimacy as a result of psychological, emotional, or existential struggles are also losses to a relationship that prior to the combat experience may have been perfectly healthy. These kinds of issues for the couple threaten the solidity of their marriage or covenant with each another. This in turn creates a fear of yet one more very significant loss.

According to Darcy Harris, "the ending of intimate relationships . . . is probably one of the most common and deeply distressing experiences that individuals in our society endure" (2011, p. 65). Harris says that relationships die essentially with the loss of the attachment bond that initially formed the relationship, regardless of whether the participants continue to exist physically or whether the legal basis for the relationship (marriage, covenant, same-sex union, etc.) remains in force. On this basis, it is fair to ask whether relationships formed before combat or deployment are still viable or whether war has already taken its toll even before the soldier returns home. Soldiers and their partners would benefit from relationship-reestablishment efforts that recognize relationship *loss* as a given and take into account what must occur as couples become familiar with one another again.

Losses of intimacy capacity and sexual functioning are as devastating as any other significant loss. These relationship losses come with some of their own unique challenges surrounding privacy, social acceptance, taboo conversations, and personal revelations. Moreover, they make for some considerable alterations of a soldier's personhood, which include changes in feelings about who they are and who they can or cannot become. It is important for the soldier and family member to adhere to the rigors of both physical therapy and any psychotherapy that would be part of any adequate treatment plan. However, there is significant and traumatic loss already in place and the potential for compounding grief to complicate any healing and transition. This is why it would be additionally beneficial for soldiers and those who care for them to find a grief counselor and put into practice appropriate protocols of grief therapy.

REFERENCES

Bruce, E. (2001). *Nonfinite loss and grief: A psychoeducational approach.* Baltimore, MD: Paul H. Brookes.

Department of Defense. (2008, September). *Active duty demographic profile.* Retrieved from SlideShare.

Ducharme, S. (2008). *The sexual consequences of polytrauma.* Retrieved May 2011 from www.stanleyducharme.com

Harris, D. L. (2011). *Counting our losses: Reflecting on change, loss, and transition in everyday life.* New York, NY: Routledge.

Price, J. L., & Stevens, S. P. (2009, September). Partners of veterans with PTSD: Research findings. U.S. Department of Veterans Affairs, National Center for PTSD. Retrieved from http://www.ptsd.va.gov/professional/pages/partners_of_vets_research_findings.asp

USACHPPM. (2007, January). Soldier combat stress reaction: A pocket guide for spouse and loved ones. *TA-056-1206.*

Wilson, J. P. (2001). *Treating psychological trauma & PTSD.* New York, NY: Guilford Press.

Worden, J. W. (2009). *Grief counseling & grief therapy: A handbook for the mental health practitioner* (4th ed.). New York, NY: Springer.

SECTION 3

Adjusting to Life's Losses by Aging or Illness or Infirmity

The chapters in this section collect thoughts and issues around what happens to us in the course of living toward our dying. This is not always synonymous or simultaneous with "aging," which in our culture comes with a kind of stigma, as if getting older were a perpetual degradation of body, mind, and spirit. This is neither factual nor true. What is true is that the more years we accumulate, the more losses we experience and the more challenges we face. Some of those challenges are to our physical and mental health. Every one of our health challenges has its own affect upon our capacity for intimacy and can bring accompanying alterations in our sexuality.

Our most common realization as we age is that we need each other: we need other people and other people need us. It is highly likely that this realization runs counter to our culture's ideology of independence and individualism, an ideology we may have found convenient to adopt personally earlier in our lives. Yet every illness, every encounter with our physical and mental limitations has at least the potential to teach us about our *interdependence*—if we are willing to learn that lesson. And as we become less rigidly independent and more cooperatively interdependent, we find ourselves learning new ways to be intimate and, very likely, new ways to be sexually expressive as well. In other words, loss of the illusion of perfect health can open us to new experiences of intimacy and sexuality, if we will mourn that loss well.

Sara Sanders, PhD, MSW, who teaches at the University of Iowa, and **Joelle Osterhaus, MSW, CSWA**, who is the bereavement coordinator for the Benton Hospice Service in Corvallis, Oregon, offer us a vivid (and well-researched) examination of the intimacy and sexuality issues that can arise for those with Alzheimer's disease and other, related, dementias—and for those who would love them. We can be so blocked by "who" this person was and shocked at who this person has become that we can miss that this "stranger" remains a person capable of love and intimacy. Theirs is a good example of people who "die twice."

Anne Katz, RN, PhD, is the sexuality counselor at CancerCare Manitoba, where she counsels men and women with a history of cancer who are experiencing sexual and relationship challenges. She travels widely, educating health care providers and cancer survivors about cancer and sexuality. She is the author of *Breaking the Silence on Cancer and Sexuality: A Handbook for Health Care Providers* (2007), *Woman Cancer Sex* (2009), *Man Cancer Sex* (2009), and *Sex When You're Sick: Reclaiming Sexual Health After Illness or Injury* (2009). Recently she has published *Surviving After Cancer: Living the New Normal* (2011) and *After You Ring the Bell: 10 Challenges for the Cancer Survivor* (2011).

Here she discusses the general physiological changes that happen to us as we age and three common illnesses (cardiovascular, diabetes, and incontinence) that affect our sexual functioning. She offers the "Good-Enough Sex" model as a framework for our considering what matters most to us in intimacy and sex.

Our time of dying is its own challenge to our networks of intimacy and to our sexual relationships. Sherri Weisenfluh, LCSW, and Vicki Merrill, LCSW, ACHP-SW, work for Hospice of the Bluegrass in Lexington, Kentucky. **Sherri Weisenfluh** is Associate Clinical Officer of Counseling for Hospice of the Bluegrass. Sherri has been with Hospice of the Bluegrass for 19 years. She is a licensed clinical social worker with the state of Kentucky and has over 25 years of clinical experience. Sherri currently serves as the Social Work Section Leader for the National Council of Hospice Professionals through the National Hospice and Palliative Care Organization and serves on the Field Advisory Committee for the College of Social Work at the University of Kentucky. She is a recipient of a Project on Death in America Social Work Leadership Development Grant from the George Soros Foundation, was honored by the National Academies of Practice, and was recently inducted into the University of Kentucky College of Social Work Hall of Fame for her national work. **Vicki Merrill** is a counseling supervisor with Hospice of the Bluegrass, where she has worked for 5 years. Prior to this role, she worked as a team social worker servicing hospice patients in the home and in long-term care facilities. She is a licensed clinical social worker in Kentucky and has worked in the field of social work for the past 34 years in Ohio, North Carolina, and Kentucky. She has been recognized for her work in community organization with the creation of a nonprofit organization focusing on substance abuse prevention in rural Kentucky. Vicki has successfully written over $25 million in grants for nonprofits, schools, and businesses. She obtained her MSSW degree from University of Louisville Kent School of Social Work.

One of their discoveries was that the intimacy needs and sexuality desires of the patients and family members under the care of Hospice of the Bluegrass were not routinely assessed. In other words, inquiries were not made. We believe that this is likely to be the case at many, if not most, hospices, not just the one where Sherri and Vicki work. We hope that what they have to say will contribute to a better appreciation of—and assessment for—the intimacy needs and sexual desires of the dying and their caregivers. Sherri and Vicki have included the assessment tool they used; other hospices would do well to adopt and adapt it.

CHAPTER 7

Birth of a Stranger: Intimacy, Sexuality, and Dementia

Sara Sanders and Joelle Osterhaus

Bob and Gloria had been married for 42 years when Gloria first started showing signs of memory loss. Gloria's disease seemed to progress quickly, and within a few years, she no longer knew Bob as her husband. Instead, she referred to him with anger as "that man." Despite Gloria's no longer recognizing their 42 years of marriage, Bob, with minimal assistance except for adult day services three days a week, provided 24-hour care for Gloria. Bob found pleasure in learning how to fulfill new roles—such as that of a cook, a hair stylist, and a social planner—and often commented on how he was surprised that he learned how to apply makeup and put nylons on his wife without a single run.

Regardless of the pride that Bob felt as a caregiver, he yearned for the intimacy and connection that he and Gloria had shared throughout their marriage. Since her diagnosis, Gloria no longer wanted to engage in any intimate contact with Bob. She resisted hugs, hand holding, and kisses and refused any form of sexual intimacy. When Bob tried to show her affection, she screamed and yelled and threatened to call the police. She indicated that "her husband" or sometimes even "her father" was going to come home and would not be happy to see "that man" in her house. Bob was heartbroken and actively grieved the many losses that accompanied this disease, including the loss of intimacy that he and Gloria once shared in their relationship. Despite his grief and feelings of inadequacy and rejection, he continued to provide her with the care he felt she deserved.

During a monthly caregiver support group meeting, Bob met another caregiver named Ann. Ann was struggling with many of the same complex issues associated with her husband's disease progression. She and Bob developed an instant relationship. They started meeting for coffee and mutual support while their spouses were at adult day care. Over a few months, Bob and Ann developed intimate, sexual feelings for each other. After discussing the implications of their feelings, they decided to engage in a dating relationship that included sexual intimacy. Both Bob and Ann maintained this intimate relationship while also providing care to their spouses at home until the final years of the disease when both of their spouses were admitted into different long-term care facilities. At this point, despite their children's objections, Bob and Ann decided to move in together as a couple. They both continued to care for and support their spouses until their deaths.

ALZHEIMER'S DISEASE AND RELATED DEMENTIA

Alzheimer's disease and related dementia (ADRD) is a growing epidemic in the United States. According to the national Alzheimer's Association (2010), 5.3 million individuals live with ADRD, with new cases being diagnosed every 70 seconds. It is estimated that by 2050, 16 million people will have ADRD, with each diagnosed person requiring at least one individual to serve as a primary caregiver (Alzheimer's Association, 2010). As of 2009, there were 10.9 million unpaid individuals providing care to people with ADRD. Caregivers consist of family members, friends, neighbors, and others who know a person with ADRD. Some estimates suggest that every family in the United States will have a member with ADRD by 2020 (Alzheimer's Association, 2010).

From diagnosis to death, ADRD progresses over a period of 3–20 years, with many factors—including type of dementia, age, race, and health status—having an impact on the rate of progression (Alzheimer's Association, 2009). Individuals with any type of ADRD progress through a series of stages, with each stage demonstrating greater impairment in cognitive and physical functioning. Additionally, with each new stage, greater assistance is required for both those individuals with the disease and those who assume a caregiving role (Borrayo, Salmon, Polivka, & Dunlop, 2002).

In the early stages, individuals with ADRD experience impairment in their overall short-term memory, their ability to recall basic information, and their ability to determine times and dates. They may also become suspicious and questioning of those around them. Individuals' ability to judge, perceive, and reason through complex tasks and situations also becomes gradually impaired. Many of these early signs of ADRD are overlooked by family and friends, often being mistakenly labeled as "old age" or "senility," or they are inaccurately attributed to other stressors occurring in one's life. By the middle stages of the ADRD, impairment can be seen in one's ability to recall more complex information, such as names, locations, and dates. In addition, overall judgment and the ability to complete complex, multistep tasks, as well as the completion of perhaps simpler but familiar tasks, become compromised. During this phase, individuals with ADRD gradually require increasing assistance with activities of daily living (ADLs), including dressing, feeding, grooming, and toileting. By the end of the middle stages, individuals with ADRD may no longer recognize themselves or others, which is particularly distressing to caregivers, who may be referred to by a different name or viewed as a complete stranger. The final stages of the disease are characterized by individuals with ADRD losing their ability to speak, walk, or sit without assistance, requiring total assistance with all activities of daily living, and becoming increasingly susceptible to secondary infections, such as pneumonia and urinary tract infections (Alzheimer's Association, 2009).

Throughout the course of ADRD, caregivers are called upon to provide more and more assistance to the person with ADRD. As aforementioned, individuals with ADRD may no longer recognize their familial caregiver, who is often a family member or friend, nor are they able to recall the history or meaning of the relationship with that individual. For many caregivers, as ADRD progresses, they watch as the individual with ADRD changes and slowly emerges as a person who no longer possesses many of the qualities or personality characteristics that once embodied the care recipient—hence, "the birth of a stranger." This often creates many emotional and psychological challenges for the caregiver as one provides care to a person who may possess attributes that are painful reminders of the impact of ADRD.

The impact of ADRD on family caregivers has been well documented for the past 30 years. This extensive body of research has identified that caregivers are susceptible to increased levels of stress, burden, depression, and other mental health complications, as well as to having an increased risk for other health complications, including premature death due to stress. Since the mid-1990s, research has expanded its focus on caregiver outcomes to include grief reactions, with some researchers hypothesizing that grief is at the heart of the caregiving experience and contributes to other adverse caregiving reactions (Meuser, Marwit, & Sanders, 2004). As suggested by Meuser, Marwit, and Sanders, the grief associated with dementia should be considered "true grief" as it resembles the grief that occurs post-death.

The purpose of this chapter is to examine grief among caregivers of individuals with ADRD, with a specific focus on the grief that stems from changes in intimacy and sexual expression with the care recipient. The chapter will be arranged to provide an overview of grief in caregivers, an overview of intimacy and sexuality as it relates to ADRD, and then practice recommendations for professionals who may interface with caregivers that are experiencing grief due to changes in intimacy and sexual expression. While it is recognized that individuals with ADRD also experience many losses throughout their own disease progress that impact intimacy with others, these losses will not be captured in this chapter given that the specific focus will be on the caregivers' experiences.

OVERVIEW OF GRIEF RELATED TO ADRD CAREGIVERS

The first mention of caregiver grief associated with ADRD was in 1981 when Nancy Mace and Peter Rabins, in *The 36-Hour Day*, indicated:

> As the person's illness progresses and the person changes, you may experience the loss of a companion and a relationship that was important to you. You may grieve the way she used to be. We usually think of grief as an emotional experience that follows a death. However, grief is a natural emotional response to loss and so is a normal experience for people who love a person with a chronic illness. (1981, p. 209)

Despite this direct reference to the grief experience of caregivers, an empirical focus on grief in caregivers did not become prominent in the literature for another 15 years.

The grief experience for caregivers of individuals with ADRD is often disenfranchised, as the losses that accompany the disease are not socially recognized and validated. As a result, caregivers struggle with how to define their grief experience given that the care recipient is still alive. The term *ambiguous loss* (Boss, 1999) has been used to characterize the grief experience of caregivers of individuals with ADRD. According to Pauline Boss, ambiguous loss occurs when a person is physically present but psychologically absent. For caregivers, care recipients may look the same, yet they may no longer possess any mannerisms, elements of their personality, or other qualities that defined them pre-diagnosis. Caregivers ask, "am I still his spouse?" or note, "she no longer acts like my mom," or lament, "they don't recognize me anymore." Therefore they experience difficulty trying to make sense of their changing roles and relationship with the care recipient. Caregivers frequently struggle to understand why the person with ADRD is behaving or communicating in a way that is uncharacteristic of the individual they have known for years. Statements such as "my mom would never say such things" or "my husband was always so patient and loving" demonstrate losses for caregivers that are created by the ambiguity that develops within the roles and relationship post-ADRD diagnosis.

Research has found that between 47% and 68% of ADRD caregivers report grief reactions (Collins, Liken, King, & Kokinakis, 1993; Sanders & Corley, 2003); however, it is estimated that these percentages are low given the stigma associated with expressing the loss of a person prior to an actual death occurring. Caregivers report that the most intense grief reactions stem from the losses associated with disease progression. A few of these losses, which will be elaborated upon hereafter, include losses associated with one's relationship with the care recipient and other support systems, roles, and responsibilities, as well as the ways in which one manages daily routines.

The grief experience for caregivers has been found to vary based on several key factors, including relationship status and stage of disease. Grief has been found to increase as the disease progresses, with some of the most intense grief occurring in the final stages of ADRD (Meuser & Marwit, 2001; Ponder & Pomeroy, 1996; Sanders & Adams, 2005). Meuser and Marwit (2001) found that grief reactions for spousal caregivers are more intense than for adult child caregivers, given the nature of their relationship and in many cases the intensity of their caregiving role. For spousal caregivers in particular, change in intimacy is one area that produces intense grief reactions.

INTIMACY, GRIEF, AND ADRD

The term *intimacy* is defined as a connection, closeness, or bond between two people. It can also be defined as a sense of belonging to another individual and the choice to accept and reciprocate feelings that are associated with the relationship (*Merriam-Webster's*, 2010). Intimacy can be physical, emotional, psychological, and sexual, with the degree of connection between a person and a partner varying in each of these domains throughout the relationship. Changes within one's intimate relationship with the person with ADRD result in grief reactions that warrant exploration.

As ADRD progresses, intimacy between the caregiver and care recipient changes (Alzheimer's Society, 2010), resulting in many losses for the caregiver. For instance, caregivers experience the loss of communication, decision-making, social activities, socially and personally defined roles and relationships, past memories, and future dreams, with each of these losses representing a form of intimacy that once existed between the caregiver and care recipient. These losses may be experienced and accumulated daily as the caregiver gradually loses the ability to consult with the care recipient on decisions, share with the care recipient feelings and reactions to events, and participate in once-enjoyable activities with other family members or friends due to the isolating demands of their care-giving duties. In essence, caregivers lose the very fabric of the relationship that they once had with the care recipient. For spousal caregivers or those in a partnered relationship, a central component of that relationship may have included sexual intimacy, a topic that warrants much more clinical and empirical attention.

For spousal or partner caregivers, physical losses, those associated with sexual intimacy in particular, often create the most intense grief reactions. According to the Family Caregiver Alliance (2001), "Being sexual in a relationship . . . is part of closeness and intimacy. The loss of the sexual relationship is a major part of the grief and sense of loss that caregivers experience while caring for a loved one." Despite the grief and pain that develops from the losses that surround sexual intimacy, this grief is rarely discussed by professionals or caregivers, with the Family Caregiver Alliance (2001) noting that even physicians are "reluctant" to address this topic. Additionally, changes in sexual intimacy raise many challenging and ethical questions as husbands, wives, and life partners try to maintain the closeness and bond that existed prior to disease onset, continually adapting to the changes in sexual intimacy that accompany the disease progression.

SEXUAL INTIMACY AMONG SPOUSES AND PARTNERS OF INDIVIDUALS WITH ADRD

Within clinical practice and empirical research, the topic of sexuality and aging has received minimal empirical attention, with issues specific to ADRD receiving even less attention (Burgess, 2004). The topic of sexuality is negatively laced in ageist stereotypes and values about older adults as sexual beings, with some viewing older adults as asexual and uninterested in maintaining sexual relationships as they age (Masters & Johnson, 1966). However, there are no known age limits to the interest in, expression of, and need for sexuality (Edwards, 2003; Kaplan, 1974; Lopater, 2005; Masters & Johnson, 1966; Richardson & Lazur, 1995). Research has consistently found that older adults who are in relatively good health are interested in and able to maintain an active sex life throughout their older adult years (Capuzzi & Friel, 1990). According to the National Council on Aging, people 60 and older typically enjoy sexual relations at least once a month (Johnson & Scelfo, 2003). The Sexuality Survey commissioned by the AARP and Modern Maturity in 1999 found that sexuality plays an important role in the lives of older adults (Feldkamp, 2003; Willert & Semans, 2000).

While sexual intercourse is one component of sexual activity for older adults, research has also found that other forms of sexual intimacy—such as romance, companionship, personal grooming, the need to feel attractive, mutual caressing, handholding, kissing, and cuddling—are also important avenues for sexual expression (Burgess, 2004; Hajjar & Kamel, 2003). In addition, the quality of the intimate experience rather than the frequency of an intimate act may be viewed as more important. For those older adults who maintain a healthy pattern of sexual behavior, research has found that it enhances psychological and physical well-being, which in turn positively influences the overall mental health of the older adult (Burgess, 2004).

Part of the veil covering some of the controversial topics associated with sexual intimacy and ADRD was lifted when Sandra Day O'Connor, retired Supreme Court Justice, announced publicly that her husband, who had battled Alzheimer's disease for more than a decade, had fallen in love with another woman at the assisted living facility where he resided. O'Connor indicated that she was happy for him and that he was now relaxed and content as he sat, frequently holding hands with his girlfriend, during O'Connor's visits to him. While some may question the choices made within this particular family situation as well as express concern about the emotional toll that this could take on a caregiver and perhaps the entire family system, this case brings to light one of the most hidden challenges that caregivers face while caregiving for someone with ADRD: finding the balance between meeting the respective needs of both care recipient and caregiver with respect to sexual intimacy, grief, and care. It also illuminates one of the greatest struggles for professional caregivers: finding the balance between the needs of the person with ADRD, the family caregiver, and the professional values and ethics they are bound to.

For caregivers, particularly those of individuals with ADRD, the disease-related changes in the care recipient, combined with the challenges associated with the caregiving role, can have an impact on sexual expression within the relationship (Burgess, 2004). Providing assistance to an ill partner creates changes in the level of intimacy within the relationship because the health of the care recipient becomes the focus of the relationship (Burgess, 2004), often leaving any form of sexual expression on the back burner. According to the Alzheimer's Society (2010), "Dementia certainly doesn't have to mean the end of a happy sex life. It can lead to some big changes. . . . Many couples find that they can still be close through their sexual relationship even when other means of expression have diminished, while others find that they come to discover other forms of closeness, comfort, and intimacy." Those caregivers who try to maintain some form of sexual contact, even though sexual intercourse may no longer be an option, demonstrate sexual intimacy through kissing, massage, and other forms of caressing. While this may be possible for some caregivers and individuals with ADRD, others may find even these forms of physical intimacy overwhelming and grief provoking for several reasons.

One reason may be related to the sexual drive of the care recipient. Research has found that individuals with ADRD may either experience an increase or a decrease in their level of interest in sexual expression (Baikie, 2002). Decreases in the levels of sexual interest may be related to complicating physical health issues or depression that may present with the disease or perhaps has been a historic concern for the care recipient. For those with an increased desire for sexual relations, Baikie found that this may be related to the loss of inhibition that accompanies ADRD. Another reason for an increased sexual drive may be difficulty with cognitive sequencing. Some individuals with ADRD may "forget" that they had just asked for or participated in a form of sexual expression or may start to ask to engage in sexual acts that have not been the norm in a relationship (Davies, Zeiss, & Tinkleberg, 1992). Loss of inhibition may also create situations in which the care recipient is also interested in sexual activity with other individuals besides their spouse or life partner, as was seen in the case of Sandra Day O'Connor's husband.

Another reason for changes in sexual intimacy may stem from caregivers who experience a decrease in their feelings of attraction toward their partners with ADRD. Individuals with ADRD may lose interest in personal hygiene, or usual grooming habits, and may display personality changes, all of which may alter a caregiver's interest in intimacy (Deacon, Minichiello, & Plummer, 1995).

Caregivers may also feel that sexual activity is inappropriate due to the very nature of their role as caregivers (Litz, Zeiss, & Davies, 1990). This can frequently be coupled with feelings of guilt, shame, despair, resentment, and anger, which can impede one's interest and desire in sexual intimacy (Alzheimer's Society, 2010). These changes in the care recipient's and the caregiver's associated feelings can be difficult to accept and may contribute to the experience of grief and loss as caregivers witness their roles and relationship with the care recipient changing.

Issues of recognition can also complicate sexual intimacy. As stated earlier, within the middle stages of the disease, individuals with ADRD often cease to recognize their caregivers, referring to them by the name of another individual, such as a past partner or friend, or the name of their parent or an adult child or even someone unknown. For caregivers, this lack of recognition can create a great deal of grief as the care recipient may be asking them to participate in sexual activity but referring to them by another name. Lack of recognition can also create sexual intimacy challenges for a caregiver who may desire to maintain a sexual relationship with the care recipient but struggles with losing his or her own identity in the eyes of the person with ADRD. The individual with ADRD may reject the caregiver or express fear of them. As seen in the case of Bob and Gloria at the beginning of the chapter, caregivers have reported that care recipients accuse them of rape or of making threats toward them, as well as report that care recipients scream or become combative when any form of intimate contact is initiated, including contact that occurs during and for the purpose of personal cares. These reactions can cause additional grief for caregivers as they represent not only changes in the care recipient but also changes in the relationship that once existed (Davies & Shea, 1998; Litz et al., 1990).

Sexual intimacy can also cause grief for caregivers when the issue of competency is considered. Competency refers to the ability of an individual to make his or her own choices in an informed manner. With the progression of ADRD impairing cognitive status, individuals slowly lose the capacity to make their own choices, which raises questions about their overall levels of competency. This issue of competency calls for caregivers to explore new and difficult questions that have never before been a part of the equation of their relationship with the person with ADRD, including "Is the person able to consent to the sexual act?" and "Is the individual a willing participant in the sexual act?" For caregivers, simply considering that a lifetime partner may not be a willing participant or able to consent to sexual intimacy with them has the strong potential to produce grief reactions. Competency becomes an even larger issue for caregivers when new intimate partnerships form between the care recipients and others outside of their own partnership, such as the one that occurred in the case of Sandra Day O'Connor's spouse and another long-term care resident. Additional dynamics compound the grief experience as other family and care professionals become a part of these discussions.

All of these noted changes in sexual intimacy previously mentioned create the ambiguity in the ADRD caregiver–care recipient relationship that Pauline Boss included in the term "ambiguous loss." Changes in sexual intimacy accentuate the other losses that caregivers experience, such as the loss of communication, relationship, closeness, roles, bonds, and overall attraction toward the individual with ADRD. Caregivers are thereby forced to question how to maintain an intimate relationship, if possible, with an individual who they no longer know and recognize as their spouse or life partner, and vice versa. The term "pseudo widower" has been informally used to identify this experience for caregivers because it characterizes the process of being intimately involved with a person but recognizes that the status of that relationship is no longer clearly defined.

PRACTICE IMPLICATIONS

While all individuals with ADRD and their caregivers are likely to experience changes in sexual intimacy within their relationship, most caregivers report that helping professionals do not ask about or disseminate relevant information about the types of changes that may occur. Nor do they discuss how the disease will have an impact on the sexual intimacy in their relationship and how they can adapt and respond to the grief associated changes (Duffy, 1995). In light of the grief experienced by individuals with ADRD and their caregivers, and particularly the intensity of the grief related specifically to loss of intimacy between the two, it stands to reason that a wide range of potential practice implications across a multitude of disciplines should be considered. As the disease progresses and losses accumulate for caregivers, opportunities are present for helping professionals to intervene at all stages of the disease within the context of their respective settings, including, but not limited to, case management agencies, public health departments, geriatric healthcare clinics, adult day programs, senior centers, homecare agencies, and long-term care facilities.

Assessment

Regardless of stage of the disease, helping professionals can take the lead in providing front-line support to such couples by taking the initiative to include assessment and discussions regarding sexual intimacy and grief during routine visits and standard plans of care. This direct and open communication provides couples with the permission they may need to share their concerns, and it helps them to identify issues and match these with objectives and goals in plans of care. Sbrocco, Weisberg, and Barlow (1995) offer specific recommendations for assessing caregivers and persons with ADRD regarding sexual intimacy. They outline a four-part framework of questions for assessing sexual functioning (desire, excitement, orgasm, resolution). They prepare helping professionals for what issues may arise during such an assessment and provide suggestions for handling difficult topics such as masturbation and oral sex. Davies and Shea (1998) suggest some helpful modifications and additions to this assessment, such as ensuring a couple's willingness to discuss these issues, providing validation that this will likely be uncomfortable, and rapport building to allow for ongoing assessments and interventions as needed with the progression of ADRD. They also suggest avoiding asking questions regarding memory when assessing the person with ADRD specifically and instead focusing on general descriptions of, as well as the person's feelings and hopes around, certain issues. Davies and Shea also point to Annon's PLISSIT model[1] for responding to such assessments on four levels. The first level (P) is for giving permission to the couple to be sexual; the second (LI) is providing limited educational information about the changes they are experiencing; the third level (SS) entails offering specific suggestions to help the couple adapt to the changes identified. The final level (IT) is the recommendation of intensive therapy, if it is felt that this would be necessary for the couple.

As previously mentioned, with the progression of ADRD, an individual's capacity to consent to sexual intimacy diminishes. As a standard, the careful evaluation of an elder's decision-making capacity is considered critical, and outside consultation is highly encouraged (Feldkamp, 2003; Kamel & Hajjar, 2003; Richardson & Lazur, 1995). Lichtenberg and Strzepek (1990) suggest helping professionals and caregivers ask three questions to assess an individual with ADRD's capacity to consent to sexual intimacy both at home and in long-term care settings.

First, what is the individual with ADRD's awareness of the relationship? For example, does the person with ADRD know who is initiating the contact? Does he or she accurately or inaccurately believe the other person to be their spouse? Is he or she cognizant of their actual identity and intent? And finally, can the person with ADRD state the level of sexual intimacy they are comfortable with?

Second, what is the individual with ADRD's personal ability to avoid exploitation? For example, is their behavior consistent with their formally held values and beliefs? Do they have the ability to say no to any unwanted sexual intimacy?

Finally, is the individual with ADRD aware of the potential risks involved? Examples of this include whether they realize the relationship may be limited by time and whether they can describe how they will react when the relationship ends. These questions help to explore and identify if sexual intimacy can safely be allowed or encouraged to continue and can assist caregivers as they determine forms of sexual intimacy with care recipients.

[1] The authors of Chapter 9 also reference this model. See page 174.

Grief Work With ADRD Caregivers

Caregivers of persons with ADRD often describe themselves as being "frozen" in their grief. As the disease progresses and losses accumulate, their grief is not resolved but, rather, is suspended, with additional losses accumulating for the caregiver daily. The ability of caregivers to cope over the long term is compromised as the stress of their caregiver role mounts alongside the disease.

Helping professionals need to be cognizant of a caregiver's willingness to openly discuss and receive support for his or her grief related to the typically private and sensitive issue of sexual intimacy. The foundation of a positive rapport will be essential for any support strategies to be effective. A psycho-educational approach with caregivers is particularly effective in addressing their grief reactions. In all stages of the disease, but particularly in early stages, the provision of ample information about the disease process helps caregivers to anticipate losses, thus minimizing potential grief reactions proactively (Davies & Shea, 1998). This might include identifying how the loss of sexual intimacy now between the partners will affect future sexual health and activity (Capuzzi & Friel, 1990; Masters & Johnson, 1966).

Facilitating the exploration, identification, and acknowledgment of the losses caregivers have experienced and the grief reactions that have resulted is an essential part of the grief work of ADRD caregivers. A psycho-educational approach can be particularly effective in preventing future misunderstandings and crises, and it serves as well to decrease anxiety, stress, and the intensity of one's grief later in the disease process (Capuzzi & Friel, 1990). The psycho-educational model in support group settings for caregivers may also be effective in helping caregivers address and relieve the grief they experience (Davies, Priddy, & Tinklenberg, 1986; Sanders & Corley, 2003). They may also have a normalizing effect, countering feelings of shame and frustration that result from negative reactions from helping professionals. Through psycho-education, older adults may become empowered to advocate on their own behalf and more easily adapt to maintain satisfying and meaningful intimate relationships without other formalized interventions.

As helping professionals normalize and validate this unique grief experience by providing education on the progression of ADRD, as well as on grief, they are then poised to facilitate the caregiver's negotiation of the following paradox, which is considered key in coping with ambiguous loss: that the person with ADRD is both someone that they know and someone that they do not know. By living with this paradox, caregivers are then better able to celebrate what remains, grieve what has been lost, and better adapt to their still-changing relationship with the ADRD care-recipient. For those caregivers whose grief presents as more complicated in nature, helping professionals will need to be at the ready to refer them for grief therapy (Worden, 1991).

The opportunity for sexual intimacy between partners may at some point be determined as lost due to the progression of ADRD. There may be a variety of plausible reasons for this: (a) an individual with ADRD refuses the intimacy; (b) the individual with ADRD has been determined to lack the capacity to make such a decision; (c) the caregiver no longer feels comfortable with sexual intimacy due to changes observed in their partner; or (d) the partners are kept separate after one has been placed into a long-term care setting. Helping professionals can assist caregivers and persons with ADRD to explore alternatives for meeting their sexual intimacy needs. Satisfying alternatives to sexual intimacy with their partner may simply entail changed grooming habits, increased socialization outside of the partner relationship, or personal stimulation and release (Capuzzi & Friel, 1990; Longenberger, 1980; Malatesta, Chambles, Pollack, & Cantor, 1988; Renshaw, 1985; Richardson & Lazur, 1995; Walbroehl, 1988; White, 1982; Willert & Semans, 2000). For other caregivers, such as Bob, the gentleman in the case presented at the beginning of the chapter, beginning and maintaining extramarital relations seems like the best option for meeting sexual intimacy needs. Each one of these options should be discussed and processed with the caregiver in a non-judgmental fashion.

Impact of Long-Term Care on Sexual Intimacy and Grief of Older Adults

As aforementioned, individuals with ADRD often need more and more care, and they are commonly placed in long-term care settings. Nursing homes and other related institutions have been found to present significant barriers for caregivers as they try to maintain a level of intimacy with the care recipient. First, lack of privacy is evident in the architecture and common practices of most long-term care settings, including rooms that cannot be locked, doors being kept open, staff that do not knock on doors, and the use hired personal supervisors for individuals with ADRD (Edwards, 2003; Kelly, Gray, & Vincent, 1995; McClean, 2004; Richardson & Lazur, 1995). It is also lamentable that while heterosexual living arrangements have been found to correlate with improved behavior, self-care, and increased residential satisfaction, most long-term care settings today still segregate genders and couples and are by and large bereft of high levels of social interaction and activity (Hubbard, Tester, & Downs, 2003).

Another barrier to sexual intimacy in long-term care settings includes the attitudes and practices of staff (Richardson & Lazur, 1995). Staff in long-term care settings typically adhere to conservative, Victorian values about sexuality (Willert & Semans, 2000). More specifically, these attitudes include ageist stereotypes equating and permitting sex amongst youth only, belief that masturbation is harmful (or even sinful), and values that state women should engage in sex only for the purpose of procreation (Edwards, 2003; Longenberger, 1980; Willert & Semans, 2000).

A variety of strategies and interventions to meet the sexual needs and desires of older adults in long-term settings can be pursued. The implementation of such strategies could serve to prolong the intimate relationships of couples with ADRD and could thereby decrease the intensity of the grief experience of both partners. The most empirically supported strategy for promoting recognition and understanding of the sexual rights and needs of older adults is the creation and inclusion of staff education about respecting and being sensitive about resident choices and behavior (Edwards, 2003; Kamel & Hajjar, 2003; Roach, 2004; Walker & Harrington, 2002). Although staff training programs have been found to increase knowledge and improve attitudes (Bouman, Arcelus, & Benbow, 2007; Walker & Harrington, 2002), there is no evidence mentioned of the effectiveness of their translation into more sensitive, respectful, or even changed activities among staff. Further assessment of the impact of such curricula is needed.

Other strategies include revisions to the policies and practices of long-term care settings. Some examples of such revisions might entail allowing more private time for residents; allowing couples' room assignments; including more explicit language in policies, such as, "residents have the right to seek out and engage in sexual expression"; and permitting sexually explicit materials (books, magazines, and videos) in public and private areas. The level of staff involvement, however, is dependent upon ongoing clinical assessments about consent, mutuality, and the safety and well-being of each of the individuals involved. Some suggested materials for long-term care settings looking to develop trainings and establish updated policies include *Freedom of Sexual Expression: Dementia and Resident Rights in Long-term Care Facilities* (2002) and *A Thousand Tomorrows: Sexuality, Intimacy, and Alzheimer's* (1995), both by Terra Nova Films, and the HBO Documentary Films four-part special *The Alzheimer's Project* (2009), which also displays caregivers and individuals with ADRD maintaining strong intimate relationships. These videos display poignant vignettes as well as related materials such as manuals, study guides, and handouts. Clearly, care settings will need to be increasingly intentional about adopting safe, private, and supportive environments.

Ethical Considerations

Helping professionals will likely be called upon to navigate the ethical issues that arise as an individual with ADRD's disease progresses. Helping professionals are often committed to multiple ethical obligations concurrently, including to the person with ADRD, their family, the employing institution or agency, those served by that institution or agency, their own professional discipline, and the team of professionals with whom they work. The result is that they frequently encounter conflicts among both people and competing ethical standards. Other common complicating factors include a lack of resources to help staff navigate a variety of situations, as well as long-term care facility policies that may conflict with a staff's own moral conscience. The task of ethics very often entails discerning a caring course of action from among contradictory principles and dealing sensitively with differing values, beliefs, and practices. In a word, ADRD creates an incredibly complex practice setting for helping professionals to navigate.

With respect to sexual intimacy among persons with ADRD and their spouses or partners, ethical dilemmas arise within the realms of personhood, autonomy, self-determination, privacy, and safety. Specific changes within the intimate and sexual behavior of the person with ADRD call for a careful exploration of ethics before practice decisions are made. One's sexuality is a cornerstone to one's sense of self. Yet it is also a defining aspect in who others see one to be.

Dilemmas in the balancing of ethical obligations and values occur in both home and long-term care settings. In the case of Bob and Gloria, there are clearly some ethical concerns demanding the attention of any helping professionals involved in supporting both this couple and their children. For those working with Bob and Gloria, at the point in Gloria's disease progression when she began mistaking Bob for someone else and refusing intimacy, helping professionals would need to provide support to Bob by exploring with him his own needs and the needs of his changing wife and by helping him to process and work through his grief. For those helping professionals working with Bob, Ann, and their spouses and children, it would be important to help them to explore the intersection of all of their needs and subsequently support their decisions that demonstrated balance and safety.

An increasing number of gerontologists argue for an approach to resolving ethical dilemmas in this context that does not exaggerate the value of cognitive capacity but instead places greater value on the concept of personhood. These arguments are based mainly on findings of the differences in types of human memory and suggest that while being cognitively impaired and unable to recall past events, individuals with ADRD are still able to construct "semantic memory," which includes the ability to reproduce meaningful relationships (McClean, 1995). Proponents of this philosophy compare a person with ADRD's decision to be sexually active as equivalent to deciding on a flavor of ice cream (Richardson & Lazur, 1995).

Valuable recommendations for helping professionals looking to resolve ethical dilemmas within the context of sexuality and ADRD can be extrapolated from the research of Tabak and Shemesh-Kigli's (2006) which gives suggested actions for nurses and their related systems. They argue that four basic ethical obligations be the basis for practice: improve quality of life for persons with ADRD, avoid offense to their dignity and privacy, respect their autonomy, and dispense proper care without discrimination. Thereafter, should dilemmas arise, the helping professional may ask the following four questions: What is the source of my dilemma? What is expected of me? What can I do? What should I do? Tabak and Shemesh-Kigli point out that action will be based on individual attitudes, judgment, and experience and may incur some professional risk.

CONCLUSION

Although between the 1980s and 1990s, fewer than 5% of journal articles even remotely addressed later-life family concerns, the incidence of such research and writings is on the rise (Willert & Semans, 2000). More specifically, practitioners and researchers have historically been overlooking the sexual concerns of the elderly and its familial implications. While much research and policy has been dedicated to caregiver stress and burden, studies that examine the grief associated with the sexual lives of older adults is lacking, along with support for the perspective that sexual expression is a normal and natural part of an older adult's continued development (Capuzzi & Friel, 1990). Additional studies reaching further into the contextual issues surrounding this stressful and sensitive topic will be increasingly helpful to geriatric helping professionals, caregivers, and persons with ADRD themselves.

The present majority of proposed strategies place the responsibility for action and reform into the hands of individual service entities. This standard clearly promulgates the continued practice of ignoring the sexual desires, needs, and grief of elder caregivers and care-recipients with ADRD on the basis of ageist attitudes. All helping professionals within the field of gerontology need to understand the important role that sexuality plays in the overall mental and physical well-being of older adults, including those with ADRD. In order to support the health and well-being of caregivers and carerecipients with ADRD, it will be essential that cultural stigma and lack of education and training for helping professionals be addressed. Support for and establishment of universal guidelines must occur on multiple levels—including licensing boards, national associations, as well as others—so that it may thence be disseminated to the myriad of groups that serve older adults (Edwards, 2003). Pioneers and prominent researchers in the field of gerontology should be among those who lead advocacy efforts for such large-scale, macro-level changes, in partnership with caregivers and carerecipients with ADRD. Meanwhile, the best of these pioneers maybe simply those already caring for those with ADRD who recognize that chronic disease does not necessarily result in the loss of one's humanity, nor one's sexuality.

REFERENCES

Alzheimer's Association. (2007). Sexuality. Retrieved from http://www.alz.org/documents/ms/resourceguide_ms_2007.pdf

Alzheimer's Association. (2009). Just the facts. Retrieved from http://www.alz.org/national/documents/report_alzfactsfigures2009.pdf

Alzheimer's Association. (2010). Just the facts. Retrieved from http://www.alz.org/documents_custom/report_alzfactsfigures2010.pdf

Alzheimer's Society. (2010). Sex and dementia. Retrieved from http://www.alzheimers.org.uk

Aminzadeh, F., Byszewski, A., Molnar, F. J., & Eisner, M. (2007). Emotional impact of dementia diagnosis: Exploring persons with dementia and caregivers' perspectives. *Aging & Mental Health, 11*, 281–290.

Annon, J. (1976). The PLISSIT model: A proposed conceptual scheme for the behavioural treatment of sexual problems. *Journal of Sex Education and Therapy, 2*(2), 1–15.

Baikie, E. (2002). The impact of dementia on the marital relationship. *Sexual and Relationship Therapy, 17*, 289–299.

Beerman, S., & Rappaport-Musson, J. (2002). *Eldercare 911: The caregiver's complete handbook for making decisions*. Amherst, NY: Prometheus Books.

Blieszner, R., Roberto, K. A., Wilcox, K. L., Barham, E. J., & Winston, B. L. (2007). Dimensions of ambiguous loss in couples coping with mild cognitive impairment. *Family Relations, 56*, 196–209.

Borrayo, E. A., Salmon, J. R., Polivka, L., & Dunlop, B. D. (2002). Utilization across the continuum of long-term care services. *The Gerontologist, 42*(5), 603–612.

Boss, P. (1999). *Ambiguous loss: Learning to live with unresolved grief.* Cambridge, MA: Harvard University Press.

Boss, P. (2010). The trauma and complicated grief of ambiguous loss. *Journal of Pastoral Psychology, 59*, 137–145.

Bouman, W. P., Arcelus, J., & Benbow, S. M. (2007). Nottingham study of sexuality and ageing (NoSSA II). Attitudes of care staff regarding sexuality and residents: A study in residential and nursing homes. *Sexual and Relationship Therapy, 22*, 45–61.

Burgess, E. O. (2004). Sexuality in midlife and later life couples. In J. Harvey, A. Wenzel, & S. Sprecher (Eds.), *The handbook of sexuality in close relationships* (pp. 437–454). Mahwah, NJ: Erlbaum.

Capuzzi, D., & Friel, S. E. (1990). Current trends in sexuality and aging: An update for counselors. *Journal of Mental Health Counseling, 12*(3), 342–353.

Collins, C., Liken, M., King, S., & Kokinakis, C. (1993). Loss and grief among family caregivers of relatives with dementia. *Qualitative Health Research, 3*, 236–253.

Corbett, L. (1981). Last sexual taboo: Sex in old age. *Medical Aspects of Human Sexuality, 15*(4), 117–131.

Davies, H., Priddy, J. M., & Tinklenberg, J. R. (1986). Support groups for male caregivers of Alzheimer's patients. *Clinical Gerontology, 5*, 385–395.

Davies, H., & Shea, E. (1998). Sexuality and intimacy in Alzheimer's patients and their partners. *Sexuality and Disability, 16*, 193–203.

Davies, H., Zeiss, A., & Tinkleberg, J. R. (1992). 'Til death do us part: Intimacy and sexuality in the marriages of Alzheimer's disease patients. *Journal of Psychosocial Nursing, 30*, 5–10.

Deacon, S., Minichiello, V., & Plummer, D. (1995). Sexuality and older people: Revisiting the assumptions. *Educational Gerontology, 21*(5), 497–513.

Duffy, L. M. (1995). Sexual behavior and marital intimacy in Alzheimer's couples: A family theory perspective. *Sexuality and Disability, 13*, 239–254.

Dupuis, S. (2002). Understanding ambiguous loss in the context of dementia care. *Journal of Gerontological Social Work, 37*, 93–115.

Edwards, D. J. (2003). Sex and intimacy in the nursing home. *Nursing Homes Long Term Care Management, 52*(2), 18–20.

Family Caregiver Alliance. (2001). Sexuality and dementia. Retrieved from http://www.caregiver.org

Feinberg, R. K. (2002). Increasing need for social workers in assisted living. *Journal of Social Work in Long-Term Care, 1*, 9–11.

Feldkamp, J. K. (2003). Navigating the uncertain legal waters of resident sexuality. *Nursing Homes Long Term Care Management, 52*(2), 62–64.

Fitzpatrick, T. R. (2000). Sexuality and aging: A timely addition to the gerontology curriculum. *Educational Gerontology, 26*(5), 427–446.

Gott, M., & Hinchliff, S. (2003). How important is sex in later life? The views of older people. *Social Science & Medicine, 56*, 1617–1628.

Graham, J., & Bassett, R. (2006). Reciprocal relations: The recognition and co-construction of caring with Alzheimer's disease. *Journal of Aging Studies, 20*, 335–349.

Hajjar, R. R., & Kamel, H. K. (2003). Sexuality in the nursing home, Part 1: Attitudes and barriers to sexual expression. *Journal of the American Medical Directors Association, 4*(3), 152–156.

Hartzell, R. (2006). Senior sex: Exploring the sex lives of older adults. *Journal of Sex Research, 43*(3), 292–293.

Hillman, J., & Stricker, G. (1994). A linkage of knowledge and attitudes toward elderly sexuality: Not necessarily a uniform relationship. *The Gerontologist, 34*, 256–260.

Hillman, J., & Stricker, G. (2001). Management of sexualized transference and counter-transference with older adult patients: Implications for practice. *Professional Psychology: Research and Practice, 32*(3), 272–277.

Hubbard, G., Tester, S., & Downs, M. G. (2003). Meaningful social interactions between older people in institutional care settings. *Ageing and Society, 23* (Part 1), 99–114.

Hurley, M. (2002). On not getting it: Narration, sex and ageing. *Sexualities, 5*, 407–423.

Johnson, D., & Scelfo, J. (2003). Sex, love and nursing homes. *Newsweek, 142*, 54–55.

Kamel, H. K., & Hajjar, R. R. (2003). Sexuality in the nursing home, Part 2: Managing abnormal behavior—Legal and ethical issues. *Journal of the American Medical Directors Association, 4*(4), 203–206.

Kaplan, H. S. (1974). *The new sex therapy*. New York, NY: Brunner-Mazel.

Katz, S., & Marshall, B. (2003). New sex for old: Lifestyle, consumerism, and the ethics of aging well. *Journal of Aging Studies, 17*, 3–16.

Katz, S., & Marshall, B. L. (2004). Is the functional "normal"? Aging, sexuality and the bio-marking of successful living. *History of the Human Sciences, 17*(1), 53–75.

Kelly, C., Gray, L., & Vincent, S. (1995). The dynamics of sexual oppression in nursing homes. *Nursing Home Medicine, 3*, 56–61.

Lesser, J. M., Hughes, S. V., Jemelka, J. R., & Griffith, J. (2005). Sexually inappropriate behaviors. *Geriatrics, 60*(34), 36–37.

Lewis, M., & Trzinski, A. (2006). Counseling older adults with dementia who are dealing with death: Innovative interventions for practitioners. *Death Studies, 30*, 777–787.

Lichtenberg, P., & Strzepek, D. (1990). Assessments of institutionalized dementia patients' competencies to participate in intimate relationships. *The Gerontologist, 30*, 117–120.

Litz, B., Zeiss, A., & Davies, H. (1990). Sexual concerns of male spouses of female Alzheimer's disease patients. *The Gerontologist, 30*, 113–116.

Longenberger, R. F. (1980). Sex and the elderly. *Journal of Long-Term Care Administration, 8*(2), 13–20.

Lopater, S. (2005). Sexuality in adulthood and aging. In R. K. Westheimer & S. Lopater, *Human sexuality: A psychosocial perspective* (2nd ed., pp. 459–504). Baltimore, MD: Lippincott, Williams & Wilkins.

Mace, N. I., & Rabins, P. V. (1981). *The 36-hour day: Family guide to caring for persons with Alzheimer's disease, related dementing illnesses, and memory loss in later life.* Baltimore, MD: Johns Hopkins University Press.

Malatesta, V., Chambles, D., Pollack, M., & Cantor, A. (1988). Widowhood, sexuality, and aging: Lifespan analysis. *Journal of Sex and Marital Therapy, 14*, 49–63.

Marson, S. M. (2004). Clinical perspectives on elderly sexuality. *Clinical Gerontologist, 27*(3), 88–89.

Masters, W., & Johnson, V. (1966). *Human sexual response.* Boston, MA: Little, Brown.

McClean, A. (1995, September/October). What kind of love is this? *The Sciences,* pp. 36–39.

Menzel, J. C. (1995). *The impact of staff training in a nursing home setting on knowledge of and attitudes toward sexuality in the elderly.* [Ph.D. thesis]. Indiana, PA: Indiana University of Pennsylvania..

Merriam-Webster's Online Dictionary. (2010). Retrieved from http://www.mirriam-websters.com

Meuser, T. M., & Marwit, S. J. (2001). A comprehensive, stage-sensitive model of grief in dementia caregiving. *The Gerontologist, 41*, 658–670.

Meuser, T. M., Marwit, S. J., & Sanders, S. (2004). Assessing grief in family caregivers. In K. Doka (Ed.), *Living with grief: Alzheimer's disease.* Washington, DC: Hospice Foundation of America.

Mezey, M. D. (Editor in Chief); Berkman, B. J., Callahan, C. M., Fulmer, T. T., Mitty, E. L., Paveza, G. J., Siegler, E. L., et al. (Eds.); Bottrell, M. M. (Managing Ed.). (2001). *Encyclopedia of elder care: The comprehensive resource on geriatric and social care.* New York, NY: Springer.

Ponder, R. J., & Pomeroy, E. C. (1996). The grief of caregivers: How pervasive is it? *Journal of Gerontological Social Work, 27*, 3–21.

Reingold, D., & Burros, N. (2004). Sexuality in the nursing home. *Journal of Gerontological Social Work, 43*(2/3), 175–186.

Renshaw, D. C. (1985). Sex, age, and values. *Journal of the American Geriatrics Society, 33*, 635–643.

Rentz, C., Krikorian, R., & Keys, M. (2004–2005). Grief and mourning from the perspective of the person with a dementing illness: Beginning the dialogue. *Omega: Journal of Death and Dying, 50*, 165–179.

Richardson, J. P., & Lazur, A. (1995). Sexuality in the nursing home patient. *American Family Physician, 51,* 121–124.

Roach, S. M. (2004). Sexual behaviour of nursing home residents: Staff perceptions and responses. *Journal of Advanced Nursing, 48,* 371–379.

Robinson, L., Clare, L., & Evans, K. (2005). Making sense of dementia and adjusting to loss: Psychological reactions to a diagnosis of dementia in couples. *Aging & Mental Health, 9*, 337–347.

Sanders, S., & Adams, K. B. (2005). Grief reactions and depression in caregivers of individuals with Alzheimer's disease: Results from a pilot study in an urban setting. *Health and Social Work, 30*, 287–295.

Sanders, S., & Corley, C. (2003). Are they grieving? A qualitative analysis examining grief in caregivers of individuals with Alzheimer's disease. *Social Work in Healthcare, 37*, 35–53.

Sanders, S., Marwit, S. J., Meuser, T. M., & Harrington P. (2007). Caregiver grief in end-stage dementia: Using the Marwit and Meuser Caregiver Grief Inventory for assessment and intervention in social work practice. *Social Work in Health Care, 46*, 47–65.

Sanders, S., Ott, C. H., Kelber, S. T., & Noonan, P. (2008). The experience of high levels of grief in caregivers of persons with Alzheimer's disease and related dementia. *Death Studies, 32*, 495–523.

Sbrocco, T., Weisberg, B., & Barlow, D. (1995). Sexual dysfunction in the older adult: Assessment of psychosocial factors. *Sexuality and Disability, 13*, 201–218.

Silverberg, E. (2006–2007). Introducing the 3-A grief intervention model for dementia caregivers: Acknowledge, assess, and assist. *Omega: Journal of Death and Dying, 54*, 215–235.

Sweeting, H., & Gilhooly, M. (1997). Dementia and the phenomenon of social death. *Sociology of Health and Illness, 19*, 93–117.

Tabak, N., & Shemesh-Kigli, R. (2006). Sexuality and Alzheimer's disease: Can the two go together? *Nursing Forum, 41*, 158–166.

Walbroehl, G. (1988). Effects of medical problems on sexuality in the elderly. *Medical Geriatrics, 43*, 63–67.

Walker, B. L., & Harrington, D. (2002). Effects of staff training on staff knowledge and attitudes about sexuality. *Educational Gerontology, 28*(8), 639–654.

White, C. B. (1982). Sexual interest, attitudes, knowledge, and sexual history in relation to sexual behavior in the institutionalized aged. *Archives of Sexual Behavior, 11*(1), 11–21.

Willert, A., & Semans, M. (2000). Knowledge and attitudes about later life sexuality: What clinicians need to know about helping the elderly. *Contemporary Family Therapy: An International Journal, 22*(4), 415–435.

Worden, W. (2009). *Grief counseling & grief therapy: A handbook for the mental health practitioner* (4th ed.). New York, NY: Springer.

Yahnke, R. (2002). Intimacy, sexual expression, and dementia. *The Gerontologist, 42*, 873–874.

difficult to accept and may also fear that they are no longer sexually attractive to their partner with the appearance of wrinkles and perhaps some weight gain. The messages in the media and society in general are negative concerning the aging person, and middle-aged adults are often portrayed as being sexually unattractive and in need of plastic surgery, medications, hair dye, and makeup to appeal to others. If this message is internalized, it can have deleterious results of self-image and self-confidence.

Our negative social messages about our bodies' natural changes as we age become amplified in the cases of the newly single middle-aged persons who may not feel that they are capable of attracting someone new. In many, their apprehension about their ability to attract a new sexual partner combines with emotions related to how their grief over their loss has resolved. The middle-aged person who has lost a partner to death has likely already provided end-of-life care and may be ambivalent, at best, at the prospect of having to provide it again. Yet, in that context, they are also acutely aware of their own mortality and their own need to be cared for. The illness-related risks of beginning new relationships at this time in life present a range of personal dilemmas to face.

On the other hand, individuals in new relationships often find that their passion and sexual energy is rekindled with a new partner. The strongest predictor of sexual health for midlife adults remains the presence of a loving partner who is interested in sexual activity; poor health of the partner is the main reason that sexual activity ends (Kontula & Haavio-Mannila, 2009).

A recent study of sexual activity in middle to later life (Lindau & Gavrilova, 2010) examined data from two cross-sectional population surveys in the United States, comprising over 3,000 adults. The results suggest that men at age 55 will experience an additional 15 years of sexual activity while women can expect only 10.6 more years of sexual activity. The study suggests that these extra years of sexually active life are due to medications (such as the erectile aids Viagra, Cialis, and Levitra), the use of the Internet to find new partners, and improvements in overall health and access to care. However, compared to life expectancy, both men and women will experience years (8 to 9 years for men and 17 to 18 years for women) where sexual activity is absent, and demographic life expectancy exceeds sexually active life expectancy. The major reason for the gender difference is, of course, that men die younger than women do, so there will be a surplus of older women who are not sexually active. But there are other factors too. Physical changes in women's bodies, such as urinary incontinence, can render women reluctant to be sexual. And there are attitudinal differences that may influence this as well: men tend to have more positive and permissive attitudes toward sex than women do (Waite, Laumann, Das, & Schumm, 2009). DeLamater and Moorman (2007) concluded from their study of 1,384 men and women aged 45 and older that illness and treatments are generally unrelated to frequency of sexual activity and that satisfaction with the physical relationship with one's partner is strongly correlated to behavior. Noncoital activity well into old age may maintain physical closeness and be highly satisfying for both partners, especially after illness (DeLamater & Karraker, 2009).

CHRONIC ILLNESS AND SEXUALITY

Certain chronic conditions have a direct affect on sexual functioning. These conditions are extremely common and occur across the lifespan but are particularly prevalent in middle-aged and older adults. These conditions include cancer, heart disease, kidney disease, diabetes, arthritis, chronic lung disease, and multiple sclerosis. Even more common in today's society is obesity, which both has an impact upon body image and contributes to other chronic diseases. Urinary incontinence is another common complaint in women in midlife that has very real sexual effects.

Four of these chronic conditions have been chosen for explication: cardiovascular disease, diabetes, incontinence, and obesity. In what follows, implicit interconnections among these conditions can be seen. Each one, on its own or in conjunction with others, influences the sexual functioning of people over 50. As losses of physical health, they also influence emotional choices made in mourning relational losses.

Cardiovascular Disease

One in every three American adults suffers from one or more types of cardiovascular disease (CVD) in their lifetime, according to the American Heart Association (AHA) (www.heart.org). Due to advances in treatment, many individuals with cardiac disease are able and encouraged to maintain an active lifestyle, including sexual functioning, for the rest of their lives. Cardiovascular disease includes the following conditions: coronary heart disease, angina pectoris, myocardial infarction (heart attack), acute coronary syndrome, hypertension (high blood pressure), and heart failure. In addition, stroke (CVA) and transient ischemic attacks (TIA) are also caused by changes in the cardiovascular system. Cardiovascular disease is caused by narrowing of the blood vessels, which causes decreased blood supply to various organs. If the heart is affected, the person may have a heart attack. If the vessels to the brain are affected, a stroke may result. When the tiny blood vessels in the penis are affected, often years earlier than the larger vessels in the rest of the body, erectile difficulties are the result.

Hypertension (high blood pressure) is a cause of erectile dysfunction (ED) in men, and some men may not take their prescribed medication to treat this condition since the treatment may actually worsen their sexual difficulties (Doumas & Douma, 2006). Women with hypertension may also have sexual problems that are often ignored or not reported to health care providers (Schwarz, 2007). Individuals who have had a stroke experience global problems with sexual functioning from loss of libido to alterations in orgasmic capacity. The psychological consequences are also important since many stroke patients feel sexually unattractive (Jung et al., 2008). Relationship distress and breakdown is not uncommon after a stroke, and altered sexuality may play a role in this (Murray & Harrison, 2004).

In men, erectile dysfunction may be an early sign of cardiovascular disease, and it is important that any complaint of ED be followed up carefully with appropriate investigations (Jackson, Rosen, Kloner, & Kostis, 2006). The use of the oral medications commonly used to treat erectile dysfunction are contra-indicated in men who are taking nitrates to treat chest pain; however, men not taking these medications may be helped by the oral erectile aids. It is unclear if sexual difficulties in women are also an early sign of cardiac disease. This may hold true, but there is insufficient evidence to support or refute this. The analogue of ED in women is lack of vaginal lubrication; this is experienced by many women as a result of menopause and is also influenced by other factors, such as the relationship with their partner, so a direct link to cardiovascular disease is more difficult to establish.

Medications used to treat cardiac disease may cause sexual difficulties for some people (Steinke, 2000). Many of the medications used to treat cardiac disease (such as β-blockers, angiotensin-converting enzyme (ACE) inhibitors, calcium channel blockers, and anti-hypertensives) may cause sexual difficulties. These include decreased interest in sex, problems getting or maintaining an erection, changes in ejaculation for men, and decreased lubrication for women. Both men and women may experience the inability to have orgasms. Using alcohol in combination with these medications may increase the risk for sexual difficulties.

Couples are significantly affected by a cardiac event. A study of 24 couples suggests that three outcomes are possible after a diagnosis of heart disease (Mahrer-Imhof, Hoffmann, & Froelicher, 2007). The first outcome is that some couples see the diagnosis of cardiac disease as a transformative and positive experience that brings them closer. The second outcome is that the experience of heart disease is assessed as a threat that imposes fear on the couple and the couple works together to make changes in their lifestyle. The third outcome is when the couple fails to make any changes, becomes dissatisfied with each other, and goes back to their old ways of functioning. Each outcome indicates how the persons in this partnership are choosing to face this time in life.

Diabetes

Diabetes is an extremely common disease affecting many millions of Americans. Diabetes causes problems in many body systems, including the cardiovascular system, the kidneys, and the nervous system. Diabetes has also been linked to the epidemic of obesity in North America. It is an insidious disease, sometimes labeled “the silent killer” since the damage to organs occurs over time. Many with the disease are diagnosed only once significant damage has been done.

It is well known that men with diabetes experience erectile problems (Eardley et al., 2007), but less is known about women with diabetes (Enzlin, Mathieu, Vandershueren, & Demyttenaere, 1998). The erectile response in men is in part vascular, as blood fills the spongy tissue of the penis, and in part neurological, as this filling is dependent on messages from the nerves supplying the penis. It is easy to see how nerve and blood vessel damage would then result in erectile difficulties. The same vascular influences occur in women (Rutherford & Collier, 2005); women with diabetes report decreased lubrication (alterations to blood supply to the vaginal tissue results in less lubrication), which is an important part of sexual arousal. Lack of lubrication tends to cause pain with intercourse that then lessens desire for sex. About 50% of people with diabetes will experience neuropathy as a result of their diabetes. This can cause pain, tingling, and numbness of the hands and feet, which in turn can interfere with sexual pleasure and desire. The skin is also a large erogenous zone, and these altered sensations can be a powerful challenge to being sexual.

Women with diabetes, particularly type 2 (or adult onset) diabetes, have higher levels of androgens, which may affect sexual functioning in a negative way. Women with poor control of their blood glucose levels also have urinary tract infections more frequently, and these can cause irritation of the vulva and pain with sex.

Depression is common among people with diabetes (Enzlin, Mathieu, Ven Den Bruel, Vanderschueren, & Demyttenaere, 2003), and the effects of depression on sexual functioning result in sexual problems that may then be compounded by treatment with SSRIs (selective serotonin reuptake inhibitors) that themselves cause problems with desire and orgasm. People with diabetes often gain weight, and the associated body image changes may have a negative impact on sexual self-concept and on their attractiveness to their partner. The high blood levels of glucose experienced by diabetics with poor control negatively affect energy and mood. Irritability does not encourage feelings of well-being in diabetics or their partner and may be a detractor.

Early diagnosis of diabetes is important, and tight control of blood glucose levels may help to minimize organ damage that can affect sexuality. Exercise not only will help to control levels of glucose in the blood but can help alleviate depression and control weight, both of which are known to affect body image and sexuality. Just like a physical work out, sex has its impact on blood glucose levels, and some diabetics may find that they need to have a snack handy if their glucose levels fall during or after sex. Those people who have an insulin pump can leave it on during sexual activity or remove it completely, or just the tubing can be removed and the infusion set left in place as long as it is well anchored. Stopping the infusion for up to an hour is probably safe, but each person should be aware of the signs of high blood glucose and be prepared to restart the pump immediately after sex.

The treatments for arousal difficulties are the same as with anyone who has problems in this area. Oral medications for erectile dysfunction are moderately useful (Safarinejad, 2004). The vacuum pump and penile injections also work for those who cannot take the pills or who do not respond to them. For women, vaginal moisturizers and lubricants can be effective in treating vaginal dryness. Caution should be used with glycerin-based lubricants, which may increase yeast infections. It may take longer for both men and women with diabetes to become aroused.

Extra time should be spent kissing, touching, and actively stimulating the penis and scrotum in men and the clitoris in women. This may be tiring for both those with diabetes and their partner. Using a vibrator can really help with this, and the extra stimulation from the vibrations may be very pleasurable even without intercourse.

Incontinence

Incontinence, the involuntary loss of urine, is fairly common among women and increases with age (Barber, Mullen, Dowsett, & Viktrup, 2005). The two most common kinds of incontinence are *stress* incontinence, in which loss of urine occurs with sneezing, coughing, or exertion, and *urge* incontinence, where the loss of urine occurs after a sensation of urgency but follows it so very quickly that the woman is not able to get to the toilet in time. Both forms of incontinence are associated with sexual problems.

For women who experience incontinence, great effort is commonly made to conceal this fact (by using pads and sprays or washing frequently to minimize odor) or to control it (by frequent visits to the restroom, which leads some women to avoid social situations where they are not sure of their access to a restroom, or by avoidance of physical exercise, which has the secondary effect of weight gain and perhaps negative body image). In other words, incontinence has its own as well as secondary effects, that "domino" into other areas of life. Women go to great lengths to cover up their incontinence with frequent showers, having intercourse only in the shower or bath to mask any leakage, using feminine sprays to mask odor, or padding the bed with sheets or towels. While some of these coping mechanisms may be effective, seeking help is ultimately more sensible.

Women with stress incontinence often experience leakage during sexual activity (Barber et al., 2005). This leakage is more likely to occur with penetration, in contrast to women with urge incontinence, who tend to experience leakage with orgasm. But the consequences of this go much further than what happens in the bedroom (Urwitz-Lane & Ozel, 2006). Women who have incontinence often lose desire for sex. This is in part due to embarrassment but also because the leakage of urine at all times alters the environment of the vagina and may cause painful intercourse. When aroused, many women find it difficult to relax and will often go to the bathroom multiple times during foreplay to ensure that their bladder is empty and to preempt involuntary leakage. Sexual activity can become fraught with anxiety: fear of leakage also leads to problems with orgasm; knowing that orgasm will cause leakage, many women do not relax and in fact hurry their partner to finish; this in turn can cause problems for the partner, who may develop premature ejaculation from the pressure to get it over with. When sexual activity is affected by incontinence, the usual response is to avoid sex, which in turn leads to relationship distress (Coyne et al., 2007). This avoidance can influence choices in mourning. Many women choose not to pursue another relationship after losing a sexual partner, some expressing relief that they no longer are in a relationship with sexual expectations.

Male urinary incontinence is less common and may be a side effect of surgery to the prostate or urethra. When involuntary leakage occurs during sexual activity, often during arousal or orgasm, it may cause the same consequences for the man as it would for a woman: embarrassment and avoidance of sexual activity or even erectile dysfunction due to fear of it happening again.

Fecal incontinence, the involuntary loss of feces or stool, is another condition that causes great shame, perhaps even more so than urinary incontinence (Wilson, 2007). Sexual avoidance is very common, and surgical treatment seems to offer little relief. Perhaps the patterns of avoidance set up before surgery continue despite improvements in symptoms.

There are a number of treatments for urinary incontinence that, if successful, will also treat the sexual dysfunction associated with it. For instance, there are oral medications that are effective in treating urge incontinence. Though many of these have side effects, there are different types that can be tried, and a consultation with a physician can be the first step.

Pelvic floor physiotherapy, where the muscles of the pelvic floor are strengthened through exercises, has been shown to be effective in both controlling leakage and improving sexual functioning (Zahariou, Karamouti, & Papaioannou, 2008). Both men and women see improvement after learning and doing the prescribed exercises. Using electrical stimulation of the muscles of the pelvic floor is also helpful, although slightly more invasive (Giuseppe, Pace, & Vencentini, 2007). For those who are not helped by medication or exercise, surgery is usually the next alternative, and in this there are different options for both men and women.

A major challenge in the treatment of incontinence is that many people with this condition are reluctant to seek help. This may in part be due to embarrassment or to resignation, seeing incontinence as an inevitable aspect of aging.

Obesity

Obesity has been associated with sexual dysfunction (Kolotkin et al., 2006). Obese individuals are more likely to feel unattractive, experience less enjoyment from sexual activity, have more difficulty with the performance of sexual acts, and avoid sexual activity. Obese men are also more likely to have erectile dysfunction than their normal-weight counterparts, but obese women are more affected by poor body image, lowered desire for sex, and avoidance of sexual encounters.

Much of the research on obesity and sexual difficulties has been done with individuals who have had gastric bypass surgery for morbid obesity, where they need to lose a substantial portion of their body weight (Kinzl et al., 2007). Less is known about those who are only slightly or moderately overweight. Given that people who are overweight often have a negative body image, and since we know that body image has an impact on sexual self-concept and confidence as well as desire for sex, then it is perhaps not unreasonable to recognize that even moderate obesity can affect sexual functioning. Obesity is often linked to cardiovascular disease, which is in turn linked to erectile dysfunction in men.

Lifestyle changes such as diet and exercise are the cornerstones of treatment of mild to moderate obesity, and these changes have been shown to improve sexual function in about a third of men with ED (Esposito et al., 2004). Loss of weight should equate to improved self-image and increased sexual confidence, but the evidence in the scientific literature is lacking. There is, however, strong evidence for improvement in sexual functioning among the morbidly obese who lose significant amounts of weight following gastric bypass surgery.

THE "GOOD-ENOUGH SEX" MODEL

Because of the physiological changes and challenges faced by people over 50, it is important for them to alter their attitudes toward sex and sexuality as they age. What was appropriate for them when they entered adulthood ill-fits them in middle adulthood. Metz and McCarthy (2007) propose a unique model for increasing sexual satisfaction in couples that is based on realistic expectations with intimacy as the ultimate focus. In this model, sex is not an isolated factor in the life of the couple but, rather, an integrated event in daily life; in turn, daily life is integrated into the couple's sex life. The aim is for the couple to create its own, unique sexual style.

The model is based on cognitive, behavioral, emotional, and relationship factors. These promote cohesion, cooperation, and intimacy for the couple. There are 12 key elements in the model:

1. **Make the affirmation that sex is a good element in life, an invaluable part of an individual's and a couple's long-term comfort, intimacy, pleasure, and confidence.** This principle relies on a positive attitude about sex. Couples need to value sex as inherently good and must counter negative thoughts and attitudes.
2. **Relationship and sexual satisfaction are the ultimate developmental focus and are essentially intertwined.** The couple is an "intimate

team." The authors suggest that sex does not exist in a vacuum and requires cooperation, mutual conflict resolution both inside and outside of the bedroom, and a sharing of emotional empathy.

3. **Realistic, age-appropriate sexual expectations are essential for sexual satisfaction.** The model challenges couples to set realistic and positive expectations of their bodies and their minds. It also challenges the popular images of sexual attractiveness that dominate media messages and suggests that healthy couples will appraise these messages and reject them as hype or "too good to be true."
4. **Good physical health and healthy behavioral habits are vital for sexual health.** Individuals value their own body and their partner's body. Wellness is seen as an important goal because ill health will impact negatively on sexual health. Medical interventions for sexual problems are integrated into the couple's sexual style and are not a quick fix.
5. **Relaxation is the foundation for pleasure and function.** There are many different areas of life where relaxation can help sexual functioning. These include physical, mental, and relationship areas and are important as couples age. Anxiety about health and sex has a negative impact upon sex and its enjoyment. Relaxation promotes sexual enjoyment and counteracts worries about sexual performance.
6. **Pleasure is as important as function.** In this model, touch and pleasure are seen as just as important as erections and orgasms. This allows for relaxation and lessening of pressure to perform. Valuing variable, flexible sexual experiences and abandoning the need for perfect performance inoculates the couple against sexual dysfunction by overcoming performance pressure, fears of failure, and rejection.
7. **The "Good-Enough" model recognizes that in sexually satisfied couples, there is a great deal of variability in the quality of sex.** Research and clinical experience suggest that for satisfied couples, sex is very good about 20%–25% of the time, good about 40%–60% of the time, fair but unremarkable 15%–20% of the time, and dissatisfying about 5%–15% of the time. Acceptance of this variance helps to set realistic expectations.
8. **The five purposes for sex are integrated into the couple's sexual relationship.** These purposes are (a) reproduction (which is, generally speaking, not a factor for people over 50), (b) tension and anxiety reduction, (c) sensual enjoyment and pleasure, (d) self-esteem and confidence, and (e) relationship closeness and satisfaction. There is variation in the setting of priorities for each individual in the couple, and the priorities can change on a daily basis.
9. **Integrate and flexibly use the three sexual arousal styles.** These styles are (a) partner interaction, where the focus is on the partner and

each partner's arousal plays off the other's; (b) self-entrancement, where the focus is on one's own body and sensations and on relaxation and accepting touch; and (c) role-enactment, where arousal focuses on fantasy, variety, and experimentation.

10. **Gender differences are respectfully valued and similarities mutually accepted.** Celebrating the differences and similarities between men and women allows the couple to enjoy the "Good-Enough" approach to sexual satisfaction.
11. **Sex is integrated into real life, and real life is integrated into sex.** Sexuality is developing, growing, and evolving throughout life. Sex changes over the life of the couple, and "Good-Enough Sex" meshes with the couple's relationship style, making it unique to that couple at that particular stage of life.
12. **Sexuality is personalized: sex can be playful, spiritual, and/or special.** This model challenges couples to recognize not only sexual skills and performance but also the emotion and meaning in their relationship. Sex is different at different times, but when the focus is on the relationship, intimacy results.

The "Good-Enough Sex" model is particularly useful in helping couples to understand and weather the changes that occur as a result of aging, ill health, and chronic conditions. The focus is not on sexual performance or unrealistic standards set by the media or culture but on meaningful interactions that promote closeness, are realistic, and have an ultimate goal of intimacy and enhanced couple functioning.

CONCLUSION

For the adult over the age of 50, physical changes are inevitable. Speaking about sex after 50 has been a taboo subject in our culture. Instead, the assumption has been perpetuated that older couples are either not interested in sex or not able to have sex or both. The results of some recent studies turn those assumptions firmly on their heads. **The basic needs we have for touch and affection are not mitigated by age and may in fact be more meaningful with the years.** Older women report that as the years progress they are more interested in physical touch, kissing, and hearing loving words from their partner than they are in penetrative intercourse. This may be of some comfort to the older man who is having difficulties with erections. Older couples also report that the intimate connection grows deeper with the years and that the relationship takes on a deeper spiritual quality than before.

One of the most challenging aspects of sexuality in middle age (50–75) is that adults that age are already seen to be "old" by health care providers. Health care providers generally lack recognition that older people have sex and may not ask about this important aspect of quality of life when counseling the older adult about newly diagnosed medical conditions or prescribed medications. Many health care providers either assume that older adults are not sexually active or are themselves embarrassed to talk about a topic with someone the same age as their parent or grandparent. This effectively leaves the older person or couple to raise the topic, and they may be as embarrassed also. This shame-motivated silence stifles candor in treatment conversations and increases the older the patient becomes.

Moreover, in the United States and Canada large segments of the population are being medically cared for by people not of those cultures. Non-Western cultural prohibitions inhibit patient/provider discussions about sexuality and intimacy. It is around the age of 50, as they are entering middle age, that people begin to notice that most of their health care providers are younger than they and that many are from cultures different from theirs. Yet it is precisely then, when they are increasingly vulnerable to injury and illness, that they most need to be able to speak with their health care providers about sexuality and intimacy.

These are conversations they need to have because there is important information for them to be given about how to adapt their sexual behaviors and expectations and develop relationships of satisfying intimacy. The "Good-Enough Sex" model, for example, posits that meaningful interactions that promote closeness, are realistic about sexual functioning, and have an ultimate goal of intimacy can enhance a couple's relationship. Ultimately, it is intimate relationships that provide healing and hope with the challenges of aging.

REFERENCES

Barber, M., Mullen, K., Dowsett, S., & Viktrup, L. (2005). The impact of stress urinary incontinence on sexual activity in women. *Cleveland Clinic Journal of Medicine, 72*(3), 225–232.

Coyne, K., Margolis, M., Jumadilova, Z., Bavendam, T., Mueller, E., & Rogers, R. (2007). Overactive bladder and women's sexual health: What is the impact? *Journal of Sexual Medicine, 4*, 656–666. doi: 10.1111/j.1743-6109.2007.00493.x

DeLamater, J., & Karraker, A. (2009). Sexual functioning in older adults. *Current Psychiatry Reports, 11*, 6–11.

DeLamater, J., & Moorman, S. (2007). Sexual behavior in later life. *Journal of Aging and Health, 19*(6), 921–945. doi: 10.1177/0898264307308342

Doumas, M., & Douma, S. (2006). Sexual dysfunction in essential hypertension: Myth or reality? *Journal of Clinical Hypertension, 8*, 269–274.

Eardley, I., Fisher, W., Rosen, C., Niederberger, C., Nadel, A., & Sand, M. (2007). The multinational Men's Attitudes to Life Events and Sexuality study: The influence of diabetes on self-reported erectile function, attitudes and treatment-seeking patterns in men with erectile dysfunction. *International Journal of Clinical Practice, 61*, 1446–1453. doi: 10.1111/j.1742-1241.2007.01460.x

Enzlin, P., Mathieu, C., Vanderschueren, D., & Demyttenaere, K. (1998). Diabetes mellitus and female sexuality: A review of 25 years' research. *Diabetic Medicine, 15*, 809–815.

Enzlin, P., Mathieu, C., Vanderschueren, D., Van Den Bruel, A., & Demyttenaere, K. (2003). Prevalence and predictors of sexual dysfunction in patients with type 1 diabetes. *Diabetes Care, 26*, 409–414.

Esposito, K., Giugliano, F., Di Palo, C., Giugliano, G., Marfella, R., D'Andrea, F., et al. (2004). Effect of lifestyle changes on erectile dysfunction in obese men. *Journal of the American Medical Association, 291*(24), 2978–2984.

Giuseppe, P., Pace, G., & Vicentini, C. (2007). Sexual function in women with urinary incontinence treated by pelvic floor transvaginal electrical stimulation. *Journal of Sexual Medicine, 4*, 702–707. doi: 10.1111/j.1743-6109.2006.00318.x

Jackson, G., Rosen, R., Kloner, R., & Kostis, J. (2006). The second Princeton consensus on sexual dysfunction and cardiac risk: New guidelines for sexual medicine. *Journal of Sexual Medicine, 3*, 28–36. doi: 10.1111/j.1743-6109.2005.00196.x

Jung, J., Kam, S., Choi, S., Jae, S., Lee, S., & Hyun, J. (2008). Sexual dysfunction in male stroke patients: Correlation between brain lesions and sexual function. *Urology, 71*(1), 99–103. doi: 10.1016/j.urology.2007.08.045

Kinzl, J., Schrattenecker, M., Traweger, C., Aigner, F., Fiala, M., & Biebl, W. (2007). Quality of life in morbidly obese patients after surgical weight loss. *Obesity Surgery, 17*, 229–235.

Kolotkin, R., Binks, M., Crosby, R., Ostbye, T., Gress, R., & Adams, T. (2006). Obesity and sexual quality of life. *Obesity, 14*(3), 472–479.

Kontula, O., & Haavio-Mannila, E. (2009). The impact of aging on human sexual activity and sexual desire. *Journal of Sex Research, 46*(1), 46–56. doi: 10.1080/00224490802624414

Lindau, S., & Gavrilova, N. (2010). Sex, health, and years of sexually active life gained due to good health: Evidence from two US population based cross sectional surveys of ageing. *British Medical Journal, 340*. doi :10.1136/bmj.c810

Mahrer-Imhof, R., Hoffmann, A., & Froelicher, E. (2007). Impact of cardiac disease on couples' relationships. *Journal of Advanced Nursing, 57*(5), 513–521. doi: 10.1111/j.1365-2648.2006.04141.x

Metz, M., & McCarthy, B. (2007). The "Good-Enough Sex" model for couple sexual satisfaction. *Sexual and Relationship Therapy, 22*(3), 351–362. doi: 10.1080/14681990601013492

Murray, C., & Harrison, B. (2004). The meaning and experience of being a stroke survivor: An interpretive phenomenological analysis. *Disability and Rehabilitation, 26*(13), 808–816. doi: 10.1080/09638280410001696746

Rutherford, D., & Collier, A. (2005). Sexual dysfunction in women with diabetes mellitus. *Gynecological Endocrinology, 21*(4), 189–192.

Safarinejad, M. (2004). Oral sildenafil in the treatment of erectile dysfunction in diabetic men: A randomized double-blind and placebo-controlled study. *Journal of Diabetes and Its Complications, 18*, 205–210. doi: 10.1016/S1056-8727(03)00056-4

Schwarz, E. (2007). Sexual function in women with heart disease and coronary artery disease. *International Journal of Impotence Research, 19*(4), 341–342.

Steinke, E. (2000). Sexual counseling after myocardial infarction. *American Journal of Nursing, 100*(12), 38–43.

Urwitz-Lane, R., & Ozel, B. (2006). Sexual function in women with urodynamic stress incontinence, detrusor overactivity, and mixed urinary incontinence. *American Journal of Obstetrics and Gynecology, 195*, 1758–1761. doi: 10.1016/j.ajog.2006.07.028

Waite, L., Laumann, E., Das, A., & Schumm, P. (2009). Sexuality: Measures of partnerships, practices, attitudes, and problems in the National Social Life, Health, and Aging study. *Journal of Gerontology Social Sciences, 64B*(Supplement 1), i56–i66. doi: 10.1093/geronb/gbp038

Wilson, M. (2007). The impact of fecal incontinence on the quality of life. *British Journal of Nursing, 16*(4), 204–207.

Zahariou, A., Karamouti, M., & Papaioannou, P. (2008). Pelvic floor muscle training improves sexual function of women with stress urinary incontinence. *International Urogynecology Journal, 19*, 401–406.

Joe and Marie

Joe, a patient accompanied by his wife, Marie, is being admitted to a hospice inpatient unit. The conversation centers on managing the patient's symptoms and a review of Joe's current medications. Joe asks, "Can I get my prescription for Viagra refilled?" While the question is aimed at the hospice physician, a hospice nurse and a social worker are also present. No one directly answers Joe, and the conversation seems to move smoothly into other areas. Not one team member comes back to the question or asks Joe about his concern for getting his Viagra refilled. Later, privately, Marie tells the hospice social worker that she hopes the doctor will not take her husband's request for Viagra seriously. The social worker agrees to convey Marie's message back to the doctor.

HOSPICE

A part of the Lexington, Kentucky, community for over 30 years, Hospice of the Bluegrass (HOB) is a private nonprofit organization with offices in eastern, central, and northern Kentucky. HOB serves an average of 1,000 patients per day. The organization has inpatient facilities and hospice home care services and operates a palliative care program. Both adult and pediatric patients are served.

To the general public, palliative care is perhaps an unfamiliar specialty within health care, but it is now considered the umbrella term for a variety of programs aimed at managing symptoms in patients with serious illness. Hospice care is palliative in that patients in hospice programs either wish to forego aggressive treatment and receive symptom management or do not have the choice because a cure does not currently exist. The *Clinical Practice Guidelines for Quality Palliative Care* (National Consensus Project, 2009) define hospice as both a philosophy of care and an organized model of care, usually provided by an interdisciplinary team that includes a nurse, a chaplain, a social worker, certified nursing assistants, and a hospice medical director. In order to be eligible for care under the Centers for Medicare and Medicaid Hospice Benefit, the patient must have a prognosis of 6 months or less. Hospice care can be provided in a home, a nursing home, an assisted living facility, a residential facility, or an inpatient unit. Both the patient and the family are the focus of care, and the relief of suffering and improved quality of life is the goal. Hospice clinicians utilize a comprehensive assessment to better understand and identify patient and family needs.

Hospice is a form of care that is based on preserving dignity and the belief that patients have a right to determine the type of care they want to receive at the end of life. The care is directed by the patient and the family and is frequently delivered in the patient's home. The home setting allows for needed privacy to lead to the type of conversations illustrated in the case examples. During visits with patients, a form of intimacy is created between the patient and the professional caregivers by the sharing of displayed family photos and treasured possessions and by the meeting of family and friends. As the following case examples show, regardless of the setting, with awareness of the need for privacy, personal conversations about intimacy can and do occur.

Cindy

A hospice social worker makes an initial home visit to Cindy, a new patient, 37 years old, who has been battling ovarian cancer for the past 8 years. Cindy is married and has 2 young children. During the visit, the social worker asks, "What is the hardest part of this for you?" Cindy responds tearfully, "Leaving my family." Cindy expresses how important it is for her to keep the family bed and not have a hospital bed: "I need to keep my family close, to hold my girls, and to have my husband to hold me. I need to stay in this bed." The hospice team is able to manage Cindy's symptoms without the use of a hospital bed and honor her request.

Jessie

Jessie, the wife of a 45-year-old patient, wants to know if a bigger hospital bed can be provided so she and her husband can sleep together.

Married 50 Years

"I'm lonely and miss my husband," says a wife married 50-plus years when her husband is placed in a nursing home. "I miss him being next to me. It just doesn't feel right."

SEXUALITY AND INTIMACY DURING THE LAST PHASE OF LIFE

"No one can dispute the importance of love" (Barusch, 2009, p. 13). We are sexual beings regardless of our age, physical status, or stage of life (Cort, Monroe, & Oliviere, 2004). We have a need for personal contact, tenderness, and love. Sexuality is a vital and defining part of the human experience. Hearing the word *sex* usually brings to mind young, attractive, healthy individuals. Sex, however, is not exclusive to those with youth, vitality, and health. Terminal illness does not prevent the desire or need for sexuality and intimacy. In fact, Wallace (2008) suggests that both become even more important during the last phase of life. During the most stressful times in our lives, we usually search for comfort from those we love. Should we not expect that loving relationships are significant for the hospice and palliative patient? The following cases clearly indicate how intimacy remains important as terminal disease progresses.

Jim

Jim, a hospice patient with head and neck cancer, tells staff he fears his wife won't ever want to kiss him because of his disfigurement. Jim tells staff he is aware of how he looks and worries his wife will be repulsed even as he explains he knows she still loves him.

Betty

Betty is 67 years of age and has been in treatment for breast cancer for 5 years. Recently she stopped treatments and began home hospice care. "I no longer want my husband to have intercourse with me, but I do still need him to make love to me in other ways. I am so tired all the time, but I need him to just hold me and talk to me like he used to. I feel him pulling away when I need him the most." Her husband tells the team social worker that he doesn't know how to be with his wife. "I'm losing my best friend. When I'm alone with her I want to cry. I don't want her to see me like that."

The World Health Organization (2004) defines sexual health as a state of physical, emotional, and mental social well being related to sexuality; it is not merely the absence of dysfunction or infirmity. Gilly (1988, p. 121) defines sexuality in the context of palliative care as "the capacity of the individual to link emotional needs with physical intimacy, the ability to give and receive physical intimacy at all levels, from the simplest to the most profound." A survey of palliative patients on the meaning of sexuality provides a third definition:

> Sexuality encompassed many things but was centered on emotional connectedness. Their experience of sexuality changed over time . . . to one of intimacy through close body contact, hugging, touching of hands, kissing, "meaningful" eye contact and other non-physical expressions of closeness and companionship. (Lemieux, Kaiser, Pereira, & Meadows, 2004, p. 634)

All three definitions use a broad range of human behaviors to describe sexuality and intimacy. It is especially significant that the survey by Lemieux et al. indicated that when asked, palliative care patients were willing to discuss sexuality.

One of the primary goals of palliative care is improving the patient's quality of life. "As quality of life includes sexuality, a fundamental and enduring aspect of life, it follows that palliative care should address this aspect of the human experience, even at the end of life" (Lemieux et al., 2004, p. 630). Researchers in the past decade have drawn conclusions that sexual contact, intimacy, and loving relationships are important aspects of overall quality of life during terminal illness. Supporting data appear in studies by Gianotten (2007), Horden (2008), Panke and Farrell (2004), Singer, Martin, and Kelner (1999), and Zeiss and Kahl-Godley (2001). The following patient's comments relate to quality of life.

Tom

> Tom, a married, 34-year-old palliative care patient, has lost functioning from the waist down due to an industrial accident. He has chronic pain and experiences a wide range of debilitating symptoms. His wife wonders if their sex life is over. She asks the nurse how to still be intimate. Tom looks away and says, "I love my wife and still want to be with her, but I don't feel like I can please her."

Sexuality clearly means different things to men and women at various stages of their life. An individual's unique approach to sexuality is with them from birth till death, and despite the difficulty of talking openly about intimacy and dying, sexuality doesn't go away when a person receives a terminal diagnosis. Redelman (2008) believes the sexuality of patients is largely determined by their sex life before the diagnosis and their beliefs about sexuality during this time in their life. The manner by which a patient's partner responds to the situation may also have an effect.

Receiving a terminal diagnosis may be followed by what Sudnow called a "social death"—a marked social withdrawal (as cited in Cagle & Bolte, 2009, p. 229). Friends and sometimes family members often do not know how to respond or what to do when faced with a crisis having terminal implications. As a result, friends and family may withdraw, treating the person as though he or she has already died. Even strong, dependable family members sometimes crumble emotionally, feeling helpless as the disease progresses and they watch their loved one die. During the early stages of the illness, the patient may cope with the loss of closeness by focusing all energy on treatment and managing acute symptoms. Health professionals may assume that the patient is correct on focusing on survival and that intimacy and sexuality are unimportant (Redelman, 2008). Sam, a pediatric hospice patient, in a poignant visit, illustrates how important sexuality remains in the face of disease.

Sam

> In many ways Sam is a typical 17-year-old—interested in cars, school, and girls. Sam's terminal illness, however, separates him from others, and he openly grieves the loss of activities. During a chaplain's visit, Sam expresses a desire to have sex just once before he dies. Sam asks the chaplain how to get a date.

Often as a patient's journey brings them closer to death and there are fewer distractions, the loss of intimacy is felt more intensely. There is also the possibility that fighting the disease can put a strain on existing close relationships (Cort et al., 2004). Patients may struggle as they begin to sort out their own intimacy needs.

RELEVANT RESEARCH

In the next 20 years the population over 65 years of age will increase by more than 70% (Burman et al., 1998). Perhaps related to the impending demographic shift, there has been an explosion of palliative research, textbooks, and journal articles in the last 10 years. Despite the increased focus on improving quality of life for patients and highlighting the need for providing holistic care, few palliative care articles or texts discuss sexuality. *Living With Dying: A Handbook for End-of-Life Healthcare Practitioners* (2004), edited by Joan Berzoff and Phyllis Silverman, is an excellent resource for social workers and other health care practitioners. At close to 900 pages, the book shows breadth and depth on the subject of palliative care. However, only one reference to sexuality is included in the index. *Grief, Dying, and Death: Clinical Interventions for Caregivers* (1984), written by Therese Rando, a pioneer author and researcher in end-of-life care, devotes fewer than 3 pages out of a 444-page book to sexuality and the dying patient. *Palliative Medicine* (2009), a much-anticipated and respected comprehensive text on palliative care, has 1,435 pages and devotes a chapter of 5 pages to sexuality. A similar scarcity of information on sexuality and end-of-life care is found in much of the literature devoted to hospice and palliative care.

While many authors have ignored or downplayed the importance of sexuality, some work has been done. Research in 1991 (Waterhouse & Metcalfe) found that 92% of patients interviewed would want a nurse to initiate a conversation and address sexuality concerns.

Fortunately, many prominent organizations dedicated to end-of-life care—such as the National Hospice and Palliative Care Organization, the National Association of Social Workers, and the National Consensus Project for Quality Palliative Care—agree that sexuality is a fundamental part of a palliative comprehensive assessment (Cagel & Bolte, 2009). Kern (2009) lists five common myths surrounding terminal illness and sexuality:

1. Critically ill people, particularly older people, are no longer interested in sexual activity.
2. Caregivers should never address sexual issues, except when asked to do so.
3. Sexual issues are to be discussed with a gynecologist, urologist, or psychologist (e.g., family therapist) but not with palliative care physicians or nurses.
4. If a patient has a serious disease-related sexual problem, he will talk about it.
5. Loss of sexual activity is a self-evident and unavoidable result of a life-limiting advanced illness.

Dying individuals are sexual beings, but they may assume that their sexual desires are irrelevant. Patients that internalize these feelings may experience decreased sexual activity and interest, reduced displays of affection, and emotional disengagement (Cagel & Bolte, 2009). Redelman (2008) describes the benefits of sexuality and states that sexuality is vital to a patient's self-concept, which sustains adaptability and resiliency, enabling the patient to cope with adverse circumstances and work out personal solutions. Adaptability and resiliency is critical for many patients to find peace, acceptance, and contentment at the end of life.

Davies, Zeiss, Shea, and Tinklenberg (1998) examined how cognitive changes such as those occurring in dementia patients can affect sexuality and intimacy. These authors offer compassionate approaches to assessment and interventions that take into account the patient's ability to grant permission for sexual encounters. In conclusion, they note that "healthcare professionals' willingness to address sexuality issues with older adults can reduce patient and caregiver stress and improve couples quality of life" (1998, p. 202). As the cases below indicate, long-term care patients may create special concerns for hospice staff and nursing home administrators.

John

A 74-year-old patient, John, makes sexual innuendos during nursing visits and has inappropriately touched several female hospice staff. Nurses are reluctant to visit the patient, and the hospice team wonders if the patient should be discharged from the hospice program.

Jim

Jim, a hospice patient residing in a nursing home, develops a relationship with Sandra, another resident. Jim uses a wheelchair to visit Sandra in her room. He has been seen kissing and touching Sandra. Some staff members in the nursing home want to limit the couple's time together.

Rose

Rose is 88 years old and resides in a nursing home. She tells her hospice social worker that she is lonely. Rose says, "I wish I had a boyfriend. I miss having a companion."

Frank

Frank had end-stage dementia, and his wife, Marie, is debilitated from a stroke. They shared a room together in a long-term care facility until the facility decided to move Frank to another floor when his needs required a different level of care. Marie is nonverbal but still expresses her sadness about being apart for the first time in their 60 years of marriage. The hospice staff advocated for Marie to be taken daily to Frank's room, where they took meals together, listened to music, and visited with family. Marie was able to hold Frank's hand and be with him at the time of his death.

HOSPICE OF THE BLUEGRASS SURVEY

A 2010 survey (Appendix A) administered to HOB interdisciplinary staff confirms that healthcare professionals remain uncomfortable with the topic of sexuality. Despite the encouraging research cited, hospice health care workers still seem reluctant to initiate conversations around intimacy and sexuality. Fifty staff members, out of a possible 54, responded to the survey, which asked them to respond to the following questions about sexuality and intimacy:

1. Have patients and family members ever asked you about this topic before?
2. How important do you think this issue is for your patients and families?
3. Do you have conversations with your patients/family members on this topic?
4. How often do you initiate conversations with your patients or families on this topic?
5. What is your level of comfort in discussing this topic with patients and families?
6. Please describe any situation where this topic has been identified as an issue by the team or by the patient/family and how it was addressed.

Demographic information was collected—staff members' length of work experience in hospice and their profession (nurse, social worker, chaplain, bereavement counselor, certified nursing assistant). In an effort to gain an understanding of staff educational needs, the survey asked staff to identify training or information that might increase staff comfort level with the topic. In response to a survey question asking staff to list any barriers to discussing sexuality and intimacy, responders overwhelmingly answered that patients and families are uncomfortable discussing the issue. See Tables 1 and 2.

SUGGESTIONS FOR IMPROVEMENT

Sexuality and intimacy are important facets of a patient's quality of life, but a literature review, along with the HOB staff survey, indicates that team members are generally unaware that patients want and expect health care professionals to bring up the topic of sexuality and intimacy. Furthermore, some survey responders

Table 1. Staff Responses When Asked to List Any Barriers to Having a Discussion ($n = 50$)

Patient/family is uncomfortable.	84.0%
Patients are asexual due to illness.	15.5%
One member of the couple is open to have discussion but the other member is not.	0.5%

Table 2. Staff Responses When Asked What Training or Information Would Increase Their Comfort (n = 50)

Training or in-service	50%
How to start a conversation	25%
Discussion to raise awareness	25%

describe being ill-equipped to discuss sexuality and report having a lack of knowledge on how to initiate a conversation. HOB staff members admit to being uncomfortable and embarrassed to have these conversations with patients. Being aware of this barrier is essential in the development of staff training. Routinely assessing sexual concerns and exploring how sexuality affects a patient's quality of life should be encouraged. Hospice employees also need to recognize their own biases, feelings, and thoughts about sexuality. Training can help develop the ability to have open discussions with patients at the end of life.

To ensure that sexuality and intimacy needs are assessed, the interdisciplinary team members should discuss how they will complete a patient assessment and how to address intimacy issues. The team may choose to designate one team member to complete a sexual assessment to avoid a diffusion of responsibility. Some hospice teams may choose to have each team member complete a sexual needs assessment, utilizing the perspectives and expertise of each profession. The value of the interdisciplinary team is that no matter who completes the assessment, there is a collaborative process to address any sexual needs identified.

Hospice and palliative care teams must become comfortable in having difficult conversations with patients and know how to incorporate patient sexuality and intimacy into routine, ongoing assessments so that every patient has an opportunity to explore these issues. In the survey of HOB staff and team members, a consistent theme was identified. Team members want assistance in knowing how to have these conversations. Providing scripted openings for discussion should increase the staff's comfort level. "Do you feel that your sexuality has changed since your diagnosis?" is a question suggested by Spaulding (2006) for nurses to use during initial assessments. Nurses are told to explain that this question is asked of all patients. According to Spaulding, this approach helps increase the patient's and the practitioner's comfort level.

Hordern and Currow (2003, p. 9) have devised specific phrases to help health care staff open the door for discussion with patients who face terminal illness. These are not direct questions but are phrases that help patients hear that others with similar illnesses have issues with sexuality and intimacy. This approach can frame a patient's worries as normal and legitimate.

Suggested phrases include the following:

- "Some people who are going through an illness like yours have been concerned about their sexuality."
- "You have been through so much since your diagnosis. This may affect the way you see yourself as a woman/man."
- "You might be wondering how all of this will affect your sexuality or intimacy. Let's talk about that."
- "This illness may have impacted your relationship and other intimate areas of your life."
- "Other women who have been given this treatment have experienced a dry vagina." "Some men taking this medication have problems having an erection."

There are several models of assessment available for interdisciplinary team members to consider when assessing the sexual-related needs of patients. The widely referenced PLISSIT model[1] (Annon, 1976) has been recommended as a useful template that provides a general framework on how to initiate and further conversations about sexual issues. Cagle and Bolte (2009) write that this approach is versatile and can be applied to a range of situations, illnesses, and settings—both inpatient and outpatient. The PLISSIT model stands for four steps or levels: permission (P), limited information (LI), specific suggestions (SS), and intensive therapy (IT). The latter steps build on previous ones, but the team members can move back and forth between the levels based on the patient's and partner's needs.

The first step in using this model is to ask permission (P) to begin the sexual assessment of the patient by communicating a willingness to discuss sexuality and intimacy. This is followed with open-ended questions designed to elicit the patient's concerns about sexual health and is an invitation to further the conversation. One example of such a question is "Those in similar situations have expressed concerns about intimacy and sexuality. What concerns are you having?" This question offers the patient permission to both have and discuss sexual concerns (Cagle & Bolte, 2009, p. 227).

Next, the team member provides limited information (LI) or education to patients about normal and pathological changes that may affect sexual health and tries to dispel any misconceptions (Wallace, 2008). Limited information may be given in a short period of time or over several brief meetings to provide accurate and relevant information (Cagle & Bolte, 2009).

At the third step, patients are given concrete specific suggestions (SS) on how to cope with the effects of the illness. These suggestions are tailored to address the patient needs that were identified from the open-ended questions

[1] The authors of Chapter 7 also reference this model. See page 140.

of the assessment. The final step calls for intensive therapy (IT) to address ongoing concerns and may involve a referral for additional counseling. It is estimated that only a small minority of cases may require this type of intervention since the majority of sexual function problems can be resolved with providing permission, limited information, and specific suggestions (Derogatis & Kourlesis, 1981).

Whatever model or type of questions that the interdisciplinary team chooses to utilize, the patient needs to feel comfortable about discussing his or her sexual needs. The team needs to create a safe, open, confidential environment for these conversations to occur.

THE NEED FOR A NATIONAL CHANGE

Given the myths and the reluctance of staff to bring up the topic of sexuality, there is little doubt that other hospice programs may face similar barriers to those found at Hospice of the Bluegrass. There is a need to develop leadership awareness, offer training on national and state levels, and develop quality improvement measures to assure ongoing progress.

Strategically, the most important step for hospice and palliative care leadership is to acknowledge that barriers exist in addressing patient's sexuality. Once barriers are acknowledged and identified, significant change can occur. An obvious approach would be to highlight the intimacy and sexuality needs of palliative patients at state and national conferences. Attendees can be encouraged to go back to their organizations and replicate the survey used by Hospice of the Bluegrass or devise one of their own to gather information on their staff's attitudes regarding sexuality and intimacy at the end of life. Experiential workshops can help identify attitudinal barriers and also help identify regional or cultural factors that could be integrated into training programs. The national leadership network needs to take on the task of assuring that hospice organizations across the country realize and accept the challenge to educate their staff on how to assess and address the sexual health needs of patients that enter hospice and palliative care.

Like other providers of health care, the hospice industry has been encouraged to develop a set of quality measures to safeguard the public and show evidence of improved patient outcomes. Standardized measures that show how pain is rated, treated, and reassessed until the patient is comfortable is a common quality assurance process utilized by many hospice programs. To make a sustained improvement, hospice programs would need to develop a standardized set of measures to indicate that sexuality was assessed and addressed within a specified amount of time. Chart audits of other data collection measures could be utilized to assist staff and managers and track improvements.

A majority of the Hospice of the Bluegrass staff that completed the survey believe that patients and their families are uncomfortable talking about sexual needs. Staff also identified that they felt uncomfortable and ill-prepared to engage in such discussions. This combination almost ensures that few patients are asked about their intimacy needs and that concerns are not being addressed. Barriers exist, but implementing training can increase staff confidence and improve staff's willingness to address intimacy concerns. Sensitivity and thought are also required when bringing a hospital bed into a patient's home. Patients and their family members deserve our compassion and our respect. The end of life should be a time for the exchange of loving words, touching, and any form of consensual sexual contact that brings comfort. Hospice needs to bring sexuality into the definition of holistic care.

CONCLUSION AND GROWTH

Hospice was formed in response to the recognition that illness was more than a medical event. Patients are affected emotionally and spiritually as well as physically by disease.

Hospice patients are facing multiple challenges as they approach the end of their lives. Faced with distressing symptoms, decreased mobility, and at times isolation, hospice patients deserve the best care possible. While the physical care of terminally ill patients is important, spiritual and psychosocial concerns are equally deserving of the best hospice can offer. Reviewing research on intimacy and conducting the HOB staff survey, led us to believe that hospice patients are not getting their sexual needs fully addressed or assessed. Belief in the myth that patients are uncomfortable talking about sexuality has allowed hospice staff to ignore patients with legitimate intimacy concerns.

The process of writing this chapter has been enlightening and provided us with an opportunity to put Hospice of the Bluegrass, the health care organization we work for, under a microscope. The process involved examining our own perspectives, as well as those held by the agency and clinical staff, as they pertain to the sexual and intimacy needs of patients and families. With over 19 years of end-of-life care experience to draw from, we found ourselves engaged in animated conversations and examining memories of patients and their families. Our dialogue led to a dual process of writing and making changes in practice to impact the care patients receive.

Intimacy and sexuality are part of life. It is time to talk about it. As John A. Simone Sr. says, "the key to wisdom is knowing the right question" (Simone, 2012). To serve patients better, end-of-life care professionals need to grow in the wisdom of asking the right questions about the intimacy and sexuality needs of their patients and families.

APPENDIX A

Sexuality and Intimacy at End of Life—Staff Survey

Please take a few moments to complete this survey on your thoughts about sexuality and intimacy at the end of life. For the context of this survey, sexuality is defined as a type of emotional closeness, which may include physical and non-physical expressions such as intercourse, close body contact, hugging, touching of hands, kissing, meaningful eye contact, and other non-physical displays of closeness and companionship.

1. Have patients/family members ever asked you about this topic before?
   ____ Yes ____ No

2. How important do you think this issue is for your patients and families? (Please Circle One)
   1. Very Important
   2. Important
   3. Moderately Important
   4. Of Little Importance
   5. Unimportant

3. Do you have conversations with your patients and families on this topic? (Please Circle One)
   1. Very Frequently
   2. Frequently
   3. Occasionally
   4. Rarely
   5. Never

4. How often do you initiate conversations with your patients or families on this topic? (Please Circle One)
   1. Very Frequently
   2. Frequently
   3. Occasionally
   4. Rarely
   5. Never\

5. What is your level of comfort in discussing this topic with your patients and families? (Please Circle One)
   1. Very Comfortable
   2. Comfortable
   3. Minimally Comfortable
   4. Uncomfortable
   5. Very Uncomfortable

6. What training or information do you feel would increase your comfort level?

7. Please list any barriers you can identify to having a discussion on this topic with your patients and families.

8. Please describe any situation where this topic has been identified as an issue by the team or by the patient/family and how it was addressed.

Staff Position: ___________ Number of Years Providing Hospice Care: _____

REFERENCES

Annon, J. (1976). The PLISSIT model: A proposed conceptual scheme for the behavioural treatment of sexual problems. *Journal of Sex Education and Therapy, 2*(2), 1–15.

Barusch, A. S. (2009). Love and ageism—A social work perspective. *Social Work Today, 9*(1), 12–17.

Burman, L., Penner, R., Steuerle, C., Toder, E., Moon, M., Thompson, L., et al. (1998, May). *Policy challenges posed by the aging of America.* Discussion briefing prepared for the Urban Institute Board of Trustees, Washington, DC.

Cagle, J. G., & Bolte, S. (2009). Sexuality and life-threatening illness: Implications for social work and palliative care. *Health and Social Work, 34*(3), 223–233.

Cort, E., Monroe, B., & Oliviere, D. (2004). Couples in palliative care. *Sexual and Relationship Therapy, 19*(3), 337–354.

Davies, H. D., Zeiss, A. M., Shea, E. A., & Tinklenberg, J. R. (1998). Sexuality and intimacy in Alzheimer patients and their partners. *Sexuality and Disability, 16*(6), 193–203.

Derogatis, L., & Kourlesis, S. (1981). An approach to evaluation of sexual problems in the cancer patient. *CA: A Cancer Journal for Clinicians, 31*, 41–50.

Gianotten, W. L. (2007). Sexuality in the palliative-terminal phase of cancer. *Sexologies, 16,* 265–266.

Gilly, J. (1998). Intimacy and terminal care. *Journal of the Royal College of General Practitioners, 38,* 121–122.

Hordern, A. J. (2008). Intimacy and sexuality after cancer: A critical review of the literature. *Cancer Nursing, 31*(2), E9–E17.

Hordern, A. J., & Currow, D. C. (2003). A patient-centered approach to sexuality in the face of life-limiting illness. *Medical Journal of Australia, 179*, S8–S11.

Kaeton, E. (1998). Pastoral care at the end of life: Listening for the question beneath the question. *Journal of Palliative Medicine, 1*(3), 285–289.

Kern, M. (2009). Sexuality and intimacy in the critically ill. In K. Murphy, C. Carroll, P. Hetherington, & J. Bartz (Eds.), *Palliative medicine* (1st ed., pp. 355–359). Philadelphia, PA: Saunders.

Lemieux, L., Kaiser, S., Pereira, J., & Meadows, L. M. (2004). Sexuality in palliative care: Patient perspectives. *Palliative Medicine, 18*, 630–637.

National Consensus Project for Quality Palliative Care. (2009). *Clinical Practice Guidelines for Quality Palliative Care* (2nd ed.). Pittsburgh, PA: Author.

Panke, J. T., & Ferrell, B. R. (2004). Emotional problems in the family. In D. Doyle, G. Hanks, & N. Macdonald (Eds.), *Oxford textbook of palliative medicine* (3rd ed., pp. 985–991). Oxford, England: Oxford University Press.

Redelman, M. J. (2008). Is there a place for sexuality in the holistic care of patients in the palliative care phase of life? *American Journal of Hospice & Palliative Medicine, 25*(5), 366–371.

Shell, J. A. (2008). Sexual issues in the palliative care population. *Seminars in Oncology Nursing, 24*(2), 131–134.

Simone, J. Retrieved June 26, 2012 from http://www.brainyquote.com/quotes/authors

Singer, P. A., Martin, D. K., & Kelner, M. (1999). Quality end-of-life care: Patient's perspectives. *Journal of American Medical Association, 281,* 163–168.

Spaulding, S. (2006). No patient assessment is complete without asking one question. *ONS Bewsm, 21*(9), 6-7.

Wallace, M. A. (2008). Assessment of sexual health in older adults. *American Journal of Nursing, 108*(7), 52–60.

Waterhouse, J., & Metcalfe, M. (1991). Attitudes toward nurses discussing sexual concerns with patients. *Journal of Advanced Nursing, 16*(9), 1048–1054.

World Health Organization. (2002). Sexuality—Working definition. *Sexual Health.* Retrieved from http://www.who.int/reproductive-health/gender/sexual_health.html

Zeiss, A. M., & Kahl-Godley, J. (2001). Sexuality in older adults' relationships. *Generations, 43*(2), 18–25.

SECTION 4

Religious Bases for Understanding Intimacy, Sexuality, and Healing After Loss

This section both brings us back to basics about the origins of many of our attitudes toward intimacy and sexuality and prescribes what might change within our sociocultural life for us to provide better comfort and support for ourselves as we mourn.

Given the contemporary skepticism and suspicion about religion and its institutions in our culture, we may underestimate the significance of religion in our mourning practices. Religious writing and principles have shaped our concepts of intimacy and sexuality, and therefore our intimate and sexual behaviors. Whether we are aware of it or not, we often find, especially in our vulnerable times, that our self-understandings are shaped by our culture's religious conceptualities. Mourning is just such a vulnerable time.

Likewise, as we find in our mourning that we are all the more adrift because our society simply provides inadequate institutional support for us, we also discover that many of us turn to religious concepts and institutions for that support. That is, as we mourn, we are likely to surprise ourselves in discovering to what social institutions we turn to seek solace. However else we may feel about them, we still expect religious institutions to provide a sense of *community*. It is togetherness with others that we seek when we are mourning, and we seem to know that we will not find it in psychological or medical institutions, where we sense we will be "singled out." Beyond the boundaries of psychology, religion continues to offer us promise of consolation.

Daniel A. Roberts, DMin, DD, FT, takes us inside a class he teaches on Judaism and sexuality to remind us how deeply ingrained in our Western culture are our concepts of intimacy and our attitudes toward sexuality. He is rabbi emeritus of Temple Emanu El in Cleveland, Ohio, where he served for over 30 years. He is also a Fellow in Thanatology in ADEC, has done extensive work on the subjects of bereavement and mourning, and has produced a video on teenage suicide entitled *Inside I Ache*, which has had national distribution.

David Daubert, PhD, and **Robert D. Machamer, DMin, LMFT**, work together with Day 8 Strategies, a team of consultants who evaluate church leadership and building healthy congregations; Dave serves as Lead Consultant and CEO. Both are ordained ministers. Dave, a Lutheran pastor, serves a congregation in Elgin, Illinois, doing lifebuilding in a fast-changing community. A measure of his success: the once-struggling church is today a vibrant presence in the community. Dave has published several books and has worked in national and regional church leadership positions as well as in the parish. He is a frequent keynote speaker at conferences across the United States and Canada.

For his part, in addition to being a church growth consultant, Bob is a licensed marriage and family therapist. He completed his undergraduate degree at Grove City College and graduated from the Lutheran Theological Seminary at Philadelphia (MDiv) and Eastern Baptist Theological Seminary (DMin). He completed a postgraduate program in marriage and family therapy with a specialty in couples and sex therapy at Penn Council for Relationships in Philadelphia. He is a clinical member of the American Association of Marriage and Family Therapy. He has additional training in intentional interim ministry, mediation, and coaching. He currently serves as pastor of St. Paul's Evangelical Lutheran Church in Fleetwood, Pennsylvania.

Dave and Bob share a hope for the Church and a desire for it to have a positive, supportive, and compassionate place in contemporary society. The hope they have for the Church is analogously applicable to other religious institutions struggling both to remain true to their principles and to create communities hospitable to those who grieve.

When we think of ways to celebrate our intimacy and bless our sexuality, we turn to religions for their rituals and rites (for instance, weddings and funerals). Religions can serve to help us define our values and thus can define the purpose and the "acceptable expression" of intimacy, sexuality, and loss. Religions will always play a significant role in our cultures and our lives.

CHAPTER 10

Living, Loving, and Losing: A Spiritual Reflection Through the Eyes of a Rabbi

Daniel A. Roberts

"I know, I know," I remarked to the members of my class on Judaism and sexuality while pacing back and forth, a microphone in my hand. "I know you *think* you know about the creation of man and woman, that it took place in the Garden of Eden. You've heard the story of Adam and Eve over and over again. But you're taking the story too literally and have never read the accompanying commentaries. The blustering words of William Jennings Bryan in the play *Inherit the Wind* or the literalist preachers make you think that the myth is a factual account of the origin of man and woman, their disobedience of God, and their eventual expulsion from the Garden of Eden. However," I postulated, wandering from one side of the room to the other, "there is an underlying message hidden in the narrative that relates to Judaism, intimacy, and loss."

"If this were just a simple historical account of how humans were created, then why are there conflicting creation stories? In Bereshit (Genesis) 1:27, we find: 'And God created man in His image, in the image of God He created him; male and female He created them' (Lieber, Harlow, United Synagogue of Conservative Judaism, & Rabbinical Assembly, 2001). How did we come to think that Eve was created out of Adam's rib? Why does it suggest that they were created *together* at one time?" I left the question lingering in the air as I walked to the whiteboard and scribbled the words *endogenous* and *Lilith*.

I turned around and commented, "As a modern, liberal rabbi who is open to various interpretations, I suggest that there were two different creation myths that were edited into the first two chapters of Genesis. One version leads some commentators to advocate that the first humans were endogenous,[1] created back-to-back or side-to-side. In a Jewish folk tale, it is suggested that Adam had a first wife, Lilith, who was created from the same earth as he. According to the legend, she was haughty and refused to become subservient to him. She left him and would not return to the Garden of Eden. Later she mated with the archangel Samael (*Encylopedia Judaica*, 1972, p. 719). The resulting Lilith saga is still commonly used as source material in modern Western culture, literature, occultism, fantasy, and horror, and Lilith is presently the name of a women's magazine. What I love about this version is that all men and women are created in the image of God, thus making all human beings equal. No one can say, 'I am better than you.'"

Still pacing, I continued, "Now, no matter what the answer is regarding this first allegory, you then have another, more powerful and memorable tale in Chapter 2. You know it well. Adam is feeling lonely, and God understands this and thus fashions from his rib a helpmate. Upon her creation Adam states, 'This one at last/ Is bone of my bones/ And flesh of my flesh/ This one shall be called Woman/ For from man was she taken' (Genesis 2:23). Adam gives her the name *Chava*, which is Hebrew for 'life.' But you probably have missed the most important verse in this account, which ends with these words: 'Hence a man leaves his father and mother and clings to his wife, so that they become one flesh' (Genesis 2:23–24).

"Here is my point!" I exclaimed, waving my finger rapidly in the air. "This tale is a *myth* designed not to teach us the history of the creation of man and woman but, rather, to elucidate a new, needed approach to sexuality and intimacy."

THE NEW APPROACH

I stopped pacing and hypothesized the following theory to the class: "Prior to the second biblical account, one can imagine that sexuality was an imitation of the animal world. When a man saw a woman who was attractive and desirable, he simply grabbed her and engaged in sex."

"That sounds good to me!" mumbled one of the male students.

I continued without acknowledging him, "He probably assumed the same position and manner that an animal would assume. Since, for the most part, monogamy is not common in the animal world, we can assume that humans were

[1] According to the commentary, "The Midrash (Gen. R. 8:1) alludes to a legend, also found in Plato's *Symposium* and in other ancient traditions, that the first human being was actually a pair of twins attached to each other, one male and one female. God divided them and commanded them to reunite, to find the other person who will make each of them complete again, in order to reproduce and attain wholeness. . . . This would imply that Eve was not fashioned out of Adam's rib as an afterthought but was created at the same time as Adam, as half of the first human creature" (Lieber et al., 2001, p. 10).

not monogamous either. With no moral code to prohibit a person from acting in such an animalistic manner, there would be no need to establish a committed relationship. Since sex was just a response to an inner drive, there would not be any concern as to the woman's enjoyment."

Then I shared a quote from Dennis Prager:

> Human sexuality, especially male sexuality, is polymorphous or utterly wild (far more so than animal sexuality). Men have had sex with women and with men; with little girls and young boys; with a single partner and in large groups; with total strangers and immediate family members; and with a variety of domesticated animals. . . . There is little, animate or inanimate, that has not excited some men to orgasm. Of course, not all of these practices have been condoned by societies—parent-child incest and seducing another's man's wife have rarely been countenanced—but many have, and all illustrate what the un-channeled, or in Freudian terms, the "un-sublimated," sex drive can lead to. (Prager, 1993, p. 1)

"This is the animal world," I concluded. I gestured to a picture of dogs copulating that I had placed on the whiteboard. "It is purely a physical experience. This is vividly illustrated in the observation of Julian Huxley, the eminent British biologist:

> Many birds will attempt to mate with a stuffed dead female as readily as with a real live one . . . provided that it is set up in a certain pose; and the sperm for artificial insemination in cattle and horses can be obtained because the mating urge of bulls and stallions is aroused by suitable dummies as well as by live cows or mares. (Gittelsohn, 1969, p. 120)

"Certainly, for some men, intercourse means little more than ejaculation and a warm body part in which to deposit their semen. It is the one-night stand or a visit to a prostitute.

"Why do you think," I proposed, "that there are laws against bestiality in the Torah? One must assume that people were engaged in such sexual exploits. If they were not, then there would be no need for such a law. So the concept of becoming *one flesh* moved humans from imitating the animal world into the world of humanity, civility, compassion, and respect.

"So," I continued, pointing to a student, "what makes human beings superior to animals when it comes to sex? After all, both engage in the sexual act for the purpose of procreation and the continuance of life. What is the difference between the two?"

"Love," said one student.

"Communication and commitment," said another.

"Exactly!" I remarked. "You know as well as I do that for human beings there is more to the sexual experience than procreation. There is recreational sex for pure pleasure." I heard a nervous laugh from the members of the class and a "yeah" from somewhere near the back. "There is sex that expresses love and compassion for the other and a sense of fulfillment for both," I continued. "With this latter relationship comes a spiritual aspect, a feeling akin to holiness. It encompasses a sense of a caring, a sense of concern for the other's enjoyment, and an emotional commitment. It is the ultimate giving of oneself to another that brings one closer to holiness.

"People have a basic need for stability and order. A world that is chaotic is impossible for a person to live in. The one thing that a human being cannot grasp is chaos. We have evolved into a disciplined world out of need. We eat at regular hours, go to sleep at a set time, and easily settle into a new routine when dropped into a new setting. Thus, for this need of stability to be fulfilled, sexuality had to be bridled as well. Actually, bridled sexuality made the creation of Western civilization possible. In societies where there were no boundaries, development was stymied. Prager (1993) proclaims that women, one of society's most important assets, were relegated to the periphery for they became only an instrument for sexuality. With sexuality forced into the marital bottle, human beings could fulfill their greater need for constancy. In ancient Israel, monogamy became the standard as people began to reserve sexuality and their deepest emotional experience for their mates and for them alone. Adultery became a 'sin,' for it is a breaking of trust, a loss of stability, and an undermining of the family unit. Rabbi Roland Gittelsohn gives us an insight into the difference between the animal world and the human one:

> With us, if we wish, intercourse can be an expression not only of physical desire, but of emotional tenderness, yearning, compassion, and love. It can leave husband and wife not merely satisfied and spent physically, but more closely bound to one another in their pursuit of the true, the beautiful, and the good. (1969, p. 121)

Gittelsohn continues:

> [The] foregoing distinctions mark human sex life as superior to that of animals. There is one respect, however, in which it can be more degrading and depraved. We seem to be the only species in which it is possible for the male to overpower the female, forcing himself upon her sexually against her will. In short, only among human beings do we find the contemptible practice of rape. Our sex life can be either incomparably more glorified or unconscionably more debased than that of any other creature on earth. The choice is our own to make. (1969, pp. 121–122)

"So the difference between the two worlds," I remark, "is in the choices you make. You can allow your own needs to rule your sexual responses and engage in nonemotional sex to the detriment of your partner. You can engage in the mutual consent of a hookup or one-night stand where both use the other for a few minutes of lustful satisfaction. Or you can choose the emotional and physical elevation of love and devotion to be your driving force.

"I hope you understand that the stories of creation in the Bible are more than the history of how human beings were made. They are stories of humans being lifted above the animal world with regard to sexuality and intimacy. The Torah elevates the sexual experience. Sexuality was now considered 'holy,' 'spiritual,' and 'special.' I love the mystical story[2] that God takes a soul at birth, splits it in half, and places one half in a male and one half in a female. They then spend their early days looking for their other half. Upon finding their *soul mate*, the two halves reunite in the sexual act, becoming whole once again. Look at the sexual apparatuses of the two and you see how nicely they fit together. The sexual act was to be an intimate relationship in which two humans care about each other and *become one flesh*—reunited.

"We are taught that we are to struggle against our sexual impulses and make sex truly unique. As indicated before, what might once have been considered an act of bestiality acquires a sense of holiness. The male impulse to bed any woman must now be restrained and controlled. Most societies developed ceremonies that made public a man and woman's intent to be a sexually involved family unit with the purpose of procreation.

"I find it interesting," I remark, "that in the Bible it is only the male who is commanded to take *leave* of his mother and father and cleave unto his wife (Lieber et al., Genesis 2:24). Leave-taking is a loss: a loss of security and a loss of closeness with parents."

"Why is only the *man* commanded to undergo this change of relationship and not the woman?" asked a male student.

"I suspect," I responded, "that one reason is the polymorphous sexuality previously mentioned. The primitive man did not freely commit to monogamy. However, the Torah's prohibition of nonmarital sex led to a revolution that demanded men control their libido and commit to only one woman. Virtually all of society changed through this directive.

"Another reason might be that in ancient societies a woman joined her husband's world and was subjected to the whims of the male and his family. If divorce happened, she would be forced to leave with her few possessions. If he should die in a hunting accident or in war, his family could dismiss her and she would have to seek refuge in another place with no inheritance. To quote Eskenazi: 'Perhaps it is because of the capriciousness of the male's family that this law is commanded. Now she is free of the control of his family' (Eskanazi, 2008, p. 13).

[2] Referenced above, page 184. See also Aristophanes' speech in Plato's "Symposium." A significant difference between Plato and Judaism is that Plato countenances same-sex unions. But the "soul mate" pursuit of reunification is similar: "And the reason is that human nature was originally one and we were a whole, and the desire and pursuit of the whole is called love" (Plato, 1956 version, pp. 353–357).

"A third reason, I would postulate, is that I believe women by nature find commitment easier. Women, not to raise feminists' ire, generally have a greater need for security and safety than men do. Females, far more than men, enjoy being held and cuddled. Men, on the other hand, are more focused on the completion of the sex act. Also, women are generally far more loyal to their men than men are to their women. For the most part, women have far fewer sexual encounters than their male peers. A woman gives her body to a man with whom she believes she will have a committed relationship, even if she deludes herself into believing this.

"Of course, I admit that these are only stereotypes. Not everyone fits this example, but this is what leading thinkers propose. To wit, the following:

> Men want sex, and women want relationships. Men want flesh and women want love. Just as boys want toy soldiers, cars, and carburetors, girls like to play house, share feelings with their girlfriends and dream of their weddings. The female mind is organized to place priority on relationship, the male on achievement. Men keep a tally of their sexual conquests. The female brain is not organized to keep sex in a separate compartment. This is a male model—as if his brain has a specific filing cabinet for sex, completely unrelated to emotion. (Moir & Jessel, 1992, p. 107)

"I find it fascinating," I remarked to the class, "that the Hebrew language uses different words to express the more intimate relationship between a man and his wife and those relationships that are illicit in nature. When the Torah speaks of sexual relations, as it does with Adam and Eve, it uses the Hebrew term *yadah*—'to know.' This term suggests a deep intimacy and love between the two partners. However, when it speaks of sexual relations that are conducted outside of that bond, other terms are used, like *yavo*—'to come,' which tends to be used in cases of prostitution, such as Judah and Tamar. When a man takes a concubine, as in the story of Abram and Hagar, the term *shachav*—'to lie with'—is used. *Shachav* is also used in cases of idolatrous practice, such as occurred with ancient fertility rites, improper relations between relatives (as in the story of Lot and his daughters in Leviticus 18 and 20), and cases of rape (such as the rape of Dina in Genesis 34) (Plotkin, n.d.).

The Torah and later the rabbis do not shrink from mentioning sexual relationships; rather, they recognize sexual needs as a reality of life and one of its driving forces. The fact that a sexually explicit book, *Shir Ha-Shirim* (The Song of Songs), was included in the final canonization of the Jewish Bible is revealing! This testifies to the naturalness of sexuality and the absence of prudery in classic Judaism. As Rabbi Alan S. Green writes, 'And the fact that these verses were then used in worship makes them all the more striking' (1979, p. 38). Let me read you a little bit of Song of Songs and you will understand how spiritual the sexual relationship was to the early molders of Judaism (Song of Songs 1:1–2, 13; 5:1, 6:3; 5:10–11, 14–15; 7:2–4; 8:6):

The Song of Songs, which is Solomon's:

> Let him kiss me with the kisses of his mouth
> For your love is better than wine. . . .
> My beloved is unto me as a bag of myrrh
> That lies between my breasts. . . .
> I am come into my garden. . . .
> I am my beloved's and my beloved is mine. . . .
> My beloved is white and ruddy,
> His locks are curled.
> His body is as polished ivory,
> His legs are as pillars of marble. . . .
> How beautiful are your steps in sandals,
> O prince's daughter!
> The roundings of your thighs are like the links of a chain.
> Your navel is like a round goblet. . . .
> Your breasts are like two fauns, twins of a gazelle. . . .
> Set me as a seal upon your heart,
> For love is strong as death.
> Its flashes are flashes of fire,
> A very flame of the Lord. (*Writings: Kethubim*, 1982)

"What religious tradition demands," I say as I write the word *holy* on the whiteboard, "is to make the sexual act *holy*, special, not animalistic. Traditional sources recognize that companionship, love, and intimacy are the primary purposes of marriage, noting that woman was created in Genesis 2:18 because 'it is not good for man to be alone.' *Man* here is used in the generic sense, indicating that each sex needs the other. The partner is needed not just for procreation, as in the animal world, but for companionship too. The human relationship goes beyond the simple command of being fruitful and multiplying. It is a relationship that brings comfort as well. In Genesis 24:67 when Isaac brings his wife, Rebecca, to his mother's tent, he *finds comfort after his mother's death*.

"Therefore," I repeat, "the purpose of the creation myth is not to tell about the history of mankind but to change the human sexual encounter into one that led into a new world of *civility*. In a commentary entitled *The Love of Midnight*, Sarah Zadok (n.d.) makes a beautiful observation: 'A mere physical act can produce a child, but an intimate connection performed with intention and passion can create a soul.' I think you can see that for the human being there is to be a spiritual side to intimacy."

HOLY IDEAS

"Rabbi, you talked about sex as holy," said a student. "I have always heard that sex is considered wicked in some way. Wouldn't celibacy be a holier state in some cases?"

I would guess that some of you are still seeking your destined one. I truly hope you find your soul mate."

"Yeah, but what if my soul mate just happens to be a woman too?" asked a female student. "What about committed gay relationships? After all, they are now legal in some states."

"If this is a typical class, I am sure that some of you are in a relationship with a member of the same sex. Of course, some of what I said applies to you if you are in a monogamous, committed relationship. However, I believe the married relationship to be of the highest ethical relationship because these two people are *publicly* committing themselves to each other. They pledge both legally and morally to care for the other from this day forth until either death or divorce changes the situation. When there is a wedding, it is expected that the couple is sleeping together. Unspoken though understood in the wedding ceremony is the promise of sexual exclusivity. A wedding tells the rest of the world that one person is sexually bonded to another and others should stay away. This is one significance of the wedding ring.

"As an aside, although same-sex marriages are becoming legal, there is no requirement that clergy must perform such a ceremony. All clergy may operate according to their own beliefs as to whether or not this is proper in the eyes of God. No one can mandate or require clergy to go against their conscience, and although it may be difficult, we must honor their beliefs as well. Thus, you will find that most religions, including Judaism, still do not sanction same-sex marriages. Definitely, no Orthodox rabbi would perform a same-sex marriage based on the rules of Leviticus 18:22. Likewise, I doubt very much that a Conservative rabbi would participate; however, I believe there are a few who will do a commitment service. On the other hand, in the Reform and Reconstructionist movements there are many who would perform these marriages, based on the needs of individuals and their dream of a lifelong commitment. Just know that this is not universal among rabbis and that there are still many liberal rabbis who do not perform such marriages because of their belief that it is contrary to Jewish thought and ideology and to what is best for society as a whole.

"Now, let's get back to our previous discussion about commitment and contrast this with the sleeping arrangement of a young couple who is dating. It is often done in secret with the unwritten pledge not to tell anyone. Yes, I am aware that many couples publicly acknowledge that they are living together, but since there is no public, legal, and, above all, *sanctified* commitment, the reality is that this is only an experimental relationship. Both parties are reserving the right to reject the other, to walk out without any legal consequences or spiritual necessity to try and rectify the dissolution. Should this relationship break up, the couple would be left with just the emotional adjustment of loss and the fact that they will be beginning all over again in the dating world. There are no legal consequences, no necessity to try and work things out and rectify the relationship.

So let me summarize this part of the lecture with the words of Rabbi Berel Wein (2002):

> Sexual intimacy is viewed in Judaism as an act that is to be sanctified. Just as Jews sanctify the act of eating food through the recitation of blessings before eating and of grace after eating, so too, the physical aspect of sexual intimacy requires a sacred dimension to it as well. Therefore, promiscuity, adultery, womanizing, prostitution, and all other forms of wanton sexual behavior are judged to be inherently wrong, improper and forbidden in Jewish tradition and life. The victimization of anyone, man, woman or child, in pursuing sexual pleasure or behavior is expressly forbidden in Judaism and is considered a heinous and particularly offensive transgression of Torah norms and values. Sexual relations are not only to be consensual, and even then only within the framework of marriage, but they are to be tinged with holiness and a sense of true personal bonding and the creation of a lasting mutually satisfying relationship as well.

"So mysterious is this sense of intimacy that the rabbis of the Talmud wrote that the challenge of God finding soul mates for people was as difficult as it was for God to split the Red Sea. While we do not know what attracts people to one another, the special holiness of a truly intimate relationship is a gift to behold and, perhaps, in reality, a gift from God."

RECONCILING LOST INTIMACY

A young woman asked, "Rabbi, what happens when this holy experience subsides either through a death, a divorce, or even the possibility that they no longer desire each other?"

"What a wonderful question! That is just where I was going with this lecture, for we need to talk about loss," I replied. "Loss of any intimate relationship demands some ritual to assist in adjusting to the loss and finding a balance so as to continue life. The price we pay for the blessing of having experienced a holy relationship is *mourning*. Thomas Attig writes, 'The central challenge as we grieve is moving from a life where we loved them in presence to a new life where we love them in absence. Nothing is more difficult. Nothing is more important. Nothing is more rewarding' (1996, p. 46).

"If one's significant other dies, religious rituals help guide the mourner through this chaotic time. They aid in allowing one to reconcile the death and to discover a new life in which the beloved still touches the survivor's soul. For instance, in the Jewish tradition we begin with a 7-day period (*shiva*) following the funeral, during which one is to explore the emotional catalog of regret, relief, guilt, anger, shame, self-pity, remorse, and so on. This is then followed by a 30-day period (*shloshim*) in which the mourner withdraws from all social events and begins the process of balancing the old life with the new one. Over time, the mourners slowly move from withdrawal to resocialization.

The formal mourning period concludes at the end of 30 days from the date of the death for spouses, at which time a male may marry again; a woman has to wait for three Jewish holidays."

"That's not fair!" interjected a woman. "Why are men given this privilege and women have to wait?"

"Inheritance," I responded. "In this case it's simply a matter of bloodlines. Should the woman be pregnant at the time and remarried immediately, one would not necessarily know whose child it was."

"But I believe that for the loss of a holy relationship one needs to take time to mourn and reorient oneself to a world without the intimacy known before. Life is chaotic until new order and meaning can be made of one's life alone. This takes far longer than a month, more like a year, at least. Judaism takes this into account. The ancient rabbis indicated that the mourner should say the *Kaddish* memorial prayer in a gathering of 10 adult men daily (for liberal rabbis, it would be 10 people) for 11 months. Technically, this is only recited after the loss of a parent, but I encourage it for everyone. Every day for nearly a year, you're thinking of your loss. But you are also not isolated because you are enjoined to participate with your community.

"Beyond prayer, the critical part of reconciliation will be memorialization—how one keeps alive the memory of holy moments. Memorialization can take place in a formal way, such as by returning to a sacred space, like the synagogue, several times a year when festivals are observed and the absence of a loved one is felt the most; by holding a service dedicating the grave marker; or by establishing a charitable fund in memory of the person. It can even take place by planting a tree in memory of the loved one. More informally, creating a scrapbook with pictures and mementos and telling stories about the deceased keep memories alive.

"Intimacy is a gift from God. It is beautiful when we have it, but the price of the gift is the painful journey of grief when it ends. Eventually, intimacy will be followed by the beauty of memory, of keeping our loved one 'present' even in the midst of anguish. Perhaps the single most-used word in the Torah is the word *zachor*—'remember.' It is used to describe our memory of going out of Egypt. It reminds us to observe Shabbat. It bids us to remember what our enemies did to us, and it is used as part of the command to keep alive the memory of those we love. We learn from this simple commandment to remember that mourning is never complete and literally goes on until one's own death. Finding ways to memorialize our deceased is a cathartic way of dealing with death. Some scars are bigger than others, but our loved one will remain tattooed on our soul forever. One does not get over a loss like one gets over an illness. One simply learns to maneuver around the loss every day until one bumps into it again at some sacred moment of memory.

"But you have asked an important question!" I pointed to the woman who had made the inquiry. "With the loss of intimacy through death, there are formal rituals, but what about its loss through divorce or aging—or illness, such as Alzheimer's, when 'remembering' is impaired? Here grief becomes complicated, for no one formally acknowledges the pain and suffering that the divorcee must go through. We call it 'disenfranchised grief.' Following Ken Doka's definition, disenfranchised grief is 'grief that is experienced when a loss cannot be openly acknowledged, socially sanctioned, or publicly mourned' (1989, p. 4). Doka also says, 'In short, while a person experiences a loss, the person does not have a "right" to grieve that loss since no one else recognizes a legitimate cause of grief' (2002, p. 160). Unfortunately, in divorce or aging, people usually suffer alone, often putting on a smile to mask their pain. In Judaism, the ritual of a man giving a *get*, a Jewish divorce decree, in a religious ceremony is a legitimate way to put a final punctuation mark on the intimate relationship. There are also innovative divorce ceremonies created for the woman to invite her friends to gather around her and envelop her with the love of community. The male, on the other hand, seems to have to go through this alone—or commiserate with his buddies over a few beers!

"The emotional separation that can take place as a result of aging presents another problem. Here people have choices. One or both can give into the aging process and drift away both physically and emotionally from their respective soul mate. They can consult with a doctor and elect to use one of the many enhancement drugs, like Viagra. They could plan a regularly scheduled time for intimacy. They could decide to take more time with one another during the arousal moments, using lubricants that will make the lovemaking more enjoyable and less painful. Even the elderly need to be open and discuss their sexual needs, which continue almost to the day they die. Like anyone else, an aging couple must find what works best to keep alive intimate affection and let each other know that they are appreciated and honored. For instance, they could buy each other cards or flowers, send notes in gym bags, or plan romantic nights out. They must continue to find the godliness in the other, and this must be intentional as well."

STARTING OVER AFTER THE LOSS OF INTIMACY IS DIFFICULT

I heard a male voice. "How do you know when to start looking again after death or divorce? Some people seem to cling to the past; others just rush into a new relationship."

"It's an individual choice, but I would recommend waiting at least a year," I replied. "How many times have you heard someone saying to a widow or widower—or someone who's been through a breakup or divorce—just a few months (or even weeks) after their loss, 'Are you doing better? Have you gotten over your mourning? Are you ready to date again? I have someone wonderful to fix you up with. Can I give you her number?' For widowers, a 'casserole brigade' suddenly appears at their doors, women who call and offer to bring dinner or just show up, food in hand. The widower, unlike in his single days, suddenly discovers that women can be the aggressors too. The widow too is suddenly confronted with feelings of fear. If asked out on a date, she wonders what dress to wear and how sexy it should be. If he asks for a kiss or tries to fondle her, what will she do? Both the widower and the widow must decide when they will remove their wedding ring and be prepared to date, both difficult decisions.

"I'll illustrate with the story of one of my congregants with whom I became very close after his young wife died unexpectedly. Our closeness grew as I counseled him about normal grief and what he could expect regarding mourning during the next couple of years. In turn, he shared his feelings that although some months had passed since his wife's death and though he could presumably begin to date, he had no interest in moving on so quickly. His deceased wife had been his high school sweetheart. They had grown up together emotionally, intimately, and physically. She was his first and only love. He spoke of his sense of loyalty to her and felt he would be breaking his marriage vows by moving on too quickly. He believed that he could never love another person in the same way. I told him he was right, for first loves are always that way. You never forget that first love; it is always very special.

"My congregant spoke of his anxiety of getting involved with another woman and possibly having to face another loss or death as well. He feared getting involved with someone and then either being rejected or causing her pain by telling her good-bye. He felt that he was not ready to go though that pain again. I told him that this is the risk we all take when falling in love, whether the first time or any other time. Since he was financially comfortable, gnawing at his psyche were the questions: Could these women, who were so open to romance, really love him for who he was as a person, or would they just love the lifestyle he could provide? Would they be in love with him, or were they *in love with love* and just wanted someone, anyone, to be a companion? His intimacy adventure was fraught with all these questions and qualms, let alone how he would balance a new love with his memories of his former one.

"Added to this, the young widower was dealing with his children's feelings. He understood that even though his children did not want the burden of taking care of him as he aged, and in some sense they did not want him to be alone forever, they also felt that he should remain loyal to their mother and never have another intimate relationship. Because of these conflicted feelings, he would find ways to undermine his dates. His thoughts got in the way of letting himself experience other spiritual moments. Fortunately, with time, he was able to overcome these emotional and cerebral processes, and eventually he remarried. In this new relationship he found and bonded with another aspect of his soul, for there can be several soul mates in one's life and new feelings of God's presence.

"Finding love after loss is a voyage filled with insecurities and much questioning of decisions, but the beauty of the human soul is the capacity to love and love again. Finding another soul mate can be a beautiful world of security and love and a sense of God's presence."

THE PRICE OF INTIMACY

"Let me extrapolate from what we have learned about intimate relationships," I remarked. "In every intimate relationship there will be loss, grieving that must take place, and adjustments to be made. Intimate relationships will all end at some time, through death, relocation, or through natural attrition. Mates will die or possibly divorce. No matter the reason for the separation, loss demands a period of sadness and readjustment. Friends will move, change jobs, or find other friends and desert you, or they may die before you. A change in life status like retirement causes the retiree to lament the loss of the income, routine, and meaning provided by work. For some losses there is a formal ritual that allows others to recognize that a person is mourning and experiencing grief. As already mentioned, some losses will be disenfranchised—losses that do not have accompanying established rituals—such as retirement, divorce, and children or a best friend moving to another city.

"I reiterate, the penalty we pay for being involved in an intimate relationship is the pain of grief. Through the journey of grief we move from closeness with one human being to a new relationship with that person, who no longer exists physically yet remains in our memories and continues to influence us."

CONCLUSION

"Let's return to our Garden of Eden story. There are many lessons to be learned from it. We learned more about bridled sexuality than about how human beings were created. Nobel Laureate Elie Wiesel (Downing, 2008) derives another lesson from it. He points out that although Adam and Eve were expelled from paradise, they did not give in to resignation. In the face of their new mortality, they decided to fight by giving new life and by conferring meaning to life, however finite they were. Even though they now knew that they and their children would die, they decided to still have children. To them, and to all of us, one moment of life, and each moment, contains eternity. One moment of intimacy where two lovers discover the other half of their soul may indeed be a sense of heaven and earth touching. In my mind, when God created humans, God gave them a secret—not how to begin but how to love another person completely and then, when death occurs, how to begin *again*. We do this every time we choose to defy death and find a way to go on with living (Scolnic, 1992, pp. 32–33).

"Wiesel summarizes this whole lecture best: 'Every one of us yearns to recapture some lost paradise; every one of us bears the mark of some violated stolen innocence. To turn away from death and begin again is a lesson I wish many of my contemporaries could hear'" (as cited in Downing, 2008, p. 195).

Suddenly, the bell rang, and before I could finish my sentence, the students had packed up their belongings and filed out of the room without comment. I was left to wonder how much of what we discussed will serve them spiritually as they go on in life.

REFERENCES

Attig, T. (1996). *How we grieve: Relearning the world.* New York, NY: Oxford University Press.

Doka, K. J. (1989). *Disenfranchised grief: Recognizing hidden sorrow.* Lexington, MA: Lexington Press.

Doka, K. J. (Ed.). (2002). *Living with grief: Loss in later life.* Washington, DC: Hospice Foundation.

Downing, F. L. (2008). *Elie Wiesel: A religious biography.* Macon, GA: Mercer University Press.

Encyclopedia Judaica (Vol. 14). (1972). Jerusalem, Israel: Keter Publishing House.

Eskenazi, T. C., & Weiss, A. L. (Ed.). (2008). *The Torah: A women's commentary.* New York, NY: URJ Press.

Gittelsohn, R. B. (1969). *My beloved is mine: Judaism and marriage.* New York, NY: Union of American Hebrew Congregations.

Green, A. S. (1979). *Sex, God, and the Sabbath: The mystery of Jewish marriage.* Cleveland, OH: Temple Emanu El.

Guggenheim, H. (2005). *The Jerusalem Talmud.* Berlin, Germany: Walter de Gruyter.

Lieber, D. L., Harlow, J., United Synagogue of Conservative Judaism, & Rabbinical Assembly. (2001). *Etz Hayim: Torah and commentary.* Philadelphia, PA: Jewish Publication Society.

Liebman, J. L. (1966). *Hope for man: An optimistic philosophy and guide to self-fulfillment.* New York, NY: Simon & Schuster.

Lim, I. C. (1997, October). *Is monogamy of God?* Retrieved from http://www.patriarchy website.com/monogamy/mono-history.htm

Moir, A., & Jessel, D. (1992). *Brain sex: The real difference between men and women.* New York, NY: Dell.

Plato. (1956 version). Symposium. In B. Jowett (Trans.) & I. Edman (Ed.), *The works of Plato* (pp. 353–357). New York, NY: Random House.

Plotkin, D. (n.d.). *UAHC Commentary.* Retrieved from http://urg.org/learning/torah

Prager, D. (1993, September). Judaism's sexual revolution: Why Judaism (and then Christianity) rejected homosexuality. *Crisis, 11*(8). Retrieved from http://www. orthodoxytoday.org/articles2/PragerHomosexuality.php

Scolnic, B. E. (2008). Midrash, PC, and Eve. In F. L. Downing (Ed.), *Elie Wiesel: A religious biography* (p. 195). Macon, GA: Mercer University Press.

Steinsaltz, A. (1998). *The Talmud: The Steinsaltz edition.* New York, NY: Random House.

The writings: Kethubim. (1982). Philadelphia, PA: Jewish Publication Society of America.

Wein, B. (2002, November 25). *Judaism: Intimacy.* Retrieved from http://www.israel nationalnews.com/Articles/Article.aspx/1610

Zadok, S. (n.d.). *The love of midnight.* Retrieved from http://www.chabad.org/theJewish Woman/article_cdo/aid/387256/jewish/The-Love-of-Midnight.html

CHAPTER 11

Engaging the Christian Voice in Defining (and Redefining) What Is Right

David Daubert and Robert D. Machamer

The need to love is foundational to human life. The call to love is given to all humankind. Those things that preclude it—whether that love is to be directed toward God or others—are life destroying. The Christian message is grounded in the message brought by Jesus: "I came that they may have life, and have it abundantly" (John 10:10, New Revised Standard Version).

Entrusted with this message, the Church has been charged with being a partner with God. To be sure, no single institution within Western society has had more impact on our shared understanding of the rules concerning intimacy and relationships than the Christian Church. The dominant position that the Church has held means that much of this impact goes well beyond influencing the attitudes and behaviors of Christians. The shape of culture has been influenced in such ways that people of all religious traditions and those with no religious tradition find either that their own attitudes are being shaped by the Church's position or that they respond or react to it as they live or work within other traditions.

While grief and loss are a part of many aspects of human life, they can be especially painful when they preclude the formation of new or deeper relationships. This is in part because we believe that grief and loss are best lived out in the context of deep and meaningful relationships with God and with others and therefore benefit from intimacy.

Intimacy and sexuality are intertwined. Deeply personal and yet intrinsically relational, these two subjects can be separated in many ways. Yet they are also often so closely connected as to be difficult to distinguish one from the other, for both involve connections between the self and others.

In contrast, grief and loss involve the giving up of connections—and the more meaningful the connection, the deeper the sense of loss. Often these connections involve intimacy and sexuality, such as in the death of a spouse, the divorce of a married couple, or the hiddenness of a gay or lesbian person secretly loving someone of the same gender and being unable to pursue it due to societal taboos. In each of these cases, and in many others, people are bound by various socio-cultural and emotional factors. Often they feel prevented from pursuing intimate relationships with partners with whom sexuality would be a natural part of the relationship. Many experience religions as enforcers of rules rather than encouragers of love.

The shared religious roots of many Western practices lie primarily in the traditional teachings of the Roman Catholic Church, which form a major part of the foundation for most Western Christian moral thought—even for many of those traditions that have in some way rejected or reformed the content they inherited. As a result, Roman Catholic teaching is still important (even when the Catholic link is overlooked) within many Protestant churches, either as the foundation a particular church's teaching or as the foil around which the church restates its own ethical message.

As pluralism has increased in Western societies, the Church has found increasing diversity in its teaching about marriage and sometimes has had radically divergent views. But the central teaching of almost all Christian groups is grounded in thinking that almost automatically leads to the conclusion that sexual intimacy is reserved for heterosexual people who are married. The inability to marry or remarry due to certain prohibitions or the loss of marriage—either through death or divorce—can provide serious barriers to the freedom to relate to another person on both an intimate and a sexual level. Ironically, although the Church in some way represents Jesus as an advocate of love of others, often its message or methods have been received as life-diminishing rather than as helping people live life abundantly.

INTIMACY AND SEXUALITY—SOME THEOLOGICAL ASSUMPTIONS

The theological connection between sexuality and intimacy is an important one. All people are sexual beings in some way. The ability to find others with whom to live this out is an important dimension of human existence—one that is expressed or suppressed in a variety of ways. Sexuality, while needing to find expression, is intrinsic to being human.

People are created for intimacy. The Christian understanding of intimacy is grounded in the doctrine of the Trinity—the belief that relationships and community are intrinsic to the eternal nature of God. Intimacy is also understood to be grounded in Creation, in the biblical declaration that "God created humankind in his image, in the image of God he created them; male and female he created them" (Genesis 1:27, NRSV).

While an implicit need in all people, intimacy may or may not be realized in practice. Intimacy happens in relationships where trust is built and the freedom to be one's self while being fully present to the other exists. Intimacy allows people to be who they are for each other. Sexuality, while it benefits from trust, is completely possible with no real relationship at all. Intimacy is not.

Roland D. Martinson shared a helpful view showing the connection between healthy intimacy and healthy sexuality:

> Good sexuality is nurtured through intimacy and channeled through boundaries. When sexuality becomes bad and wrong, it is through clearer boundaries and healthy intimacy that sin must be curbed and its wounds healed. Even as sexuality creates intimacy, it requires intimacy for its own formation and integration; even as sexuality produces boundaries, it requires boundaries for its own formation and integration. There are those who would have intimacy in sexuality without boundaries; there are others who would have boundaries without intimacy. However, there is finally no intimacy without boundaries; there are finally no boundaries without intimacy. Intimacy and boundaries in their delicate tensions, rhythms, and balances are constitutive of sexuality. (1990, p. 116)

How people find intimacy and express their sexuality varies. It is our contention that all people are granted the freedom to pursue intimate relationships with others, to covenant with these partners, and to participate in an intimate relationship with another that permits sexuality to be freely expressed between the partners. Grief caused by relational losses can be a barrier to people finding these relationships and experiencing the freedom to pursue them. The Church is a major influence in how people understand and deal with grief in their lives, how society views sexuality and intimacy, and what barriers or supports people encounter as they pursue intimacy and sexuality in the face of grief.

THE CHURCH AS GUIDE: RECLAIMING A LOST ROLE

How people experiencing grief and looking for intimacy and sexual expression can find helpful guidance from the Church confronts the increasing truth that many people no longer look to the Church for guidance but see it as archaic or irrelevant. The argument that follows takes into account a Church with dwindling participation and influence that is hanging on in the midst of a sea of change. However, there are many people for whom religious factors continue to play an important part in their worldview and decision-making. Our hope (and belief) is that the Church, or significant parts of it, can be seen as a valuable and helpful partner in the lives of many people as they deal with the realities of grief and seek to build new intimate relationships.

While the Church was historically a primary voice in helping people interpret grief and loss, since World War II the decline of the Church has left a void that has primarily been filled with input from psychology. This has led to a view of grief that is primarily clinical, linear, and based on scientific norms. But now new voices are challenging many of these assumptions.

A key need for people trying to live through loss and then restore intimacy to their lives is the availability of a support system that allows the process to unfold in organic and helpful ways. Historically, the Church has been one piece of that support for many people, but "our modern, atomized society [has] been stripped of religious faith and ritual and no longer provide[s] adequate support for the bereaved. And so a new belief system, rooted in the principles of psychotherapy rose up to help the experience" (Konigsberg, 2011, p. 5). Although Konigsberg's work has received significant skepticism and scrutiny, her contention that religion has been supplanted by psychology is accurate. The gap left by an increasingly irrelevant Church is notable and leaves the culture lacking the support and resources that it once had.

This is a call to the Church to become a more active and helpful voice in the lives of people who have lost important and intimate relationships in their lives. We believe that churches are the best-suited and best-poised places for the spiritual support and comforting companionship that people experiencing grief need. And the Church is the one voice that is in a prominent position to be able to publicly address the importance of forming new sexual and intimate relationships following loss (even though the Church's present voice is somewhat muted!).

New evidence shows that the research of Elisabeth Kübler-Ross and her "five stages of grief" still speaks to many, even as we move away from the terminology of "stages" and its implications. There is growing consensus that grief and loss produce a much more complex and nonlinear response in most people. Even Kübler-Ross herself, in her last book, stated:

> The stages of loss—denial, anger, bargaining, depression, and acceptance—have been widely used and misused. . . . Sometimes intervention is vital but most of the time we do not allow the normal depression that comes with grief to have its place. (Kübler-Ross & Kessler, 2005, p. 23)

Moreover, there is an increasing anecdotal awareness that these stages and the accompanying processes that arose to treat them have not always been helpful. One widower we met while writing this chapter was well read and insightful but said:

> I read all about the five stages of grief and how important each one of these is as an important part of healing. But I never have been angry about my wife's death. I have felt a lot of things—sad, surprised, and lonely. But I haven't been angry about it once—and I don't see that it is very likely that I am going to be angry about it.

In short, when we reduce grief to "stages" or other formulaic approaches, the unique ways in which each person grieves and makes new sense of his or her life after a loss is neither well understood nor affirmed. The result has been that in some cases intervening in grief has produced negative outcomes and that in some ways our culture has become less adept at living through the grief process as a result of pursuing "progress" along the way. Psychology has had a mixed impact on our collective grieving processes, often making grief into a mental health issue, whether it fits there or not.

Of concern is not just that the Church has become, and has been viewed as becoming, increasingly religiously irrelevant to the real lives of people. More important is that many no longer look to the Church for *moral* guidance, or for a sense of what is "proper." Instead, they look to psychology. This shift is not simply a choice of a new source of information (a sort of change in who is in office) but indicates a significant alteration in worldview.

Psychology defines the "proper" in terms of "health" and bases its judgments about what is "healthy" on what it deems to be "normal." Such reasoning often leads to conclusions like the above-mentioned "stages" and in other uses of language that is both inaccurate and leads people to worry about whether they are "sick" or "abnormal" just because they are different. In a word, the human *science* of psychology was never intended to provide moral guidance nor to provide ethical constructs. Ironically, the conflation of the healthy and the moral leads to its own form of contemporary ethical condemnation.

If the Church can resume a lead role in contemporary moral conversation and ground its participation in the grace-inspired voice of the gospel, it can provide an important and helpful response to the pathologizing and even pejorative terminology often used in psychology—the contemporary source of the "proper." This is the Church's chance to escape its own judgmental stance and to assume a new, gracious, and powerful voice for transformation of the culture. The Church, as an institution and/or people, can do this by advocating for broader freedom and more meaningful options for people who have experienced major losses and are now hoping to restore intimacy and be active sexually in the next chapters of their lives.

The data in the next section will show that the Church has much ground to make up—it is increasingly a minority in the culture. But we believe that the possibility still exists for a meaningful voice from at least some in the Church and that the importance of this work warrants giving significant effort to the task.

TRENDS: THE CHURCH AND SOCIETY

A significant factor influencing the Church's role in helping people navigate grief and loss in order to rebuild intimacy in their lives comes from a variety of societal trends—all of which are converging to form a consistent pressure on the Church and its message. The examples we offer are intended to be illustrative rather than exhaustive, but providing more would simply point us to the same conclusions.

We will very briefly look at three important and changing social realities that have produced a variety of responses by both society and the Church. The first example concerns heterosexual marriage. The second is the changing cultural views of same-sex relationships. And a third factor is secularization—U.S. census data from 2010 shows a radical shift happening in American culture.

Marriage practices have undergone significant changes over the last 50 years. Many researchers, however, have been surprised at how quickly certain trends have accelerated in the last decade and speculate what the long-term implications of these trends may be. These statistics have caught their attention:

> Between 2000 and 2009, the share of young adults ages 25 to 34 who are married dropped 10 percentage points, from 55 percent to 45 percent, according to ACS data. During the same period, the percentage who have never been married increased sharply, from 34 percent to 46 percent. In a dramatic reversal, the proportion of young adults in the United States who have never been married now exceeds those who are married. (Mather & Lavery, 2010)

In contrast, during the 1960s, marriage rates for those 24–35 years old were about 80%. Moreover, for the first time in U.S. history, the number of adults between 24 and 35 years of age who were married dropped below 50%; this occurred around 2005. That number has continued to drop steadily each year since then. This figure has been trending downward steadily for nearly 50 years.

If people were simply waiting to get married (and there are some), this would perhaps be less meaningful, but the following additional fact adds significance with regard to traditional Church teaching, practice, and influence on relationships:

> Many people who are classified as single are actually in cohabiting relationships with opposite- or same-sex partners. In fact, the sharp decline in marriage has been accompanied by a rapid increase in the number of cohabiting couples, as reported by the U.S. Census Bureau in September, 2010. Cohabitation has been on the rise for several decades, but the Census Bureau links the recent increase in cohabiting couples to rising unemployment rates and growing economic uncertainty, especially among young men. Given the scope of the recent recession, many more couples are likely to choose cohabitation over marriage in the coming years. (Mather & Lavery, 2010)

This indicates a significant shift in cultural values and a significant dissonance between the practices of many people and traditional Church teaching. The result for people pursuing intimate relationships is either tension between their practice in the Church—which results in some form of anxiety, shame, or guilt—or the need to dismiss the Church's voice as irrelevant and unhelpful.

Similarly, a variety of changes are occurring in the legal landscapes of state and city governments and in the corporate benefit practices of some companies, which increasingly permit family benefits to extend to same-sex couples. Gay marriage is legal in an increasing number of states, sometimes through ballot initiatives and sometimes through court decisions. Other states have approved civil unions with legal benefits and protections for same-sex couples in states where same-sex marriage has not been legalized. Frequently, backlash from these decisions leads to ballot initiatives in an attempt to create laws prohibiting gay marriage—and these are often supported by large segments of the Church while being opposed by other church groups.

This mixing of conflicting public messages adds at least three new factors that are not unique to the issue of gay marriage. First, people are often confused by differing messages coming from Christian authorities, and the loud public rancor often convinces LGBT people that the Church is hostile to their concerns, even though significant segments of the Church are not. Second, people both inside the Church and outside often find one message more acceptable than another and increasingly "pick and choose" which voice to listen to. And third, some people decide the Church is too divisive and conflicted to offer much to these discussions and thus write the Church's voice off as increasingly unhelpful or irrelevant. The result is that the Church has lost its uniform voice to the cacophony of a segregation-like model, wherein some denominations or congregations are "open and affirming" while others are decidedly not.

Both of these illustrations, changing mores regarding marriage vs. cohabitation and changing attitudes toward same-sex marriage, bring new challenges for the Church and its voice in public ethics with regard to legitimating intimacy and relationships. Confronted with a message that is increasingly at odds with public practice, the Church now needs to look again at the core of its teaching and decide what would be most helpful and faithful in this new day. Some in the Church will choose to stay the course and teach that these trends in society are simply sinful and wrong. Such a role will result in either (a) the entrenchment of the Church and its members around the traditional position and an experience of shame and guilt by those who value the Church's message at some level but are out of compliance with its teaching or (b) the rejection of the Church as archaic and no longer able to provide helpful moral guidance with regard to the formation of sexually intimate relationships. Alternatively, these changes are a chance for the Church to reshape its teaching, claim new roles in the lives of people and their relational values, and be more helpful in the years ahead.

Which path the Church takes remains to be seen, and with the diversity of Church voices in today's world, not all will take the same path. These realities do bring the Church to a crossroads. They provide an opportunity for the Church to examine and accept responsibility for its cultural role in the past, they also invite the Church to articulate an initial vision for possible paths it might take in the future.

An added factor for the Church is the reality that often the Church is finding itself speaking to a decreasing audience. Some estimates now place actual weekly church attendance at below 20% of all Americans. Attendance figures are significantly lower in Canada and even lower in Europe, and many see the trends in the United States simply following the same trajectory as these regions, which became secular earlier.

These dynamics lead to a dilemma for the Western Church. How can the Church again find a relevant, moral voice, speaking from the heart of the gospel to the hearts of those who live and love—and die—within its hearing? And how can it provide ethical guidance that is true to itself without pandering to the popular or simply trying to save itself from demise by attrition? To be a meaningful moral force, the Church must not betray itself but, rather, live up to the core of its teaching and mission.

THREE IMPORTANT EXAMPLES

Grief and loss relate to all aspects of human existence in some way. In reflecting specifically on the pursuit of intimacy and sexual partners in the wake of grief and loss, we have decided to focus our attention on three important situations that many people find themselves in. From there we want to explore how grief and loss have an impact upon our ability to enter into meaningful relationships where intimacy and sexuality can be freely and fully experienced. The three circumstances we discuss here are so broadly experienced that they can serve as examples for how all issues in intimacy and sexuality might be approached by the Church when grief and loss are present in significant ways.

These three examples are:

- those desiring to pursue new relationships following the death of a spouse;
- those desiring to pursue new relationships following a divorce; and
- those desiring to enter into meaningful relationships with same-sex partners.

Relationships After a Spouse's Death

First, we will explore the circumstances around people rekindling intimacy in their lives after a marriage ends due to the death of a spouse. In this case, the Church's teaching has generally affirmed the surviving person as being whole in some way. Their aloneness is understood to be through no fault of their own and no-fault-aloneness seems to somehow make their aloneness more acceptable. Concerning the ending of a marriage by death, the Church's teaching is more consistent and less confused than in the other areas we will explore. McMinn says:

> Death is an acceptable loss. Some losses, like those experienced because of a homosexual orientation, are hidden because of shame or fear of rejection. Other losses we cannot hide, like divorce, and we bear the shame and hope

> that acceptance will come. One does not need to hide when one's spouse dies. No sin has been committed and giving comfort is uncomplicated. (2004, p. 85)

While McMinn is perhaps overly blunt and simplistic, his basic premise is helpful. While a surviving partner of someone who died may feel guilt and/or shame about having survived, generally he or she does not experience shaming by others. People do not need to defend their status to others and generally receive expressions of sympathy as a result of their loss.

When the surviving spouse is younger, the right and ability to pursue remarriage and to find a new relationship within which intimacy can take place is affirmed by the social systems quite apart from the Church. But the Church participates through the "until death do you part" clause in wedding vows; it makes this an up-front provision of the marriage covenant. Yet in practice, this too is complex. Entering into a new relationship may provide a chance to resume intimacy with another, but there is tremendous social and personal pressure attached. Guilt creeps in here as well, regardless of wedding vows. When surviving partners wonder whether they are being "unfaithful" in some way to their late spouse, the eyes they feel upon them are personal, familial—and religious.

Age, gender, and children combine in complicating relational choices for those in mourning. When children are in the mix, their feelings and opinions carry substantial moral weight. Regarding this dynamic for widowers, Moore and Stratton (2003) wrote, "Tensions with adult children involved both sons and daughters. . . . The most common situational tension arose when the father wanted to date, or started to date, or chose a new wife" (p. 182).

Many older adults have had a spouse die, found a new person to enter into an intimate relationship with, and heard from their children, "What would mom (or dad) think?" Dealing with this can give rise to emotional conflicts. These may be caused by the children's relational insecurity, concern about changes in estates or inheritance, desire not to have to lose control of the nature of the relationship with a parent by adding a new variable into the mix, or just plain discomfort picturing mom or dad sleeping in a bed with someone other than their own parent.

In these cases, the Church's theological teaching has actually provided an adequate base for healthy restoration and wholeness for the surviving spouse's pursuit of a new and intimate relationship. Clear boundaries about marriage and clear teaching that future relationships are legitimated are present in the teaching of nearly all groups within the Church. But the surrounding social pressures provide for a more complex social reality within which the Church finds itself hard-pressed to be truly helpful. Most pastors and priests are ill-equipped either to apply the Church's teaching or to provide pastoral care in a way that would serve as an ally to the person attempting to resume intimacy. Combine that with their own family systems issues, and many clergy find themselves uncomfortable providing a sense of authoritative guidance. The gospel that addresses life becomes subsumed under a desire to be liked. It can get lost completely in the codependence between the pastor and parishioners as each are trying to remain nice, even when such niceness may lead more to spirit-deadening than life-enriching.

How this often works in practice is that pastors may encourage the surviving spouse in one conversation yet may also nod in understanding and imply agreement with the children in another conversation. Everyone may feel supported by clergy—but in ways that produce confusion and escalate unhealthy conflict. Many ministers have not previously dealt in any depth with these intrafamilial dynamics in a public setting that would set the stage for later, private conversations. They may leave examples of such relational complexities out of their preaching and teaching. This means that even when the Church might make a healthy and clear contribution toward affirming the persons involved and encouraging freedom and healing, that voice has been weakened by the interpersonal realities within the Church itself.

Relationships After Divorce

A second circumstance for our attention is that of people whose relationships end through separation or divorce. Here, there is often the added dimension that one or both of the parties involved is somehow blamed. Unlike the death of a spouse, the "death of a marriage suggests a failure in a way that a physical death does not, adding another element of pain to the process of adjusting to the loss through divorce" (McMinn, 2004, p. 86). Faultfinding supports the conclusion that the parties involved have failed and are not only now incomplete (that is, lacking the partner required to make them whole in the way they were when they were married) but also now *culpable* for that fact. Culpability is often identified as sinfulness by the Church. Prohibitions from large segments of the Church against remarrying, for example in Roman Catholic teaching and in many strands of conservative evangelical teaching, add a sense of permanence to the feelings of failure and fault. These portions of the Church, in remaining static in their teaching, make themselves irrelevant to many people's contemporary situations. (As a side note, the standards are higher and the judgments heavier when the divorcing couple includes a minister.)

Take, for example, the story of Ben. Ben was divorced and then remarried. The evangelical church Ben attended before his remarriage forbid Ben from leading in any form—as a divorced person he was a permanent "sinner" and marked as beyond restoration to a position of usefulness. Although he had served on the congregation's board, after his divorce he was ruled ineligible to continue in church leadership. Since Ben's new wife had been Roman Catholic prior to their marriage, he could not worship in her church with her either; as divorced persons, without having their previous marriages annulled, they were excluded from the Eucharist. Barred from converting, Ben was functionally excommunicated even prior to attempting to enter the system. Neither of the religious traditions from which Ben and his new wife came permitted them any readily available, accepting, legitimate, and healthy option. The result was a sense of guilt and shame that imprisoned Ben. He and his new wife eventually left both of their traditions in search of a new place where they could continue to be healed from the events they had experienced. They wanted Church support in reframing their understanding of God and God's role in their life and decisions. They sought a religious understanding that they could healed and freed to pursue a relationship that permitted intimacy and wholeness for them as they continued their spiritual journey.

Situations like this raise a question for the Church: When people find themselves in broken and unhealthy relationships that are then terminated, how are they to be helped to restore intimacy in their lives? Or are people in such circumstances permanently forbidden from the possibility of a healthier intimate relationship, regardless of how long the remainder of their life may be?

Rosemary Radford Ruether makes the following case:

> Every covenanting relationship, particularly those envisioned as long-term, must deal with failure, with the possibility of brokenness, the outgrowing of a relationship, or the inability to shape the sort of deeper union to which one may aspire but which one nonetheless finds oneself unable to attain. This is the moment when those who are covenanted together to be partners often find themselves most abandoned by community, most isolated, and silenced. (2000, p. 217)

This isolation can become an issue in divorce in ways that are not the case when a partner is dealing with the death of a spouse. While most people who are part of a faith community are able to maintain relationships within that faith community when a spouse dies, the divorce of a couple can make this awkward. Divorce means separation from one another, and it may not be possible for both parties to attend the same congregation to which they belonged as a couple. "Custody campaigns" over which spouse "gets" the church can ensue. One or both parties may be more likely to disconnect from their faith community, even if (or because) it was an important part of their shared life together. Not only may the theological teachings of some Church traditions make healing difficult, the social systems within the Church may disintegrate, together with the marriage, for people going through divorce. The impact of individual church members going through death and divorce is not just a private affair. It tears at the very fabric of the shared communal identity of the Church.

The work of the Church must hold two truths in some form of integrated tension. Kysar and Kysar capture this well: "It is in part at least the old question of how the Church offers forgiveness without implying approval of the wrong that has been committed." "How does the Church fly with both wings—God's will for creation and his redemptive grace?" (Kysar & Kysar, 1978, p. 95).

Same-Sex Relationships

A final example of the moral dilemmas the contemporary Church faces can be found in how it regards same-sex relationships. Without a doubt, almost no aspect of the discussions about intimacy and sexuality produce more contention and emotions than those concerning same-sex relationships. Within the Church these discussions have produced significant conflict; this seems likely to continue in many traditions for some time to come. In the Evangelical Lutheran Church in America (ELCA), accepting same-sex relationships was voted on and approved following the passage of a social statement and a change in the policy concerning ordination of gay and lesbian people at the 2009 ELCA Churchwide Assembly. While this decision made space for affirming gay and lesbian people in their same-sex relationships, it also continued equally to allow and affirm a place for other leaders within the same denomination to oppose these and teach in opposition to them publicly—a compromise based on the admitted lack of uniformity regarding the teaching and practices of the Church regarding same-sex relationships. ELCA appealed to the deeply held convictions of people on both sides of this issue and the "bound conscience" of people holding these competing views. This has resulted in an ongoing public and theological conflict that has drawn the energy and attention of many within that tradition.

Underneath these tense theological and ecclesiastical debates are the lives of real people. For a variety of reasons gay and lesbian people come to grips with their sexual identity in many ways. Some become aware at relatively early ages and live their lives with a clear orientation. Others are aware early, but social and familial pressures push them to pursue heterosexual relationships in order to try to be "normal." Some of these relationships last despite the underlying sexual identity issues. Others dissolve as men and women come to grips with their identities and find the need and the courage to step out in new ways. In some cases, the above issues regarding divorce are present and further complicated by the realities of gay and lesbian relationships.

One example here will suffice. Janice and Tammy were both raised in heterosexual families and eventually married men. Both had children as a part of those marriages. Both struggled in different ways within their marriages for many years. As coworkers they became friends and discovered that there was something different in their relationship than they had ever experienced with men. Eventually both were divorced from their husbands, and Janice and Tammy moved in with each other.

Within the state in which they live, same-sex marriage is not legally recognized. Within the church denomination in which they participated, there was no sanction for blessing their relationship using the church's official rituals. While there were many within their church tradition who were willing to do so, the tradition as a whole was still unable to bless their union. This meant that both the state and the Church were in a position of saying that this was not a relationship in which sexuality and intimacy was to be found. It was not legally recognizable. And it could not be religiously blessed either—in fact, its mere existence was deemed by many Christians to be an overt expression of sin.

What Janice and Tammy did was pursue their own rite of blessing. Gathering friends and family—from both within the Church and outside it—they shared a wedding service and exchanged rings. It was their belief, and the belief of those gathered there for this service, that God had indeed blessed this relationship—even though society and the Church had not. Despite their commitment, they live constantly reminded that many in the Church would prefer to find ways to prevent this relationship and others like it.

Much of the public rhetoric concerning gay and lesbian marriages is driven by Christian voices who are working to make marriage not only not legally available but even illegal or permanently prohibited. For Janice and Tammy and others like them, those parts of the Church that are changing their theological underpinnings and their practices will need to be more publicly outspoken.

WHAT IS THE CHURCH TO DO?

We have seen that the Church provides an important but changing base for the work of grief and loss and that the foundations are often present for that work to be helpful and effective. If the Church is to play a real role in the transformation of people experiencing pain, brokenness, guilt, and shame, then certain healthy practices need to be adopted. It is our observation that everything being suggested in this section is being done effectively by someone in the Church already. We also have witnessed in many settings that this work of strengthening the Church's moral voice in ways that are constructive and not merely condemning will take implementing some of the following suggestions. We are under no illusion that all parts of the Church will pursue the course described herein, but we do believe that our suggestions provide a direction that would strengthen the Church's role in influencing what is proper within the culture. At the same time, they underscore the Church's compassion and care.

The Church's Role: Relationships After a Spouse's Death

We will first deal with the Church's role in the situation regarding the death of a spouse and the ensuing healing and fostering of new intimate relationship. Here the Church's theological foundation has been somewhat consistent and generally helpful. Rituals like funerals provide a common base for acknowledging the loss of the deceased and for gathering people for support. There is generally little shame and much sympathy in such gatherings (although specific exceptions can be found in many families!). Still, our vision for strengthening the work of the Church includes the following.

The Church, when it has been at its best, has generally done a good job of accompanying people during the initial bereavement period. The time immediately surrounding the death of the spouse often results in focused pastoral attention and the mobilization of laity to provide support and care for the surviving partner. But in practice this attention often tapers off relatively quickly. Clergy and lay leaders would do well to note in their planners times to call or visit over the first few months and to be more intentional about longer periods of increased awareness. Friends in previous situations need to be equipped to be friends in new ways and to maintain intentionality about those friendships. To be sure, these friendships and pastoral visits need not be thought of as more than supportive—the need for focused counseling in most cases seems to be minimal. But these connections can and should provide new ways for the surviving partner to reframe his or her relationship to the Church community and the clergy serving it.

Another very important piece involves affirmation as the grieving person begins to rebuild his or her relationships in new ways. Doing this will involve making adjustments in the relationships already in place but now changed by the death of one partner. These may include trying to maintain relationships with close friends from when both spouses were still alive and working to reorder them in this new situation. They may also include a once-casual friendship with someone else who has also lost a spouse becoming deeper and more intimate. Of course, many people who remarry after the death of a spouse remarry someone who has also been previously married and has experienced the death of a partner as well. These relational changes may, in many cases, also involve the beginning of some new relationships—which may provide new avenues for intimacy and commitment. Here, the Church would do well to be supportive in the processing of any guilt that may arise in the course of these new relationships. There is little theological baggage here, but many people still feel somehow unfaithful to their previous spouse as such relationships become intimate. Clear communication and helpful pastoral care here can help a person heal and be in a better position to make healthy choices.

A third element of this work will be to think about how interactions with other family members affect the healing and rebuilding of a grieving person's life. The presence of adult children in the same faith community can provide avenues for pastors and others to relate to the larger family system. As we noted, often pastors and others have been able to affirm the viability and ethical basis for developing new intimate relationships when speaking to the grieving parent. But they have also often been awkward in their ability to be consistent in their message when confronted with the grief and emotional pain and confusion being experienced by children from that relationship. Here religious leaders would do well to confront their own experiences and feelings and find ways to provide more helpful, direct messages to those processing these feelings.

To be fair, many clergy are working in dysfunctional congregational settings, and their economic survival can too easily hang in the balance. Training in processing of such issues and emotions would be important aspects of helping clergy be more aware, helpful, and effective in these circumstances. Continuing pastoral education and support efforts from both academic institutions and denominations would also be important.

Finally, it is our belief that the majority of these suggestions should begin being implemented in pastoral practice *before* being confronted with providing care for people in crisis. Pastors and priests would do well to explore their own preaching and teaching on these subjects and create conversations with images and illustrations that show the rebuilding of lives after loss. A story in a sermon, for example, about a widower who remarried and found stability and happiness in a new chapter of his life told *before* a particular family experiences this may open doors for imagination in the midst of grief. Examples of people who have experienced tragedy, grief, or loss and who have come out the other side whole and vibrant can give people, perhaps decades away from experiencing that in their own life, the tools they will need to be better prepared when life brings loss and the challenges of mourning to them.

The Church's Role: Relationships After Divorce

As we consider the situation concerning divorce, the issues become more complex and the role that the Church should play becomes more ambiguous. This ambiguity has its roots in the variations in theology and practice within the Church. It is our belief that those churches who have been most helpful in providing support for struggling couples prior to divorce have been able to state both sides of the matter clearly. On the one hand, that divorce is something less than God's desire for people who are married. And on the other hand, that the mission of the Church is to provide grace and support a healing that allows people to move forward, rekindle intimacy, and consider remarriage within the framework provided by the Church. Those traditions that either gloss over divorce as "no big deal" or who see it as an almost-unpardonable sin would do well to revisit their teaching and move toward a mission that is more honest about sin's reality while also being fully committed to furthering life in its fullness.

One place where we see a significant societal need for a change from the Church has to do with the role of ritual in divorce. While many in Western culture get married in the Church—even if for sentimental reasons in many cases—divorces happen in civil courts. The Church would do well to recognize this disparity and provide for a ceremony of confession and release from the covenant of marriage. As Ruether has suggested:

> Here the spiritual community must find forms of healing ceremony that can help partners who are dissolving a relationship work through the transition to new lives, new ways to be friends, ways to continue to parent their children together even if they themselves are no longer a couple. (2000, p. 217)

If the formation of a formal covenant is worthy of ritual and the Church's attention, then certainly also is the dissolution of that same covenant. If the Church could and would help people deal with their realties (good and bad) in more transparent ways, both the integrity of the Church's ministry and the helpfulness of that work would benefit.

A second concern we have is for the number of people involved in divorce from within faith communities who are cut off, not only from their spouse but also from their faith community. Few couples who attended church together while married are comfortable attending the same church together after divorce. Even sitting at opposite ends of the sanctuary provides no help here. Relationships are awkward and overlap. Feelings of failure are already present for many people when they enter the Church. Seeing their former spouse rekindles these feelings repeatedly. Churches wanting to be helpful in providing a faithbase for divorcing people would do well to sit down with both partners and talk through this situation, with the purpose of keeping both people connected to the faith community—or facilitating their individual searches for another, if they wish. When people simply drop out after divorce, it is a sad loss indeed. Church leaders need to be willing to be more intentional in helping people grieve and rebuild their lives, especially when children are involved. This will require courage, truthfulness, and integrity on the part of pastors and priests. It will also call for these aspects of ministry to be given more attention in seminaries, in continuing education, and from the leadership throughout the Church.

Frank Honeycutt shares these helpful words to pastors:

> Though they may not know it at the time, parishioners come to pastors not just for affirmation and a listening ear. They want to know what we think of their lives in the context of a very old, competing narrative, much of which may be long buried. Like it or not, we are called upon to do more than listen. We are called to speak the truth in love. Learning to do so is a lifelong task. Spoken truth will require immense energy and courage and may cause undesirable responses or require explanations. (2011, pp. 104–105)

He goes on to talk about how trust and time are essential parts of pastoral work. Effective pastors will need to invest real energy in their work in order to be able to withstand the pressures of simply living in codependent relationships with church members. They will also need strength and support in order to be able to be an assertive and positive influence in the midst of pain and dysfunctions in the lives of others.

Another matter to be addressed is the upfront treatment of these issues in preaching and teaching. As we discussed above, the teaching of the Church can provide a framework from which people shape their worldview and cultivate options for their lives. Even in a declining church, a relevant framework can provide the basis for people of faith to "be yeast," effectively and legitimately, within the wider culture. Indeed, for churches to see themselves this way, as preparers of Christians, may be one of the principle sources of church renewal.

Yet many pastors shy away from this kind of advocacy. One of the authors of this chapter was recently at a gathering of pastors the week after the Gospel lessons from the lectionary were from Jesus' Sermon on the Mount; included in the lectionary reading were verses linking divorce, improperly pursued and based, to adultery. When asked about whether they had used that occasion to speak about divorce, the pastors at the gathering laughed! They had steered away from the subject of divorce because it was too hot to handle. The irony was, these pastors were from a tradition that has, for the most part, been non-judgmental about divorce. One would have thought that, as a result, there would have almost surely been several divorced and remarried people present in each of their congregations. Those who were present heard Jesus' words about divorce when the Gospel lesson was read and may well have been uncomfortable with the implications. They would have been helped had their pastors explained that since marriage opens a covenant with God, a way needs to be found to close that covenant when divorcing. Instead, none of the pastors there had chosen to deal with divorce and remarriage in the teaching that day. Quite likely, one result was that many people left worship that day confused and concerned about the disconnect between their perceived acceptance as persons by the congregation and the biblical text they heard that day. Others probably left assuming that the connection between Jesus' teaching and their lived reality was minimal at best. Neither avoidance nor denial was a healthy approach, but every pastor in the room had apparently made those choices anyway. How much better it would have been to speak about the nature of sin and the assurance of grace!

The Church's Role: Same-Sex Relationships

Finally, concerning same-sex marriages and relationships, the Church has an important opportunity to reframe itself in ways that promote life. Although within particular denominations discussing same-sex relationships and marriage cannot be done without considerable emotion and stress, it is our belief that it is both necessary and constructive for the Church not to turn away from these challenges. The Church's mission is not to reinforce the status quo but to be a leader in personal and social transformation. A clear and gracious voice is needed here. Grace, which is at the center of the Church's message, needs to shape its policy and practice as well. The LGBT community is a social reality. Attempts to ostracize, shun, or ignore LGBT people through moral pronouncements have produced few good results and done significant damage, not only to personal lives but also to widespread perception of the Church.

When the Church withholds God's grace, or is silent about its free and abundant gift, it furthers the societal impression that it condones bullying, teen suicide, and interpersonal violence. When the Church puts forth messages condemning

LGBT people, it risks giving explicit sanction to such violence and easy pardon to the persecutors. Moreover, it withholds the compassionate support it could and should provide to victims of violence and grieving parents, relatives, and friends.

Pastors are called to proclaim courageously and forthrightly God's message of grace and love for all people. With this comes the call to all people of faith to love others and to act lovingly toward others—even those (perhaps especially those) who are different from the majority. Churches that are hospitable and affirming need to find ways to be publicly clear about this rather than simply feeling progressive or tolerant inside their own walls.

One congregation we worked with in Florida was, like many mainline congregations, aging and declining. Traditional challenges for them to "redevelop" were increasingly difficult as there were not many members and not much energy among those who remained. One day a community group that worked with youth asked if they could use the building for afterschool gatherings. When the board first heard this, they were excited at the chance to have young people in the church. But then it came out that the program was for gay and lesbian youth to provide support for them as they worked out their identities through their teenage years. The discussion became more mixed and anxious. They wondered whether their church could support something like this.

Then one woman shared how her own daughter had struggled with her sexual identity growing up. Looking back, she wished there had been someone there to help her. The tone of the conversation changed, and others were able to share their own struggles or the struggles of someone they knew—some related to homosexuality but many others related to other situations where someone had been ostracized or bullied or was hurting and found no support. The church decided the group could use the building and that each time the group met, members of the church would stop by and bring homemade cookies or some other treats.

When we heard this story, this congregation had been significantly transformed already. The woman who told us this story shared that the tradition of this congregation was to leave their pews and gather in a circle around the sanctuary for the closing prayers and blessing. For many years they had done this, but due to the decline in numbers, there had been too few to actually join hands and connect the circle for a long time. With tears in her eyes she shared that a few weeks earlier, for the first time in years, there had been enough people present to complete the circle and for everyone to join hands. The aging little group now was more eclectic and diverse. They had discovered that the one thing they had to offer was a genuine willingness to love everyone—even those who were different from most of them. That decision had brought a vehicle for hope for young people wrestling with their sexual identity. It had also become an experience of hope for a congregation that had been in decline.

All of this points to an absolutely essential dimension of this subject. Changing the *practices* that the Church carries out surrounding grief requires changing the *picture* that many in the Church have been given about God. A legalistic God who is most concerned with right and wrong and calls people to pursue moral perfection in order to be acceptable is often behind many of the worst of the practices described above. Yet in Jesus we meet a Son of God who is more gracious, more loving, and more forgiving than the God many in the Church cling to. In order to deal better with the losses people are experiencing in their lives, the Church will have also to *cause* some grief by encouraging people to let go of previously held images of God, especially those that have preferred to reinforce the powerful links between Church and societal power more than proclaim how God is revealed in and by Jesus Christ. Whether the Church can be a viable voice for many will be determined by how open they are to wrestling with and letting go of the images of God that ground the Church's former status in our society.

This may sound like a small thing. Who would be put into a state of crisis because they have discovered that God is more gracious, more forgiving, and more present in suffering than they previously believed? But the answer is, quite surprisingly, that many people find the thought that God may be different than they originally believed to be frightening and offensive. The recent furor over the release of Rob Bell's new book, *Love Wins* (2011), has shown that there are many in the Church who are angered by such a notion. Providing for a gracious, healing, and proactive stance toward the formation of new sexual and intimate relationships will require some people to let go of their thoughts about God in order to be open to and take on new thoughts. The Church should understand that transformation brings about these changes as *losses*, losses that require their own genuine grief. If the Church embraces those who are willing to lose long-held beliefs about God and to embrace new ones, the Church can move forward with confidence and new theology as a result. The Church will not be in a position to implement completely the suggestions in this chapter if it is not also willing to tackle this foundational work. A gracious voice from the Church requires the Church to have a gracious God at its core.

Ultimately, the above ideas are offered as a way to encourage people within all Christian traditions to use the best of their tradition to encourage an honest engagement with the realities of contemporary life and to do so in a way that both addresses the brokenness in the present and the grace and new life that can follow. Traditions that deal only with the brokenness and the sin without providing for helpful and legitimate ways to move forward are in danger of either damaging people or becoming irrelevant to their lives. Neither cheap grace nor legalism will do. An honest Church will not deny sin but will also declare that grace is real and that sin is not an end but a reality in every journey. Only those Christian traditions that find ways to teach and act in order to provide forgiveness, healing, and the freedom to pursue a new chapter in the lives most affected by loss will be relevant and helpful to people rebuilding their lives. It is our belief that this is the Church that God is calling forth. We look forward to those traditions that are willing to be enthusiastically and energetically led into the future God wants for the Church.

REFERENCES

Berry, C. R. (2005). *The unauthorized guide to sex and the church.* Nashville, TN: W Publishing Group, a division of Thomas Nelson.

Honeycutt, F. G. (2011). *The truth shall make you odd: Speaking with pastoral integrity in awkward situations.* Grand Rapids, MI: Brazos Press.

Konigsberg, R. D. (2011). *The truth about grief: The myth of its five stages and the new science of loss.* New York, NY: Simon & Schuster.

Kübler-Ross, E., & Kessler, D. (2005). *On grief and grieving: Finding the meaning of grief through the five stages of loss.* New York, NY: Scribner.

Kysar, M., & Kysar, R. (1978). *The asundered: Biblical teachings on divorce and remarriage.* Atlanta, GA: John Knox Press.

Martinson, R. D. (1990). Sexuality, intimacy, and boundaries. *Word and World, 10*(2), 114–123.

Mather, M., & Lavery, D. (2010). *In U.S., proportion married at lowest recorded level.* Washington, DC: Population Reference Bureau. Retrieved from http://www.prb.org/Articles/2010/usmarriagedecline.aspx

McMinn, L. G. (2004). *Sexuality and holy longing: Embracing intimacy in a broken world.* San Francisco, CA: Jossey-Bass.

Moore, A., & Stratton, D. (2003). *Resilient widowers: Older men adjusting to new life.* Amherst, NY: Prometheus Books.

Robinson, B. A. (2007). *How many North Americans attend religious services (and how many lie about going)?* Kingston, Ontario, Canada: Ontario Consultants on Religious Tolerance. Retrieved from http://www.religioustolerance.org/rel_rate.htm

Ruether, R. R. (2000). *Christianity and the making of the modern family.* Boston, MA: Beacon Press.

AFTERWORD

Toward a Spirituality of Love and Longing

Brad DeFord

> Intimate attachments to other human beings are the hub around which a person's life revolves, not only when he is an infant or a toddler or a schoolchild but throughout his adolescence and his years of maturity as well, and on into old age. From these intimate attachments a person draws his strength and enjoyment of life and, through what he contributes, he gives strength and enjoyment to others. These are matters about which current science and traditional wisdom are at one. (Bowlby, 1980, p. 442)

With this comment, John Bowlby concludes *Loss*, the third volume of his landmark trilogy, having begun with *Attachment* and proceeded through *Separation*. Curiously, through a thousand pages over three volumes, it is the first time he references *intimacy* in speaking to attachment and loss. Yet what make our attachments significant are not merely the patterns we establish or repeat in forming them, nor only the manner in which we grieve our losses, but also the processes by which they became *intimate* initially. Intimacy indicates our attachments' significance and measures their depth of meaning.

When we suffer loss—and almost no loss is merely "experienced," as if it were that simple, as if there were not pain, nor perhaps humiliation, nor a myriad of other, accompanying feelings—it is the damage done to our intimacy that is the most painful for us. Our intimate relationships are the ones we count on most for support; it is those we concentrate most on repairing after each intimate relationship we lose. In the course of mourning, as we establish new intimate relationships, we begin to feel more secure in the world again. We learn anew of intimacy's value, indeed of its necessity to our survival and our living. Intimacy—our capacity for it and our ability to overcome the relational risks of it in order to provide for ourselves the comfort we need in the company of and connections with others—is a key aspect of our response to loss, and thus to our mourning.

So is love.

Hargrave and Pfister think that what Bowlby meant by "attachment" was *love* (2011, p. 4). And many might assume that we, here, in discussing intimacy and sexuality, have also been speaking about love, albeit indirectly.

Certainly, love and sexuality and intimacy overlap in our emotional consciousness, yet love differs from intimacy in significant ways.

Rollo May opens the first part of his classic, *Love and Will*, by saying:

> There are four kinds of love in Western tradition. One is *sex*, or what we call lust, libido. The second is *eros*, the drive of love to procreate or create—the urge, as the Greeks put it, toward higher forms of being and relationship. A third is *philia*, or friendship, brotherly love. The fourth is *agape* or *caritas*, as the Latins called it, the love which is devoted to the welfare of the other, the prototype of which is the love of God for man. Every human experience of authentic love is a blending, in varying proportions, of these four. (1969, pp. 37–38)

In the same way, every human experience of authentic intimacy has elements of all of these forms of love, in differing degrees and balances—just as every human experience of authentic mourning is its own seeking to reestablish in our relationships the appropriate balances of loving that our loss has disturbed. Reestablishing these balances is especially important when someone we *loved* has died. During mourning, the imbalances in our loving make us emotionally vulnerable. They deeply affect both our intimacyseeking and our choices for sexual expression—each of which probably has "love" in some way at its core.

However, just as we often confuse and conflate different forms of love, we also tend to confuse love and intimacy. Although we may have as wide a variety of experiences of intimacy as we do of love, we do not have as wide a variety of words to describe them. In several significant respects, intimacy and love differ; it is important to distinguish between them.

First, as with intimacy, it is in our families that we first learn what love means. In a manner that resonates with Bowlby, Donald Nathanson writes that "in the affective interaction between the needy infant and the solacing parent we may find the nidus of love" (1992, p. 243). Clearly, we speak easily, sometimes perhaps too easily, of love when we are describing familial relationships, such as those between spouses or between parents and children. When it comes to families, we assume that "love" is the proper description for the nature of the relationship. In that way, love takes many forms—some of which we might not name as "love," were it not for the family name of the relationship.

In this respect, intimacy adds a descriptive affirmation of the family relationship, such as when family members say they are "close." In human relating, intimacy exceeds love, blesses love, and proclaims a positive dimension to love, one which may actually be lacking in what is otherwise called "love" itself.

Second, if in our families' interactions are the origins of our senses of both love and intimacy, love and intimacy have different meanings, and we hold that difference in "tension" in our relationships. To reiterate a point we made in the Introduction, Fossum and Mason tell us that our "*family* intimacy is the experience of closeness and familiarity between two or more family members in a variety of contexts, with the expectation that the experience and the relationship will *persist over time*" (1986, p. 158). We concluded that intimacy has a horizon of promise, a hope of continuing. Intimacy inspires in us a sense that the relationship will "go on."

Love, on the other hand, embraces our mortality. May says, "Love is not only enriched by our sense of mortality but constituted by it" (1969, p. 102). And he quotes from a letter Abraham Maslow wrote while recuperating from a heart attack: "'Death, and its ever present possibility makes love, passionate love, more possible. I wonder if we could love passionately, if ecstasy would be possible at all, if we knew we'd never die'" (May, 1969, p. 99).

This is the paradox: Intimacy seeks to ignore ending or loss with the promise of continuity. Love depends on death to be meaningful. The death of someone with whom we have been intimate is an affront. The death of someone whom we have loved is a confirmation of that love itself. Since love embraces death and intimacy ignores or rejects it, as we mourn we find ourselves living into the emotional consequences of this conflict. Our letting go of the relationship and our holding onto it are shaped by how we resolve this conflict between intimacy and love.

The paradox between love and intimacy enters into our sexual relationships as well. Alexander Lowen, in *Love and Orgasm*, describes the vital, life-affirming qualities of sexuality this way: "Sexuality is the expression of life and the antithesis of death" (1965, p. 69). Lowen is essentially combining what May calls *sex* and *eros*—but in those terms, he sounds more like he is speaking of "intimacy" than he is of "love." Yet if we see in our mourning a process through which we find ourselves to be "coming alive again," arising from the deadening numbness with which most mourning begins, our sexuality, especially our capacity for sexual intimacy, is its own confirmation to us that we are indeed alive—and glad to be so.

Finally, when it comes to *philia*, to friendship, it is important to underscore how important this form of loving relationship is, particularly when we are in pain and mourning, and yet, as we said in the Introduction, how difficult true friendship is to establish in today's technological world. It is probably true that women and men form friendships differently. James Nelson, for example, has written about men's difficulties with friendship—particularly with other men (1988, p. 50). Our culture's confusions about intimacy and love and the differences among *sex*, *eros*, and *philia* probably affect relationships between men, and between men and women, more than they do relationships between women. Yet there is evidence that we are culturally more comfortable speaking about intimacy and friendship if *sex* and *eros* are not part of that conversation.

For example, Alan Loy McGinnis wrote a book titled *The Friendship Factor*. In the 1979 version, he included a chapter titled "Eros, Its Power and Its Problems" (p. 163ff). When it was revised in 2004, other chapters were added but that chapter was omitted. It is safe to assume that *eros* in friendships had become more problematic over those 25 years.

Intimacy and this constellation of the meanings of love matter deeply to us as we mourn—and as we die. Since, as we have said, our capacity for intimacy turns on our capacity for solitude, then at no other time in our lives does intimacy matter more to us than when we are dying, both because our dying is our consummate solitary act and because the process challenges us to experience several levels of intimacy. Dowrick speaks to dying's solitude. She says, "with solitariness, with aloneness, with loneliness, death has a very close relationship indeed" (1991, p. 158). Moreover, she adds, "*you will die alone*, no matter how crowded the room in which you die, and no matter how caring the people who have gathered to say farewell" (1991, p. 158). Yes, but if solitary, then intimate; and if intimate, then perhaps also *loving*. For it *does* matter whether we die by ourselves or in the company of those who love us. There is perhaps no greater *agape* than that shown to us by "the people who have gathered to say farewell."

In spite of their being distinct experiences, intimacy and love share our quest for what Brenda Schaeffer (1997) calls "healthy belonging." It is healthy belonging we seek to establish or reestablish as we mourn, for we cannot speak about intimacy or sexuality—or loss, for that matter—without affirming our human longing for each other. As Evelyn and James Whitehead have put it, "We long to belong. We yearn to be chosen and to be included, sensing our very survival is at stake" (2010, p. 81). Perhaps this too, along with intimacy and love, is what Bowlby meant by "attachment": this need we have for each other, this innate desire we share to be connected. During mourning, we feel this longing acutely. Grieving, we are likely to feel not only that we do not "belong," but also that we are unloved—and perhaps even unlovable. These experiences make mourning a crucial time both emotionally and spiritually.

Of course, developing completely a spirituality of love and longing is well beyond the scope of this book. Here we have had the more modest goal of inviting a conversation about an interplay of human experience that deserves more discussion. When we begin plumbing the depths of our grief, we discover that we are talking with each other about our intimacy needs and our sexual desires. Our disclosures ask for not only understanding but also a compassionate response. Only when we are honest and authentic with each other about the mutual importance to us of intimacy and sexuality can we ask for, and offer to each other, the solace that soothes our shared pain.

If in our mourning we are anticipating compassion, then we are trusting in love to encourage us to grow together in meaningful intimacy. When it is with compassion we are embraced, we no longer need to find words to explain ourselves.

For the rest is sweet communion.

REFERENCES

Bowlby, J. (1980). *Loss*. New York, NY: Basic Books.

Dowrick, S. (1991). *Intimacy and solitude*. New York, NY: W. W. Norton.

Fossum, M. A., & Mason, M. J. (1986). *Facing shame: Families in recovery*. New York, NY: W. W. Norton.

Hargrave, T. D., & Pfitzer, F. (2011). *Restoration therapy*. New York, NY: Routledge.

Lowen, A. (1965). *Love and orgasm*. New York, NY: Signet Books.

May, R. (1969). *Love and will*. New York, NY: W. W. Norton.

McGinnis, A. L. (1979, 2004). *The friendship factor*. Minneapolis, MN: Augsburg.

Nathanson, D. (1992). *Shame and pride: Affect, sex and the birth of the self.* New York, NY: W. W. Norton.

Nelson, J. B. (1988). *The intimate connection: Male sexuality, masculine spirituality*. Philadelphia, PA: Westminster Press.

Schaeffer, B. (1997). *Is it love or is it addiction?* Center City, MN: Hazelden.

Whitehead, E. E., & Whitehead, J. D. (2010). *Transforming our painful emotions*. Maryknoll, NY: Orbis Books.

Bibliography

Richard B. Gilbert

This bibliography is intended to assist further research in the various topics covered in this book. Its scope exceeds the specific focus of the authors to provide a wider view of the literature.

Death, Grief, and Differences of Sexual Orientation

Albers, R. (1995). *Shame: A faith perspective*. New York, NY: Haworth (Routledge).

Boyd-Franklin, N., & Lockwood, T. (1999). Spirituality and religion: Implications for psychotherapy with African American clients and families. In F. Walsh (Ed.), *Spiritual resources in family therapy* (pp. 90–103). New York, NY: Guilford.

Bushfield, S., & DeFord, B. (2010). *End-of-life care & addiction*. New York, NY: Springer.

Byock, I. (2004). *The four things that matter most: A book about living*. New York, NY: Simon & Schuster.

Carnes, P. (1989). *Out of the shadows: Understanding sexual addiction*. Minneapolis, MN: CompCare.

Carnes, P. (1991). *Don't call it love: Recovery from sexual addiction*. New York, NY: Bantam.

Chapple, H. (2010). *No place for dying: Hospitals and the ideology of rescue*. Walnut Creek, CA: LeftCoast Press.

Corless, I. (2002). The HIV-AIDS patient: Holier than thou. In R. Gilbert (Ed.), *Healthcare and spirituality: Listening, assessing, caring* (pp. 189–200). Amityville, NY: Baywood.

Corr, C., & Balk, D. (Eds.). (2010). *Children's encounter with death, bereavement, and coping*. New York: Springer.

DeFord, B. (2010, April 7). *Transforming shame: Understanding how stories heal*. Presented at the Association for Death Education and Counseling 32nd annual conference, Kansas City, MO.

De la Huerta, C. (1999). *Coming out spiritually: The next step*. New York, NY: Jeremy P. Tarcher/Putnam.

Doka, K. (Ed.). (1989). *Disenfranchised grief: Recognizing hidden sorrow*. Lexington, MA: Lexington Books.

Doka, K. (2007). Challenging the paradigm: New understandings of grief. In K. Doka (Ed.), *Living with grief: Before and after the death* (pp. 87–102). Washington, DC: Hospice Foundation of America.
Figley, C. (1997). *Death and trauma: The traumatology of grieving*. Bristol, PA: Taylor & Francis.
Fitzgerald, H. (1992/2003). *The grieving child: A parent's guide*. New York, NY: Fireside.
Gamino, L., & Ritter, R., Jr. (2009). *Ethical practice in grief counseling*. New York, NY: Springer.
Gilbert, R. (1995). Protestant perspectives on grief and children. In E. Grollman (Ed.), *Bereaved children and teens: A support guide for parents and professionals* (Chap. 8). Boston, MA: Beacon.
Gilbert, R. (2003a). *Healing the holy helpers: Healthy clergy for the third millennium*. Unpublished dissertation available electronically from the Graduate Theological Foundation.
Gilbert, R. (2003b). Living, dying, and grieving in the margins. In G. R. Cox, R. Bendiken, & R. Stevenson (Eds.), *Making sense of death: Spiritual, pastoral and personal aspects of death, dying and bereavement* (pp. 191–203). Amityville, NY: Baywood.
Gilbert, R. (2012). *Heartpeace: Healing help for grieving folk* (2nd ed.). Omaha, NE: Centering.
Goldman, L. (2001). *Breaking the silence: A guide to helping children with complicated grief—Suicide, homicide, AIDS, violence, and abuse* (2nd ed.). Philadelphia/London: Jessica Kingsley.
Goldman, L. (2006). *Children also grieve: Talking about death and healing*. London/ Philadelphia: Jessica Kingsley.
Goldman, L. (2008). *Coming out, coming in: Nurturing the well-being and inclusion of gay youth in mainstream society*. New York, NY: Taylor & Francis.
Goldman, L. (2009). *Great answers to difficult questions about death: What children need to know*. London/Philadelphia: Jessica Kingsley.
Goldman, L. (2010). *Great answers to difficult questions about sex: What children need to know*. London/Philadelphia: Jessica Kingsley.
Grollman, E. (Ed.). (1995a). *Bereaved children and teens: A support guide for parents and professionals*. Boston, MA: Beacon.
Grollman, E. (Ed.). (1995b). *Living when a loved one has died*. Boston, MA: Beacon.
Hall, L. (2011). *Counseling military families*. New York, NY: Routledge.
Harvey, S. D. (2011). Working with the loss of one's faith community. In D. Harris, *Counting our losses: Reflecting on change, loss, and transition in everyday life* (Chap. 12). New York, NY: Routledge.
Hill, C. (2008). *Human sexuality: Personality and social psychological perspectives*. Thousand Oaks, CA: Sage.
Holloway, K. (2002). *Passed on: African-American mourning stories*. Durham, NC: Duke University Press.
Houppert, K. (2005). *Home fires burning: Married to the military—for better or worse*. New York, NY: Ballantine.
Irish, D., Lundquist, K., & Nelsen, V. (Eds.). (1993). *Ethnic variations in dying, death and grief: Diversity in universality*. New York, NY: Taylor & Francis.

Jeffreys, J. S. (2005/2011). *Helping grieving people when tears are not enough: A handbook for care providers*. New York, NY: Brunner-Routledge.

Jelinek, S. (2002). The gay-lesbian-bisexual-transgendered patient. In R. Gilbert (Ed.), *Healthcare and spirituality: Listening, assessing, caring* (pp. 153–162). Amityville, NY: Baywood.

Johnson, J. (2004). *Keys to helping children deal with death and grief*. Omaha, NE: Centering.

Johnson, T. (2000). *Gay spirituality: The role of gay identity in the transformation of human consciousness*. Los Angeles/New York: Alyson.

Kaufman, G., & Raphael, L. (1996). *Coming out of shame*. New York, NY: Doubleday.

Klass, D., Silverman, P., & Nickman, S. (Eds.). (1996). *Continuing bonds: New understandings of grief*. New York, NY: Routledge.

Klein, S. (1998). *Heavenly hurts: Surviving AIDS-related deaths and losses*. Amityville, NY: Baywood.

LaGrand, L. (2011). *Healing grief, finding peace: 101 ways to cope with the death of your loved one*. Naperville, IL: Sourcebooks.

Marcus, E. (2000). *What if someone I know is gay? Answers to questions about gay and lesbian people*. New York, NY: Price Stern Sloan.

McNish, J. (2004). *Transforming shame: A pastoral response*. New York, NY: Haworth.

Nadeau, J. (1998). *Families making sense of death*. Thousand Oaks, CA: Sage.

Neimeyer, R. (2001). *Meaning reconstruction and the experience of loss*. Washington, DC: American Psychological Association.

Neimeyer, R. (2009). *Constructivist psychotherapy*. New York, NY: Routledge.

Parga, E. (2007). *No child should grieve alone: A guide for parents, caregivers & professionals*. Reno, NV: Solace Tree.

Parga, E. (2009). *Kids can cope: An activity book from children for children who are living with change and loss*. Omaha, NE: Centering.

Rando, T. (1993). *The treatment of complicated mourning*. Champaign, IL: Research Press.

Sanders, C. M. (1989). *Grief: The mourning after: Dealing with adult bereavement*. New York, NY: Wiley.

Scrivani, M. (1991/2005). *When death walks in: For teenagers facing grief*. Omaha, NE: Centering.

Shernoff, M. (1998). *Gay widowers: Life after the death of a partner*. New York, NY: Haworth.

Smith, H. I. (1994). *On grieving the death of a father*. Minneapolis, MN: Augsburg.

Smith, H. I. (1996). *Grieving the death of a friend*. Minneapolis, MN: Augsburg.

Smith, H. I. (2003). *Grieving the death of a mother*. Minneapolis, MN: Augsburg.

Smith, H. I. (2004). *Griefkeeping: Learning how long grief lasts*. New York, NY: Crossroad.

Snow, J. (2004). *How it feels to have a gay or lesbian parent: A book by kids for kids of all ages*. New York, NY: Haworth.

Tuber, S., & Caflisch, J. (2011). *Starting treatment with children and adolescents: A process-oriented guide for therapists*. New York, NY: Routledge.

Worden, J. W. (2009). *Grief counseling & grief therapy: A handbook for the mental health practitioner* (4th ed.). New York, NY: Springer.

Loss of Relationship and the Restoration of Intimacy in Families

Aasen, N. (2004). *Living still, loving always*. St. Peter, MN: Wilson.

Abrams, R. (2005). *When parents die: Learning to live with the loss of a parent* (2nd ed.). London/New York: Routledge.

Attig, T. (2000). *The heart of grief*. New York, NY: Oxford University Press.

Attig, T. (2011). *How we grieve: Relearning the world* (Rev. ed.). New York, NY: Oxford University Press.

Bateman-Cass, C. (2000). The loss within a loss: Understanding the psychological implications of assisted reproductive technologies for the treatment of infertility. *Dissertation Abstracts International, 61*(03), 1624B. (UMI No. 9965385)

Berger, G., et al. (1995). *The couple's guide to infertility: Updated with the newest scientific techniques to help you have a baby*. New York, NY: Main Street.

Bertman, S. (1999). *Grief and the healing arts: Creativity as therapy*. Amityville, NY: Baywood.

Bonanno, G., Nesse, R., & Wortman, C. (2004). Prospective aspects of caregiving and adaptation. *Psychology and Aging, 19*(2), 200–271.

Boss, P., Roos, S., & Harris, D. (2011). Grief in the midst of ambiguity and uncertainty: An exploration of ambiguous loss and chronic sorrow. In R. Neimeyer, D. Harris, H. Winokuer, & G. Thornton (Eds.), *Grief and bereavement in contemporary society: Bridging research and practice* (pp. 163–175). New York, NY: Routledge.

Bronner, G., Royter, V., Korczyn, A. D., & Giladi, N. (2004). Sexual dysfunction in Parkinson's disease. *Journal of Sex & Marital Therapy, 30*, 95–105.

Burns, L. (2005). Psychological changes in infertility patients. In A. Rosen & J. Rosen (Eds.), *Frozen dreams: Psychodynamic dimensions of infertility and assisted reproduction* (pp. 3–29). Hillsdale, NJ: Analytic Press.

Burns, L., & Covington, S. (Eds.). (1999). *Infertility counseling: A comprehensive text for clinicians*. New York, NY: Parthenon.

Butler, R., & Lewis, M. (2002). *The new love and sex after 60* (Rev. ed.). New York, NY: Ballantine.

Casale, A. (2009). *Distinguishing the concept of chronic sorrow from standard grief: An empirical study of infertile couples*. Doctoral dissertation, New York University, Silver School of Social Work. (UMI No. 3353016)

Cayan, S., Bozlu, M.,Canpolat, B., & Akbay, E. (2004). The assessment of sexual functions in women with male partners complaining of erectile dysfunction: Does treatment of male sexual dysfunction improve female partner's sexual functions? *Journal of Sex & Marital Therapy, 30*, 333–341.

Chatman, D., & Kenneally, W. (2001). *The death of a parent: Reflections for adults mourning the loss of a father or mother*. Chicago, IL: ACTA.

Covington, S., & Burns, L. (Eds.). (2006). *Infertility counseling: A comprehensive handbook for clinicians* (2nd ed.). New York, NY: Cambridge University Press.

Crawford, B., & Lazar, L. (1999). *In my world: A journal for young people facing life-threatening illness*. Omaha, NE: Centering.

Daniluk, J. (1997). Gender and infertility. In S. R. Leiblum (Ed.), *Infertility: Psychological issues and counseling strategies* (pp. 103–125). New York, NY: Wiley.

Daniluk, J., & Hurtig-Mitchell, J. (2003). Themes of hope and healing: Infertility couples' experiences of adoption. *Journal of Counseling & Development, 81*, 389–399.

Daniluk, J., & Tench, E. (2007). Long-term adjustment of infertile couples following unsuccessful medical intervention. *Journal of Counseling & Development, 85*, 89–100.

Doka, K. (1993). *Living with a life-threatening illness: A guide for patients, families and caregivers*. Lexington, MA: Lexington.

Doka, K. (2002). *Disenfranchised grief: New directions, challenges and strategies for practice*. Champaign, IL: Research.

Doka, K. (2008). *Counseling individuals with life-threatening illness*. New York, NY: Springer.

Donnelly, K. (1982). *Recovering from the loss of a child*. New York, NY: Macmillan.

Donnelly, K. (1993). *Recovering from the loss of a parent*. New York, NY: Berkeley.

Felber, M. (2000). *Finding your way after your spouse dies*. Notre Dame, IN: Ave Maria.

Gerrity, D. (2001). Five medical treatment stages of infertility: Implications for counselors. *The Family Journal: Counseling and Therapy for Couples and Families, 9*(2), 140–150.

Gilbert, A., & Kline, C. (2006). *Always too soon: Voices of support for those who have lost both parents*. Emeryville, CA: Seal Press.

Gilbert, R. (1999). *Finding your way after your parent dies: Hope for adults*. Notre Dame, IN: Ave Maria.

Jenkins, C., & Merry, J. (2005). *Relative grief: Parents and children, sisters and brothers, husbands, wives and partners, grandparents and grandchildren talk about their experience of death and grieving*. Philadelphia/London: Jessica Kingsley.

Katz, P., Millstein, S., & Pasch, L. (2002). The social impact of infertility. *Fertility and Sterility, 78*(Supplement 1), S238.

Klug, R. (2001). *When your parent dies*. Minneapolis, MN: Augsburg.

Koenig, H., & Herman, S. (1994). Religion and coping with sexual impotence in later life. *Journal of Religious Gerontology, 9*(1), 73–87.

Koenig, H., & Weaver, A. (1997). *Counseling troubled older adults: A handbook for pastors and religious caregivers*. Nashville, TN: Abingdon.

Leiblum, S. (Ed.). (1997). *Infertility: Psychological issues and counseling strategies*. New York, NY: Wiley.

Loe, M. (2001). Fixing broken masculinity: Viagra as a technology for the production of gender and sexuality. *Sexuality and Culture, 5*(3), 97–125.

Loehfelm, B. (2008). *Fresh kills: A novel*. New York, NY: Berkeley Prime Crime.

Miles, A. (2002). *Violence in families: What every Christian needs to know*. Minneapolis, MN: Augsburg Fortress.

Miller, R. (1999). *GriefQuest: Reflections for men coping with loss*. Winona, MN: St. Mary's.

Morgenthaler, A. (2003). *The Viagra myth: The surprising impact on love and relationships*. San Francisco, CA: Jossey-Bass.

Neimeyer, R. (2001). Reauthorizing life narratives: Grief therapy as meaning reconstruction. *Israeli Journal of Psychiatry and Related Sciences, 38*, 171–183.

Neimeyer, R. (2005). Widowhood, grief and the quest for meaning: A narrative perspective on resilience. In D. Carr, R. Neese, & C. Wortman (Eds.), *Spousal bereavement in late life* (pp. 227–252). New York, NY: Springer.

Parker-Pope, T. (2002, November 11). So many jokes, so many misconceptions: What the Viagra experience is really like. *The Wall Street Journal*, p. R3.
Parkes, C. M. (2006/2008). *Love and loss: The roots of grief and its complications*. New York, NY: Routledge.
Ragusea, A., & VandeCreek, L. (2003). Suggestions for the ethical practice of online psychotherapy. *Psychotherapy: Theory, Research, Practice, Training, 40*, 94–102.
Rohr, R. (2004). *Adam's return: The five promises of male initiation*. New York, NY: Crossroad.
Rubel, B. (1999/2009). *But I didn't say goodbye: For parents and professionals helping child suicide survivors*. Kendall Park, NJ: GriefworkCenter.
Rudman, L., & Glick, P. (2008). *The social psychology of gender: How power and intimacy shape gender relations*. New York, NY: Guilford.
Salzer, L. (2006). Adoption after fertility. In S. Covington & L. Burns (Eds.), *Infertility counseling: A comprehensive handbook for clinicians* (2nd ed., pp. 387–410). New York, NY: Cambridge University Press.
Santrock, J. (2011). *Life span development* (13th ed.). Boston, MA: McGraw-Hill.
Schachter, S., & Schachter, J. (2010). Adoption: A life begun with loss. In D. Harris (Ed.), *Counting our losses: Reflecting on change, loss, and transition in everyday life* (pp. 75–92). New York, NY: Routledge.
Schover, L., Fouladi, R., Warneke, C. L., Neese, L., Klein, E. A., Zippe, C., et al. (2004). Seeking help for erectile dysfunction after treatment for prostate cancer. *Archives of Sexual Behavior, 33*(5), 443–454.
Schultz, C., & Harris, D. (2011). Giving voice to nonfinite loss and bereavement. In R. Neimeyer, D. Harris, H. Winokuer, & G. Thornton (Eds.), *Grief and bereavement in contemporary society: Bridging research and practice* (pp. 235–245). New York, NY: Routledge.
Schuurman, D. (2003). *Never the same: Coming to terms with the death of a parent*. New York, NY: St. Martin's Press.
Shea, J. (2000). *Spirituality & health care: Reaching toward a holistic future*. Chicago, IL: Park Ridge Center.
Walter, C. (2003). *The loss of a life partner: Narratives of the bereaved*. New York, NY: Columbia University Press.

Adjusting to Life's Losses by Aging or Illness or Infirmity

Baars, J., & Visser, H. (Eds.). (2007). *Aging and time: Multidisciplinary perspectives*. Amityville, NY: Baywood.
Balk, D., & Corr, C. (Eds.). (2009). *Adolescent encounters with death, bereavement, and coping*. New York, NY: Springer.
Barusch, A. (2009). Love and ageism—A social work perspective. *Social Work Today, 9*(1), 12.
Beerman, S., & Rappaport-Musson, J. (2002). *Eldercare 911: The caregiver's complete handbook for making decisions*. Amherst, NY: Prometheus.
Berzoff, J., & Silverman, P. (Eds.). (2004). *Living with dying: A handbook for end-of-life care practitioners*. New York, NY: Columbia University Press.

Boog, K., & Tester, C. (2008). *Palliative care: A practical guide for the health professional: Finding meaning and purpose in life and death*. London/New York: Churchill/Livingstone.

Cort, E., Monroe, B., & Oliviere, D. (2004). Couples in palliative care. *Sexual and Relationship Therapy, 19*(3), 337–354.

Cox, G., Bendiksen, R., & Stevenson, R. (Eds.). (2002). *Complicated grieving and bereavement: Understanding and treating people experiencing loss*. Amityville, NY: Baywood.

Davies, H., Zeiss, A., Shea, E., & Tinklenberg, J. (1998). Sexuality and intimacy in Alzheimer patients and their partners. *Sexuality and Disability, 16*(6), 193–203.

Deacon, S., Minichiello, V., & Plummer, D. (1995). Sexuality and older people: Revisiting the assumptions. *Education Gerontology, 21*(5), 497–513.

DeLamater, J., & Karraker, A. (2009). Sexual behavior in later life. *Journal of Aging and Health, 19*(6), 921–945.

Doka, K. (2002). *Living with grief: Loss in later life*. Washington, DC: Hospice Foundation of America.

Doka, K., & Tucci, A. (2011). *Spirituality and end-of-life care*. Washington, DC: Hospice Foundation of America.

Dupuis, S. (2002). Understanding ambiguous loss in the context of dementia care. *Journal of Gerontological Social Work, 37*, 93–115.

Eyers, K., & Parker, G. (2010). *Tackling depression at work: A practical guide for employees and managers*. New York, NY: Routledge.

Family Caregiver Alliance. (2001). *Sexuality and dementia*. Retrieved from http://www.caregiver.org

Feldkamp, J. (2003). Navigating the uncertain legal waters of resident sexuality. *Nursing Homes Long Term Care Management, 52*(2), 62–64.

Graber, A. (2003). *Viktor Frankl's logotherapy: Method of choice in ecumenical pastoral psychology*. Lima, OH: Wyndham Hall Press.

Harris, D. (Ed.). (2011). *Counting our losses: Reflecting on change, loss, and transition in everyday life*. New York, NY: Routledge.

Hartzell, R. (2006). Senior sex: Exploring the sex lives of older adults. *Journal of Sex Research, 43*(3), 292–293.

Hood, R., Jr., Hill, P., & Williamson, W. (2005). *The psychology of religious fundamentalism*. New York, NY: Guilford.

Hurley, M. (2002). On not getting it: Narration, sex and ageing. *Sexualities, 5*, 407–423.

Johnson, D., & Scelfo, J. (2003). Sex, love and nursing homes. *Newsweek, 142*, 54–55.

Kern, M. (2009). Sexuality and intimacy in the critically ill. In D. Walsh et al. (Eds.), *Palliative medicine* (pp. 355–359). Philadelphia, PA: Saunders.

Lester, D. (1993). *The cruelest death: The enigma of adolescent suicide*. Philadelphia, PA: Charles Press.

Levy, J. (1994). Sex and sexuality in late life stages. In A. S. Rossi (Ed.), *Sexuality across the life course* (pp. 287–309). Chicago, IL: University of Chicago Press.

Matsakis, A. (2005). *In harm's way: Help for the wives of military men, police, EMTs and firefighters*. Oakland, CA: New Harbinger.

McMinn, L. (2004). *Sexuality and holy longing: Embracing intimacy in a broken world*. San Francisco, CA: Jossey-Bass.

Miller, M. (Ed.). (2008). Getting help for post-combat mental health problems. *Harvard Mental Health Letter, 24*(11), 5.

Moore, A., & Stratton, D. (2003). *Resilient widowers: Older men adjusting to new life.* Amherst, NY: Prometheus.
Osgood, N. (1992). *Suicide in later life: Recognizing the warning signs.* New York, NY: Lexington.
Parkes, C. (2006/2008). *Love and loss: The roots of grief and its complications.* New York, NY: Routledge.
Peck, S. (2007). Career harmony: Balancing a traditional career with transient military lifestyle. *Military Spouse, 3*(1), pp. 38–42.
Plante, T. (2009). *Spiritual practices in psychotherapy: Thirteen tools for enhancing psychological health.* Washington, DC: American Psychological Association.
Raezer, J. (2007). Ensuring quality mental health care for military families: A task for the new Congress. *The Voice for Military Families, 18*(2), 1–4.
Shell, J. (2008). Sexual issues in the palliative care population. *Seminars in Oncological Nursing, 24*(2), 131–134.
Sherman, M., Zanotti, D., & Jones, D. (2005). Key elements in couples therapy with veterans with combat-related posttraumatic stress disorder. *Professional Psychology: Research and Practice, 36*(6), 626–633.
Steen, J., & Asaro, M. (2006). *Military widow: A survival guide.* Annapolis, MD: Naval Institute Press.
Stevenson, R. (Ed.). (2002). *What will we do? Preparing a school community to cope with crises* (2nd ed). Amityville, NY: Baywood.
Sue, D. W., & Sue, D. (2008). *Counseling the culturally diverse in theory and practice* (5th ed.). Hoboken, NJ: Wiley.
Sullivan, T. (2006). He's the spouse? The most neglected military spouses—Husbands. *Military Spouse, 2*(6), 52–56.
Thompson, N. (2009). *Loss, grief, and trauma in the workplace.* Amityville, NY: Baywood.
Thompson, N. (2011). *Grief and its challenges.* Basingstoke, UK: Palgrave Macmillan.
Tomer, A., Eliason, G., & Wong, P. (Eds.). (2008). *Existential and spiritual issues in death attitudes.* New York, NY: Lawrence Erlbaum.
Vache-Haase, T., Wester, S., & Christianson, H. (2011). *Psychotherapy with older men.* New York, NY: Routledge.
Ward, K. (2004). *What the Bible really teaches about crucifixion, resurrection, salvation, the Second Coming and eternal life.* New York, NY: Crossroad.
Ward, K. (2006). *Is religion dangerous?* Grand Rapids, MI: Eerdmans.
Watts, F. (Ed.). (2007). *Jesus & psychology.* London: Darton, Longman & Todd.
Wilson, J. (2001). *Treatment psychological trauma & PTSD.* New York, NY: Guilford.
Wright, K. (2001). *Religious abuse: A pastor explores the many ways religion can hurt as well as heal.* Kelowna, BC, Canada: Northstone.

Religious Bases for Understanding Intimacy, Sexuality, and Healing After Loss

Albers, R. (1995). *Shame: A faith perspective.* New York, NY: Haworth.
Carr, W. (1989/2008). *The pastor as theologian: The formation of today's ministry in the light of contemporary human sciences.* London: SPCK.
Carr, W. (Ed.). (2002). *The new dictionary of pastoral studies.* Grand Rapids, MI: Eerdmans.

Chittister, J. (2011). *Welcome to the wisdom of the world and its meaning for you: Universal spiritual insights from five religious traditions*. Grand Rapids, MI: Eerdmans.

Ciarrocchi, J. (1993). *A minister's handbook of mental disorders*. New York, NY: Paulist.

Cox, G. (2010). *Death and the American Indian*. Omaha, NE: Centering.

Evans, A. R. (2004). *Healing liturgies for the seasons of life*. Louisville, KY: Westminster John Knox Press.

Evans, A. R. (2011). *Is God still at the bedside? The medical, ethical and pastoral issues of death and dying*. Grand Rapids, MI: Eerdmans.

Fortune, M., & Marshall, J. (Eds.). (2002). *Forgiveness and abuse: Jewish and Christian reflections*. New York, NY: Haworth.

Garces-Foley, K. (Ed.). (2006). *Death and religion in a changing world*. Armonk, NY/ London: M. E. Sharpe.

Gilbert, R. (Ed.). (2002). *Healthcare and spirituality: Listening, assessing, caring*. Amityville, NY: Baywood.

Holloway, K. (2002). *Passed on: African mourning stories*. Durham, NC: Duke University Press.

Honeycutt, F. (2011). *The truth shall make you odd: Speaking with pastoral integrity in awkward situations*. Grand Rapids, MI: Brazos.

Hood, R., Jr., Hill, P., & Williamson, W. (2005). *The psychology of religious fundamentalism*. New York, NY: Guilford.

Kaeton, E. (1998). Pastoral care at the end of life: Listening for the question beneath the question. *Journal of Palliative Medicine, 1*(3), 285–289.

Kimball, D. (2001/2005). *They like Jesus but not the church: Insights from emerging generations*. Grand Rapids, MI: Eerdmans.

Kirkwood, N. (2002). *Pastoral care to Muslims: Building bridges*. New York, NY: Haworth.

Langford, D. (1998). *The pastor's family: The challenges of family life and pastoral responsibilities*. New York, NY: Haworth.

Lehr, F. (2006). *Clergy burnout: Recovering from the 70-hour work week . . . and other self-defeating practices*. Minneapolis, MN: Fortress.

Lieber, D. L., Harlow, J., United Synagogue of Conservative Judaism, & Rabbinical Assembly. (2001). *Etz Hayim: Torah and commentary*. Philadelphia, PA: Jewish Publication Society.

Lewis, J., & Petersen, J. (Eds.). (2005). *Controversial new religions*. Oxford: Oxford University Press.

Long, T. (2011). *What shall we say? Evil, suffering, and the crisis of faith*. Grand Rapids, MI/Cambridge, UK: Eerdmans.

Magida, A. (Ed.). (1996). *How to be a perfect stranger: A guide to etiquette in other people's religious ceremonies*. Woodstock, VT: Jewish Lights.

Minor, R. (2007). *When religion is an addiction*. St. Louis, MO: Humanity Works.

Moriarity, G. (2006). *Pastoral care of depression: Helping clients heal their relationship with God*. New York, NY: Haworth.

O'Brien, M. (2000). *Lift up your hearts: Meditations for those who mourn*. Chicago, IL: ACTA.

Ritter, K., & O'Neill, C. (1996). *Righteous religion: Unmasking the illusions of fundamentalism and authoritarian Catholicism*. New York, NY: Haworth.

Roukema, R. (1997). *The soul in distress: What every pastoral counselor should know about emotional and mental illness*. New York, NY: Haworth.

Roukema, R. (2003). *Counseling for the soul in distress: What every religious counselor should know about emotional and mental stress* (2nd ed.). New York, NY: Haworth.

Scotland, N. (2005). *A pocket guide to sects & new religions*. Oxford, UK: Lion.

Sims, D. (1993). *If I could just see hope*. Wenatchee, WA: Author.

Smith, D. (1999). *Being a wounded healer: How to heal ourselves while we are healing others*. Madison, WI: Psycho-Spiritual Publications.

Smith, H. I. (2001). *When your people are grieving: Leading in times of loss*. Kansas City, MO: Beacon Hill Press of Kansas City.

Sweasey, P. (1997). *From queer to eternity: Spirituality in the lives of lesbian, gay and bisexual people*. London/Washington, DC: Cassell.

Taylor, R., Chatters, K., & Levin, J. (2004). *Religion in the lives of African Americans: Social, psychological and health perspectives*. Thousand Oaks, CA: Sage.

Theissen, G. (2007). *The Bible and contemporary culture*. Minneapolis, MN: Fortress.

Tomer, A., Eliason, G., & Wong, P. (Eds.). (2008). *Existential and spiritual issues in death attitudes*. New York, NY: Lawrence Erlbaum.

Ward, K. (2004). *What the Bible really teaches about crucifixion, resurrection, salvation, the Second Coming and eternal life*. New York, NY: Crossroad.

Ward, K. (2006). *Is religion dangerous?* Grand Rapids, MI: Eerdmans.

Watts, F. (Ed.). (2007). *Jesus & psychology*. London: Darton, Longman & Todd.

Webb, D. (2005). *The soul of counseling: A new model for understanding human experience*. Atascadero, CA: Imprint.

Whitehead, J., & Whitehead, E. (1994). *Shadows of the heart: A spirituality of painful emotions*. New York, NY: Crossroad.

Wilcock, P. (1996). *Spiritual care of dying and bereaved people*. London: SPCK.

Wilson, J. (2001). *Treatment psychological trauma & PTSD*. New York, NY: Guilford.

Wright, K. (2001). *Religious abuse: A pastor explores the many ways religion can hurt as well as heal*. Kelowna, BC, Canada: Northstone.

Index

Activities of daily living (ADLs), 133
ADLs. *See* activities of daily living
Adolescence, defined, 47–48
Adoption. *See* infertility, adoption
ADRD. *See* Alzheimer's disease and related dementia
Adult children, grieving, loss experiences
  abuse and, 90, 93–95, 97–98
  choosing survivorship grieving, 97–100
  intimacy issues, 91
  parental loss, 88–90
  relationship problems, 91
  research statistics, 93
  role alterations, 89–90
Aging Together (McFadden, S., J.), 16
Aging, togetherness issues, 16
AHA. *See* American Heart Association
Alone Together (Turkle), 10
Alzheimer's disease and related dementia (ADRD)
  activities of daily living (ADLs) and, 133
  assessment, 139–140
  care givers and, 133–135, 137–139
  clinical implications, 139–145
  early stages, 132–133
  ethical considerations, 143–144
  grief related to, 134–135
  grief work, caregivers, 141–142
  incidence of, 132
  intimacy, grief and, 135–136, 142
  long-term care, sexual intimacy, grief of older adults, 142–143
[Alzheimer's disease and related dementia (ADRD)]
  research, policy, present strategies, 145
  spouses, sexual intimacy, 136–139
American Heart Association (AHA), 153
Attig, Thomas, 193

Becker, Ernst, v
Being *vs.* having, v
Bell, Rob, 217
Berzoff, Joan, 170
Bowlby, John, 219, 222
Brindisi, Julia, 35–36
Brody, James, 58
Brown, Patricia, 45
Bryan, William Jennings, 183
Buddhism, v–vi

Caserta, Michael, 91
CDC. *See* Center for Disease Control
Center for American Progress, 55
Center for Disease Control (CDC), 89
Clinical Practice Guidelines for Quality Palliative Care (National Consensus Project), 166
Contemporary culture, 18
Control, 5
Crary, David, 57
Criminal-Justice and School Sanctions Against Nonheterosexual Youth (study), 58

Death Studies (Lund, Caserta), 91
Denial of Death, The (Becker), v
Diamond, Lisa, 58
Disenfranchised grief, 24–28
Dowrick, Stephanie, 222

ED. *See* erectile dysfunction
ELCA. *See* Evangelical Lutheran Church in America
Elder widowers
  future research, 81
  sexual disenfranchisement, 75–76
  sexuality, aging, quality of life, 71–72
  traditionalists, 72–73
  transformationalists, 74–75
  transitionalists, 73–74
End-of-life
  assessment models, 174
  Betty, case example, 168
  care improvement suggestions, 172–175
  Cindy, case example, 167
  cognitive changes and, 171
  common myths, 170, 175
  discussion barriers, treatment staff, 172–173
  discussions, 165
  Frank, case example, 171
  health care staff and, 172–173
  hospice, 166–167, 172–176
  Hospice of Bluegrass (HOB) and, 166, 172, 177–178
  hospice staff, nursing home administrators and, 171–172
  Jessie, case example, 167
  Jim, case example, 168, 171
  Joe and Marie, case study, 166
  John, case example, 171
  married 50 years case example, 167
  need for national change, 175–176
  organizations, 170
  patient care barriers, 175–176
  patient challenges, 175–176
  Permission, Limited information, Specific Suggestions, and Intensive Therapy (PLISSIT model), 174–175
[End-of-life]
  quality measures, 175
  relevant research, 170–171
  Rose, case example, 171
  sexuality, intimacy during, 167–169, 172–175
  social death and, 169
  suggested health care phrases, 173–174
Erectile dysfunction (ED), 153–156. *See also* Viagra
  cardiovascular disease (CVD) and, 154
  clinical implications, 80–81
  defined, 69
  diabetes and, 155–156
  psychological factors, 67–69
Ericsson, Stephanie, 13–14
Evangelical Lutheran Church in America (ELCA), 210
Expectations, 5–6

Fresh Kills (Loehfelm), 93–94
Friendship, 221–222
Friendship Factor, The (McGinnis), 222

Gay and Homeless: In Plain Sight, a Largely Hidden Population (Zavis), 56
Gay or Straight, Youths Aren't So Different (Brody), 58
Gender issues, young child, 43–44
Gender binary and, 44
Gender identity, loss, 45
Gender stereotyping, loss, 45–47
Gittelsohn, Roland, 186
GLSEN School Climate Survey, 49, 53–55
Green, Alan, 188
Grief
  Alzheimer's disease and related dementia (ADRD) and, 134–135, 141–143
  blindness of, 22–24
  disenfranchised, 24–28, 195
  importance of, ix
  infertility, adoption and, 114

[Grief]
LGBT community and, 33–34
religion and, 195, 202–203
sexuality, intimacy and, 12–14
stages, 202–203
Grief, Dying, and Death: Clinical Interventions for Caregivers (Rando), 170

Healthy Aging Taskforce, 76
Heavenly Hurts (Klein), 26
HIV/AIDS, 30–31
HOB. *See* Hospice of Bluegrass
Honeycutt, Frank, 214
Hospice of Bluegrass (HOB), 166, 172, 177–178
Huxley, Julian, 185

Identity and sexuality, 12
Infertility, adoption
clinical implications, 113–114
domestic *vs.* private adoption and, 110–111
forms of grief and, 114
impact, 104–108
incidence, North America, 104–105
international adoption and, 111
legacy of loss and, 112
medications, procedures, 105–107
name, validate losses, 113
practice of presence and, 114
primary *vs.* secondary, 104
professional support, informed support, 114
Rob and Susan, case study, 102–104, 108–109
social forces and, 107–108
Inherit the Wind (Bryan), 183
Intimacy
adult children, grieving, loss experiences, 91
Alzheimer's disease, related dementia (ADRD) and, 135–139, 142–143
Christian understanding of, 200–201
consent and, 4

[Intimacy]
defined, 4–8, 135
end-of-life and, 167–169, 172–175
LGBT community and, 21, 32–33
love and, 220–222
mourning and, 6–7
multiple losses and, 28–30
with oneself, 6, 8
religion and, 193–197, 199–201
risk and, 4, 7
sexuality, grief and, 12–14
soldiers, families and, 122–125
Intimacy (Nouwen), 17

Klein, Sandra, 26
Kübler-Ross, Elisabeth, 202
Kysar, Myrna, 209
Kysar, Robert, 209

Lesbian, Gay, Bisexual and Transgender Youth: An Epidemic of Homelessness (Ray), 55
Levi, Joshua, 191
LGBT community
death and intimacy, heterosexual *vs.*, 21, 32–33
gay parents, 26
grief's other appearances, 33–34
Harry and Jim, case, 23
HIV/AIDS and, 28–29
Janice and Tammy, example, 210–211
partner, friend, spouse and, 25
peer support, 25–26
religion and, 26–28
sanctions and, 19
suicides and, 33
Susan and Ellen, case, 23–24
terminology, 21
LGBT community, clinical implications, 34
adults, 37
closeted grievers, 37–38
LGBTQ teenagers, 35–37
partially out, out grievers, 38–39

[LGBT community, clinical implications]
recommendations, 39–40
support groups, 39
LGBT youth
Center for American Progress report, 55
Criminal-Justice and School Sanctions Against Nonheterosexual Youth (study), 58
discrimination, victimization, 51–52
family support and, 50–51
GLSEN School Climate Survey, 49, 53–55
helpful organizations, resources, 51, 59–60
homelessness and, 55–56
keeping secret, 50
loss, today's world, 49
losses associated, 48–49
parents, common reactions, 52–53
positive interventions, support, 54–55
psychological distress, 50
at risk factors, 49–52
schools, bullying, anti-gay slurs, 53–55
suicidal ideations in, 56–58
Trevor Project, 57–58
Lim, Israel, 190
Living With Dying: A Handbook for End-of-Life Healthcare Practitioner (Berzoff, Silverman), 170
Loehfelm, Bill, 93–94
Los Angeles Times, 56
Loss, Attachment, Separation trilogy (Bowlby), 219
Loss, defined, ix
Love and intimacy, 220–222
Love and Orgasm (Lowen), 221
Love and Will (May), 220
Love Wins (Bell), 217
Lowen, Alexander, 221
Lund, Dale, 91

Mace, Nancy, 134
Martinson, Roland, 201
May, Rollo, 220
McFadden, John, 16
McFadden, Susan, 16
McGinnis, Alan, 222
McMinn, L. G., 206–208
Meyer, Tony, 36
Middle adulthood
cardiovascular disease (CVD) and, 153–154
chronic illness, sexuality and, 153–158
depression and, 155
diabetes and, 154–156
erectile dysfunction (ED) and, 153–156
gender difference, 152
good enough sex model, 158–160
health care providers and, 160–161
incontinence and, 156–157
obesity, 157–158
sexual activity during, 152
stress incontinence, 156
stroke (CVA) and, 153
time of life, 151–152
transient ischemic attacks (TIA) and, 153
urge incontinence, 156
Mourning
defined, 1
intimacy seeking during, 6–7
paradox of, 1
physical absence, presence and, 2
positive view of, 11
relationships and, 2–3
Multiple losses, impact to intimacy, 28–30

Nathanson, Donald, 220
National Association of Social Workers, 170
National Consensus Project for Quality Palliative Care, 170
National Hospice and Palliative Care Organization, 170
New York Times, 45
Nouwen, Henri, 17

O'Connor, Sandra Day, 136
Openness, 4–5

Palliative Medicine, 170
Pfizer Pharmaceuticals, 68
PLISSIT model, end-of-life, 174–175
Post-traumatic stress disorder (PTSD), 121–124
Prager, Dennis, 185
Prayers for Bobby, 56–57
Pursuit of Loneliness, The, 9

Rabins, Peter, 134
Ray, Nicholas, 55
Religion, 16–18
  adult children, grieving, loss experiences, 91–92, 95
  Ben, story, 208–209
  celibacy and, 189–190
  Christian Church attendance and, 206
  Christian Church's role, 201–203, 211–217
  conflicting public messages and, 205
  creation stories, 183–184, 187–189, 197
  cultural values and, 204
  disenfranchised grief and, 195
  emotional separation and, 195
  holy ideas, 189–193
  intimacy, sexuality, Christian Church, 199–200
  Janice and Tammy, story, 210–211
  Judaism *vs.* Christianity, 190
  legal landscape and, 205
  LGBT community and, 26–28
  Lilith saga, 184
  lost intimacy and, 193–195
  lost intimacy, starting over, 195–197
  mourning and, 193–194
  new approach, 184–189
  original sin, 190
  price of intimacy and, 197
  purity and, 190
  reconciliation, memorialization and, 194
[Religion]
  relationships after divorce, 208–209, 213–215
  relationships after spouse's death, 206–208, 211–213
  relationships, Christian Church teachings, 204
  religious communities, 17
  rituals, 193–194
  same-sex marriage, gay relationships and, 192, 205, 210–211, 215–216
  secularization and, 204
  sexual relations and, 187–188
  stages of grief and, 202–203
  theological assumptions, sexuality and intimacy, 200–201
  trends, Christian Church and society, 203–206
  women's rights and, 191
  yadah, shachav, 187–188
Rilker, Rainer Maria, vi
Risk and intimacy, 4, 7
Ruether, Radford, 209, 213

Sanctions, LGBT sexuality, 19
Schaeffer, Brenda, 222
Self-identity, 6
Sexual health, World Health Organization (WHO) definition, 158
Sexuality, aging, quality of life
  elder widowers, 71–72
  sexuality defined, 169–169
  Viagra-users, classifications, 72–75
Sexuality, intimacy, and grief, 12–14
Shir Ha-Shirim (The Song of Songs), 188–189
Silverman, Phyllis, 170
Slater, Philip, 9
Smith, Harold Ivan, 92
Soldier Combat Stress Reaction: A pocket guide for spouse and loved ones (U.S. Army), 120
Soldiers, families
  intimacy and, 122–125
  military experience and, 119